ENRIQUE ALFÉREZ

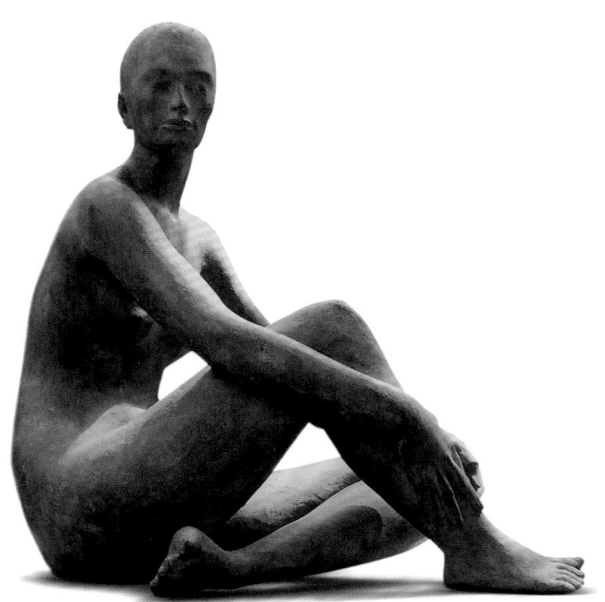

Repose in The Helis Foundation
Enrique Alférez Sculpture Garden [cast 1987–90]

photo by Alison Cody
ON LOAN FROM THE HELIS FOUNDATION

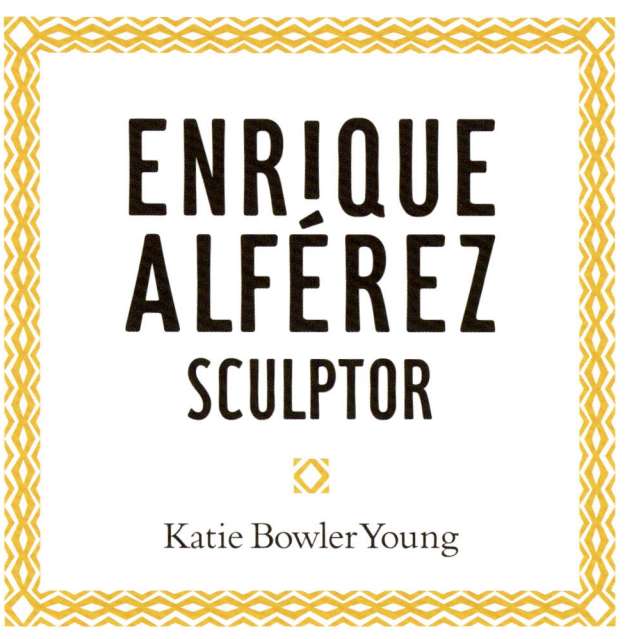

ENRIQUE ALFÉREZ

SCULPTOR

Katie Bowler Young

THE HISTORIC NEW ORLEANS COLLECTION

with the generous support of the
2019 Bienville Circle and Laussat Society

Library of Congress Cataloging-in-Publication Data

Names: Young, Katie Bowler, author.

Title: Enrique Alférez : sculptor / Katie Bowler Young.

Description: New Orleans, Louisiana : The Historic New
    Orleans Collection, [2020] | Includes bibliographical
    references and index. | Summary: "Enrique Alférez,
    born in Zacatecas, Mexico, lived nearly the entire twen-
    tieth century. After service in the Mexican Revolution
    as a youth, he emigrated to Texas; studied in Chicago;
    and, in 1929, first made his way to Louisiana. For
    almost seventy years, he worked in New Orleans. His
    lasting imprint is seen among figurative sculptures,
    monuments, fountains, and architectural details
    in prominent locations from the Central Business
    District to the shore of Lake Pontchartrain and beyond.
    Author Katie Bowler Young has gained unprecedented
    access to Alférez's personal and family holdings and
    has crafted a poetic evocation of the life and work of
    this preeminent artist. Enrique Alférez: Sculptor is
    the latest entry in the well-received Louisiana Artists
    Biography series. The book, featuring more than 100
    images of Alférez's work in New Orleans and beyond,
    will be the first in the series to center on sculpture and
    public art"-- Provided by publisher.

Identifiers: LCCN 2020020445 | ISBN 9780917860850
    (hardcover)

Subjects: LCSH: Alférez, Enrique, 1903-1999. | Mexican
    American sculptors--Biography. | Sculptors--United
    States--Biography. | New Orleans (La.)--Biography.

Classification: LCC NB237.A365 Y68 2020 | DDC 730.92
    [B]--dc23

LC record available at https://lccn.loc.gov/2020020445

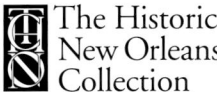
The Historic
New Orleans
Collection

The Historic New Orleans Collection is a museum,
research center, and publisher dedicated to the
study and preservation of the history and culture of
New Orleans, the lower Mississippi valley, and the
Gulf South region. The Collection is operated by the
Kemper and Leila Williams Foundation, a Louisiana
nonprofit corporation.

© 2020 Katie Bowler Young

533 Royal Street
New Orleans, Louisiana 70130
www.hnoc.org

Editor: Dorothy Ball
Director of publications: Jessica Dorman
Associate editor: Siobhán McKiernan
President and CEO: Daniel Hammer
Design: Alison Cody Design
All rights reserved.

Printed in Florence, Italy, by Conti Tipocolor

24 23 22 21 20   1 2 3 4 5

ISBN: 978-0-917860-85-0

JACKET:
Alférez in his New Orleans studio [1950s or 1960s]
COURTESY OF THE TLALOC SELWAY ALFÉREZ PAPERS

ENDPAPERS:
Symbols of Communication (detail) [1968]
photo by Max Becherer
NEW ORLEANS ADVOCATE, JANUARY 22, 2018, CAPITAL CITY PRESS/GEORGES MEDIA GROUP, BATON ROUGE, LA

In memory of Lee Ann Voorhies Vaught

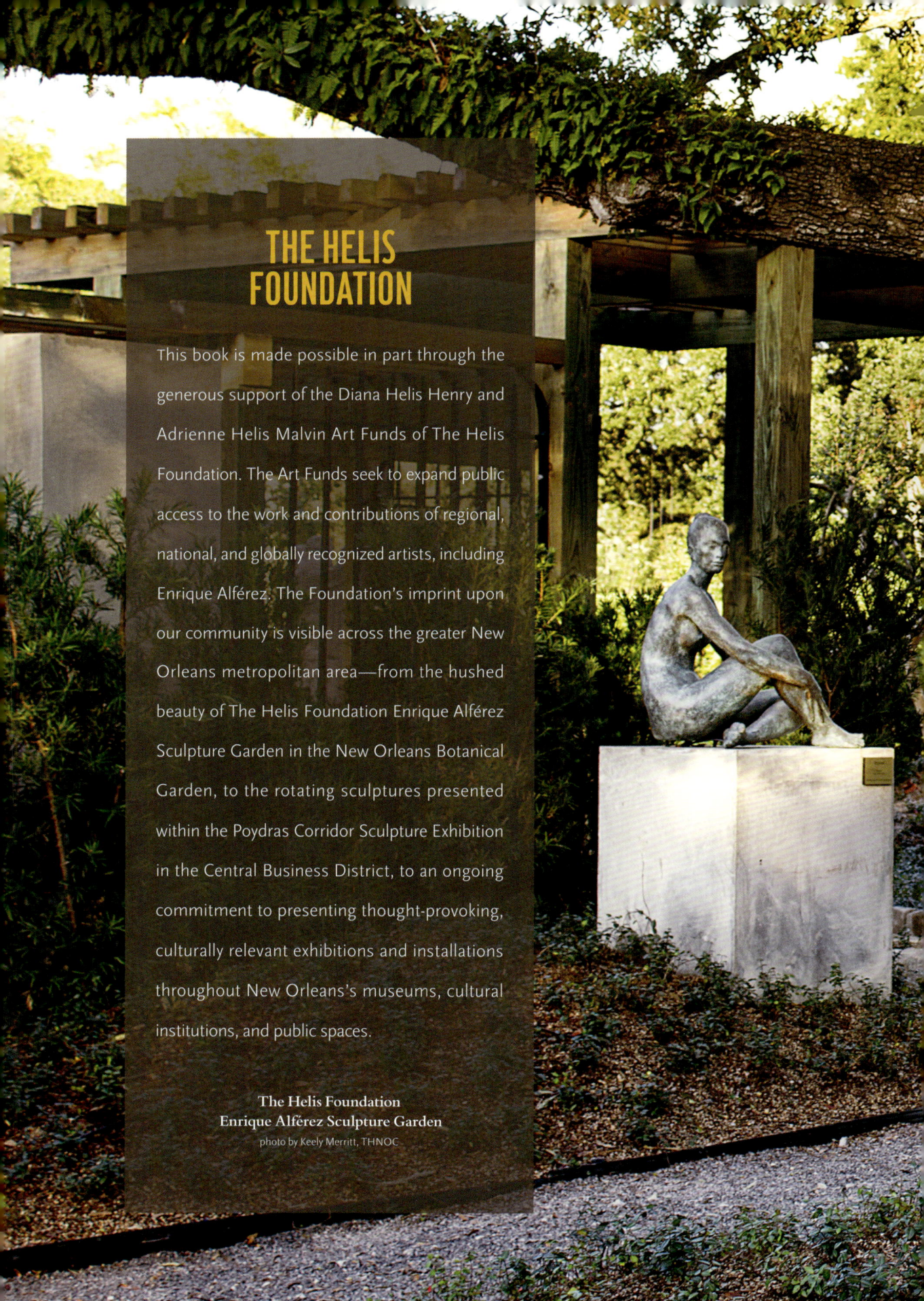

THE HELIS
FOUNDATION

This book is made possible in part through the generous support of the Diana Helis Henry and Adrienne Helis Malvin Art Funds of The Helis Foundation. The Art Funds seek to expand public access to the work and contributions of regional, national, and globally recognized artists, including Enrique Alférez. The Foundation's imprint upon our community is visible across the greater New Orleans metropolitan area—from the hushed beauty of The Helis Foundation Enrique Alférez Sculpture Garden in the New Orleans Botanical Garden, to the rotating sculptures presented within the Poydras Corridor Sculpture Exhibition in the Central Business District, to an ongoing commitment to presenting thought-provoking, culturally relevant exhibitions and installations throughout New Orleans's museums, cultural institutions, and public spaces.

The Helis Foundation
Enrique Alférez Sculpture Garden
photo by Keely Merritt, THNOC

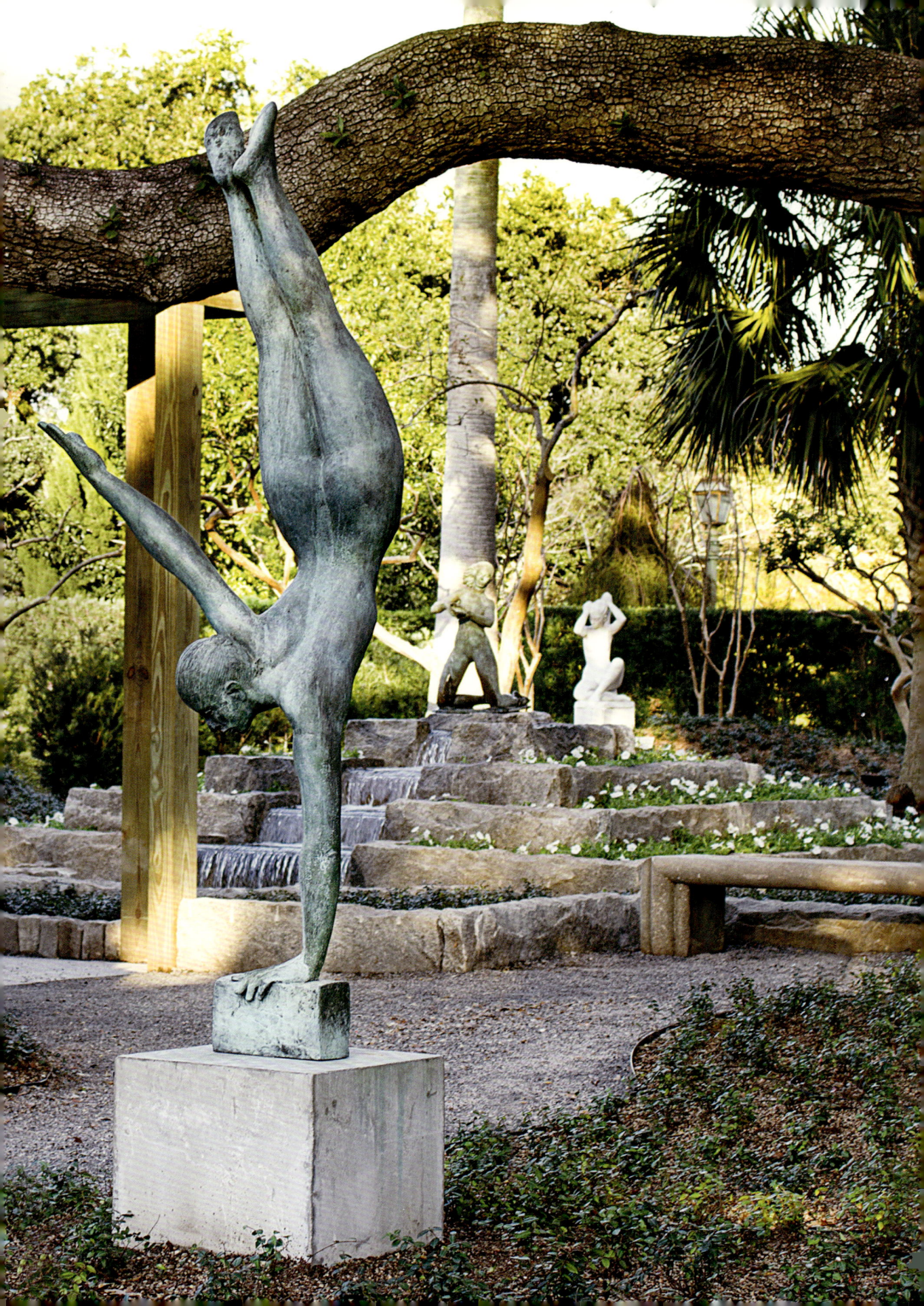

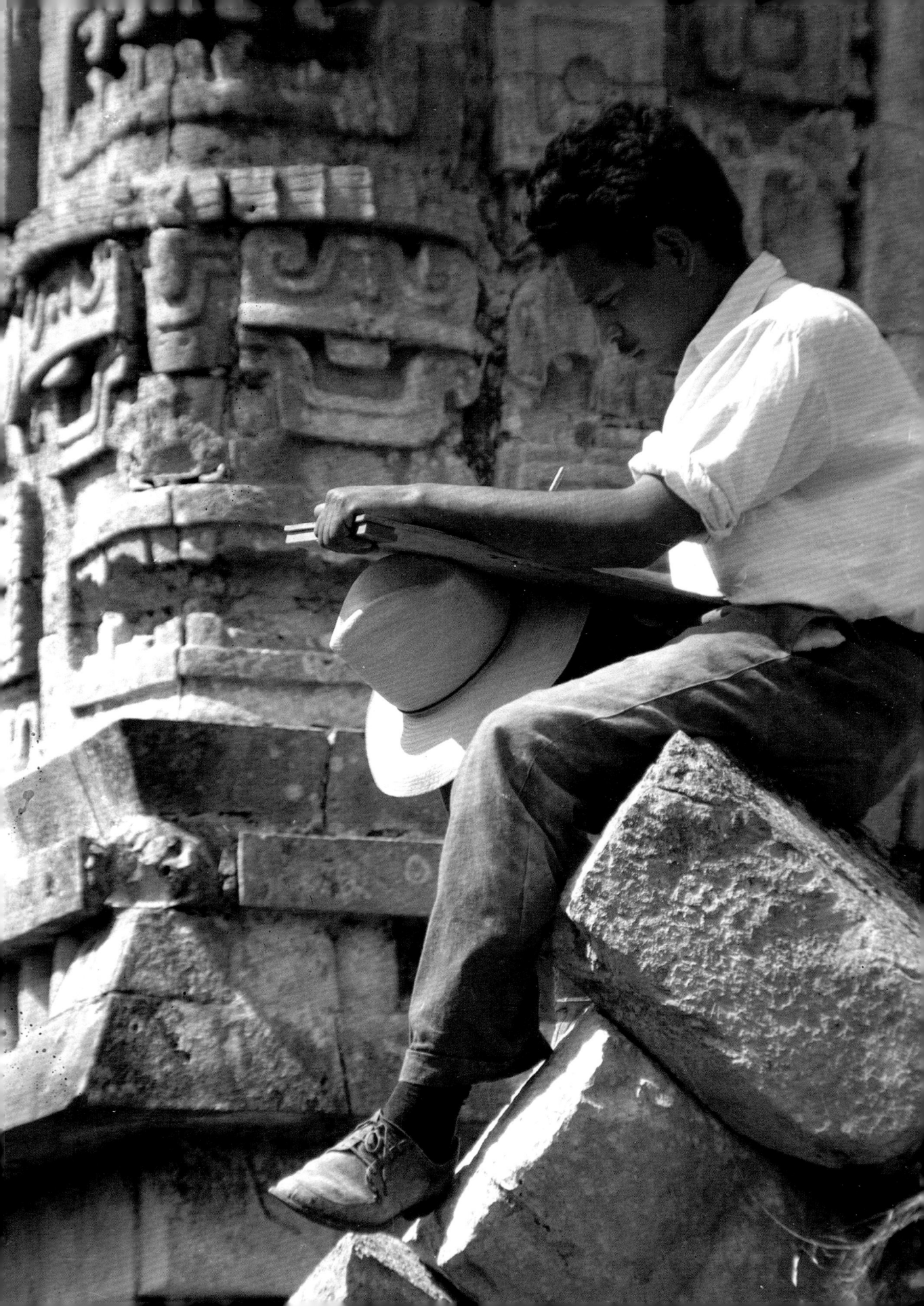

All passes. Robust art alone endures.

THÉOPHILE GAUTIER, "L'ART"

Near them, on the sand,
Half sunk a shattered visage lies, whose frown,
And wrinkled lip, and sneer of cold command,
Tell that its sculptor well those passions read
Which yet survive, stamped on these lifeless things,
The hand that mocked them, and the heart that fed…

PERCY BYSSHE SHELLEY, "OZYMANDIAS"

Enrique Alférez at work in Uxmal, Mexico [1930]

photo by Daniel Sweeney Leyrer
COURTESY OF THE MIDDLE AMERICAN RESEARCH INSTITUTE, TULANE UNIVERSITY

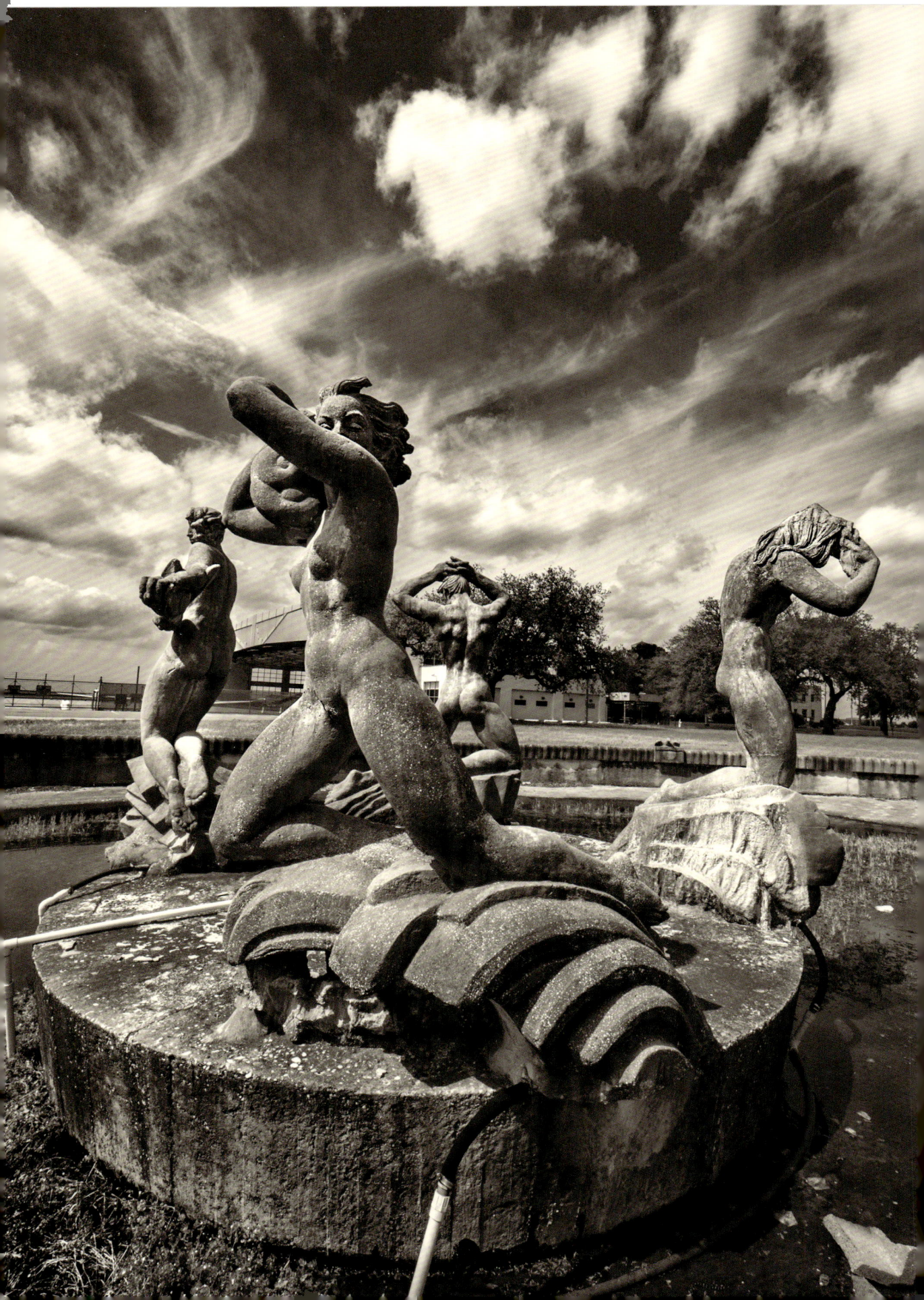

Preface

I LEARNED OF ENRIQUE ALFÉREZ through his public works of art, as many people have. I met him only once, in passing, when I was too young and shy to engage him in meaningful conversation. Since then, I have come to know him through his personal papers and drawings, as well as through the vast body of work he created in pencil, stone, wood, plaster, papier-mâché, steel, clay, concrete, bronze, lead, silver, and gold, much of which is in private collections. Although most noted for his sculpture—the primary subject driving this biography—he also created furniture, jewelry, and leather bags, belts, and other accessories. His figurative sculpture, architectural detail, and monuments can be seen throughout the United States and in Mexico.

Early encounters with his *Fountain of the Four Winds* have stayed with me nearly all my life. I have been intrigued by the fountain since I first saw it, as a girl, while riding in the back seat of my parents' car, as we approached the New Orleans Lakefront Airport for lunch and an afternoon of watching planes take off and land. Later, while studying communications at the University of New Orleans in the mid-1990s, I frequently spent time between classes visiting the *Four Winds*, just a few miles from campus. At the time, the fountain was empty of water and felt neglected, a state of decay that deepened as time passed. I was facing a turbulent period in my family, and, like many people transitioning from youth into young adulthood, I wanted to find my own place of belonging. I was also coming to an awareness that many people come to at this stage of life, starting to better understand how social structures influence the trajectories of people's lives. Feeling unsettled, I wanted a respite from worldly realities. On any day, a sweltering New Orleans afternoon or cool

Fountain of the Four Winds [1938]
photo by Donn Young

winter evening when the wind whipped off the lake and settled in my bones, I could park my car at the airport and walk toward the *Four Winds* as though they were old friends waiting for me. I'd sit down and open my literature textbook.

I sat beside the *Four Winds* while reading Percy Bysshe Shelley, reading his poem "Ozymandias," and seeing the passage of time, both on the page and in front of me. In the poem, a traveler relates an encounter with the ruined statue of "Ozymandias, King of Kings." The traveler reflects on the hand of the sculptor who created the monument. My interest was piqued by the role of an artist in leaving evidence of a passed era. As I re-read the poem near the *Four Winds,* I began to wonder who created them. Who stood beneath the arms of the West Wind and nested an owl of wisdom in her hand?

Once I made note of the marker that said *Enrique Alférez,* I returned to the campus library to find out more. Who was he? And how had Alférez arrived at that spot beside the airport? I learned about the difficult journey he traveled to obtain his education and pursue an art he loved. That his journey crossed into times and places in which he suffered the indignities of a segregated society made his path even more humbling. As I learned more in the years to follow, I felt he was walking alongside me in my own journey, prompting me back into the university, into a career in higher education, and international education in particular, out of a growing interest in facilitating connections across world regions and cultures, and into the habit of writing about artists, artisans, and their processes.

From the *Four Winds*, I began examining Alférez's work in the New Orleans area: bas-reliefs and figures throughout City Park to a Buddha statue in Greenwood Cemetery and a fountain in the Gatehouse Apartments in Metairie. I drove around with a list of places to see, checking them off as I arrived to photograph faces of Alférez's figures. I looked for consistency in his shapes and arcs, signs of the influence of art deco, level of detail in hands and feet, and consistency in the curve of closed eyes, as well as his deviations. I looked for subtle—or sometimes, not very subtle—sociopolitical messages in some of his works. His sculpture appealed to me because it revealed that he was a supporter of the everyman and everywoman. His monuments were not typically of generals or statesmen, but featured strong women, such as *Molly Marine*, the first US monument dedicated to women in the military; *Sophie B. Wright*, a monument to a champion of education who also cared for the ill and disabled; and the unnamed female figure at Shriever Fountain in the Botanical Garden at City Park, who carries a vessel of water on her right shoulder, long a symbol of female strength and responsibility for family. Other works honored laborers. I was also drawn to the metaphors, allegories, religious origins, and myths underlying his sculpture.

Over the course of the following two decades, I amassed a sizable number of articles and audio interviews and footage of Alférez, never setting out to write a biography, but wanting to understand how his life may have informed his art, how he accomplished so much despite the obstacles in his way, and how he might be remembered.

One very important source for this book has been Dr. Tlaloc Alférez, the younger daughter of Alférez. Tlaloc has stewarded her father's art since his death in 1999. During his life, alongside her mother, Peggy, she was very much a part of his creative work. In this way, his art was his family's work. Today, Tlaloc lives in an old church the Alférez family purchased in New Orleans in 1984 and converted into a home and studio. Through her, through our late conversations on her porch and days together in Alférez's studio, I finally came to call her father Rique, as his friends did.

Alférez earned acclaim for his art, but he rarely spoke publicly about his craft; when he did give interviews, he was relatively reserved about his process and sources of inspiration, which he disparagingly considered "romanticisms."[1] Despite his reservation in these areas, he was a known tale-teller, a raconteur. He embellished details about his life here and there, and once even hinted that he may have had a hand in shaping one of the most persistent myths that clings to his legacy: that he had been married as many as ten or eleven times, a detail repeated in numerous articles about him. In a 1999 interview, he stated, "I don't know who told that tale. I hope I didn't. But, of course, you never know."[2] Whether he was exaggerating or entertaining, Alférez gave fertile soil to the legends that grew around him. At best, these legends obscured his public identity and allowed him to remain a private man; at worst, the legends diverted attention from his art.

In contemplating Alférez's life and what drove him to pursue his sculpture, and in examining circumstances that influenced the figures he chose to sculpt, I often return to the writings of Lorado Taft, with whom Alférez studied in Chicago in the 1920s. Taft was not only a prolific sculptor, but also a writer and public lecturer on the arts, and he possessed deep knowledge of sculptors' craft and biographies. In his book *The Appreciation of Sculpture*, Taft expresses the value of knowing any artist as both creator and person. He suggests he is "old-fashioned enough," as though it is old-fashioned to have this desire, "to wish to know what manner of man it was who created the work which I find myself admiring. I want to know the time that he lived in; the place that he made the statue for. I am even pleased to learn that . . . he was 'good to his mother'!"[3] It is in this spirit that I was drawn to better understand the life of sculptor Enrique Alférez.

Part One

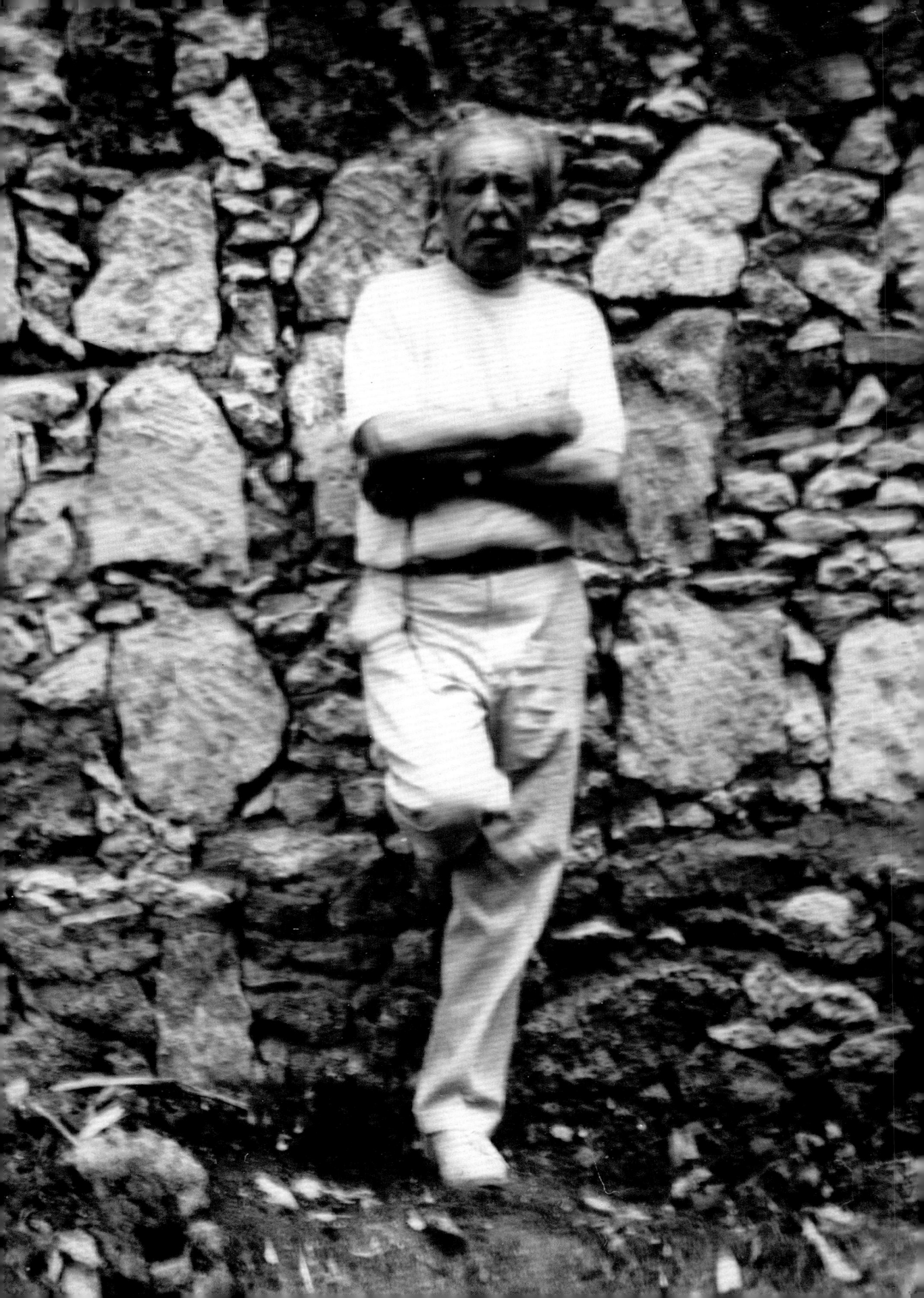

CHAPTER ONE

A Life in Brief

ENRIQUE ALFÉREZ'S LASTING imprint is seen throughout New Orleans, among figurative sculptures, monuments, fountains, and architectural details in prominent locations from the Central Business District to the shore of Lake Pontchartrain and beyond. For seventy years, from 1929 until his death in 1999, Alférez frequently had a home and studio in the city; today, this is where the majority of his artwork is on public view. He contributed to prized sites and buildings, such as City Park, the Lakefront Airport, and Charity Hospital. A number of New Orleans churches and chapels feature his wood carvings and cast religious figures. Through his art, this sculptor of Mexican origins helped shape the essence of one of the most interesting cities in the United States. "That Enrique Alférez is the premier New Orleans sculptor of this—or, indeed, of any—century is not a matter for debate," wrote journalist Don Lee Keith a few months prior to Alférez's death. "It is like the flow of the river…and the waddle of streetcars: a fact."[4]

Alférez left an imprint, albeit more modest, in other locations as well, most notably Chicago, where he began his formal study of sculpture at the School of the Art Institute of Chicago in 1924. He contributed to an architectural panel project installed on the exterior of Norton Memorial Hall at the Chautauqua Institution in Chautauqua, New York. His work is in the holdings of the Evansville Museum of Arts, History, and Science in Indiana. There are two public works in Morelia, Michoacán, Mexico, where he lived, on and off, beginning in 1969: a monument of Benito Juárez near the zoo and a *Lute Player* in a courtyard of the Conservatorio de las Rosas. His architectural details and figures appear at sites elsewhere in Louisiana, as well as in Mississippi and Alabama.

Alférez in the garden of his home in Santa María de Guido, Morelia [1971]

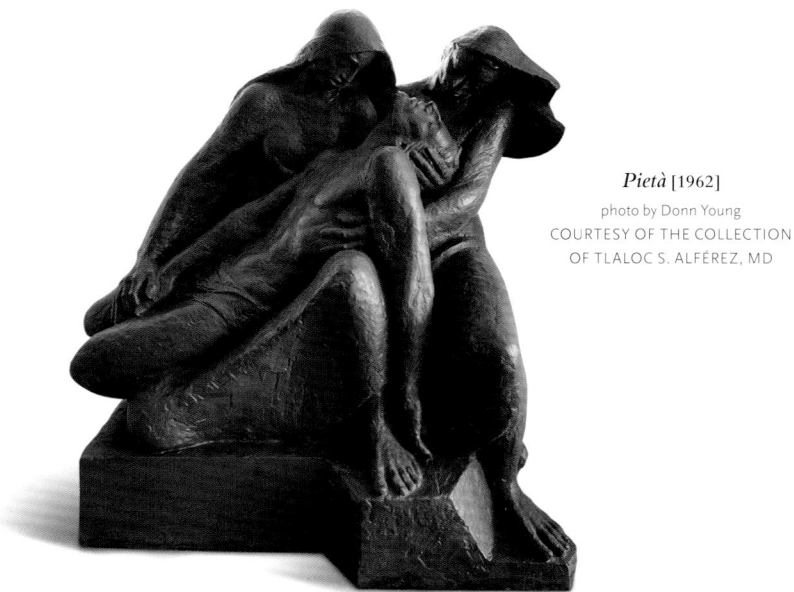

Pietà [1962]
photo by Donn Young
COURTESY OF THE COLLECTION
OF TLALOC S. ALFÉREZ, MD

Alférez's sculpture was most frequently based on the human form, primarily the female figure. He was a modernist who leaned on realism and drew extensively from classical sculpture, with careful attention to the revelation of character through physical features. He strove to better define the human figure and to capture emotion, individuality, and relationships between his subjects. Alférez also infused some of his figurative sculptures, bas-reliefs, and wood carvings with metaphor, allegory, and myth. He returned to biblical themes as well. His 1962 Christian pietà includes not only Mary, the mother of Jesus, holding her deceased son, but also Mary Magdalene. This work reflects his study of the most well-known pietà to include Mary Magdalene, *The Deposition* by Michelangelo.

Alférez thought the interpretive skill of the sculptor had advanced, almost in one gargantuan leap, from the "rather dead, lifeless" Greek interpretation of the human figure to that of the French sculptor Auguste Rodin.[5] Rodin's ability to capture human emotion in sculpture inspired him, though he still felt that "it could be better, that it could be done more honestly."[6] This led him to a study of the human condition, which he considered "so complex that it has infinite forms of expression."[7] He wasn't the only one who connected his work in some fashion to that of Rodin; scholar Judith H. Bonner, writing for the *New Orleans Art Review* in 1993, called him "a man of genius whose…reputation might one day challenge Rodin's."[8]

Realistic figurative sculpture had passed its fashionable day early in Alférez's career. By the time he was studying and working in Chicago in the mid-1920s, art was shifting toward more abstract representations of the human form; the avant-garde was influenced by art movements such as cubism and stridentism. Though he infused elements from these movements into his art, his propensity for early modern figurative sculpture went largely unchallenged throughout his career. In this way, he was not at the forefront of a new movement, but a product of his time.[9]

Alférez embraced elements of classical sculpture at a time when leading voices in Mexico's art scene, such as Diego Rivera, were discouraging the imitation of European models.[10] His work was shaped by his exposure to ancient Greek and Roman sculpture and modern European art, first through his father and then at the School of the Art Institute of Chicago. This formal training provided him with a foundation in technique, themes, and subjects. His artistic lineage contains the masters he was introduced to in Chicago, who influenced both his choice of subjects and the execution of his figures. One of Alférez's early works, the elevator door panels and wood carvings in the Palmolive Building in Chicago, bears the evidence

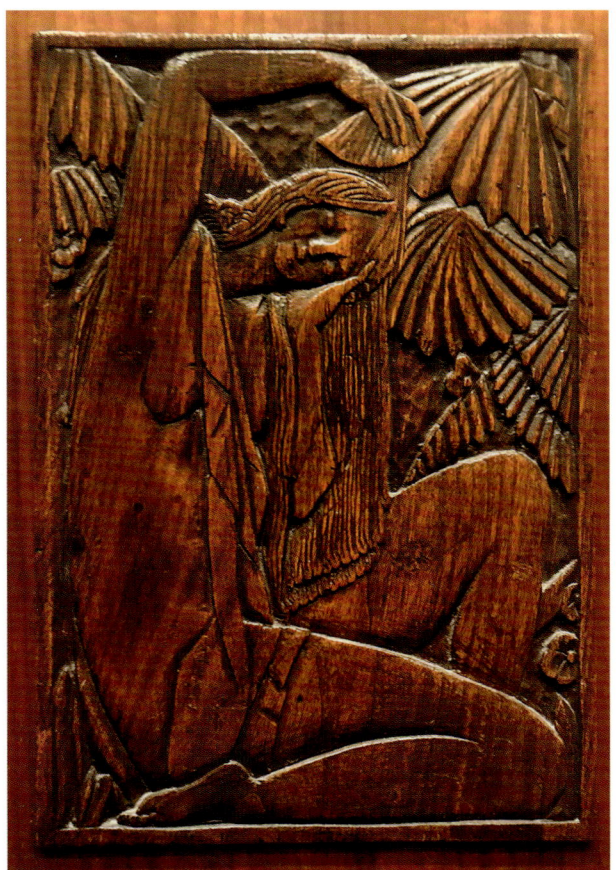
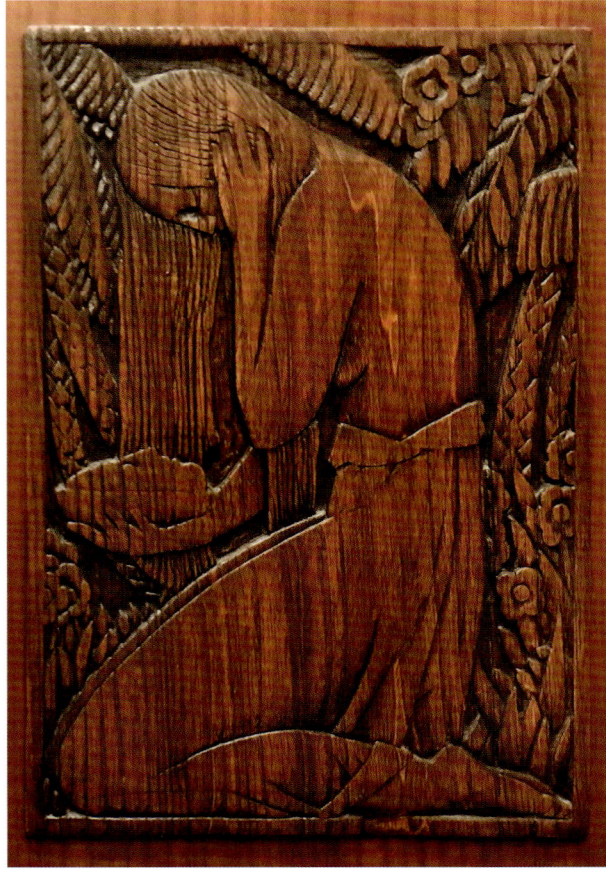

Interior decoration of Palmolive Building elevator [1928]
photo by Lynn Stephens
COURTESY OF THE PALMOLIVE BUILDING

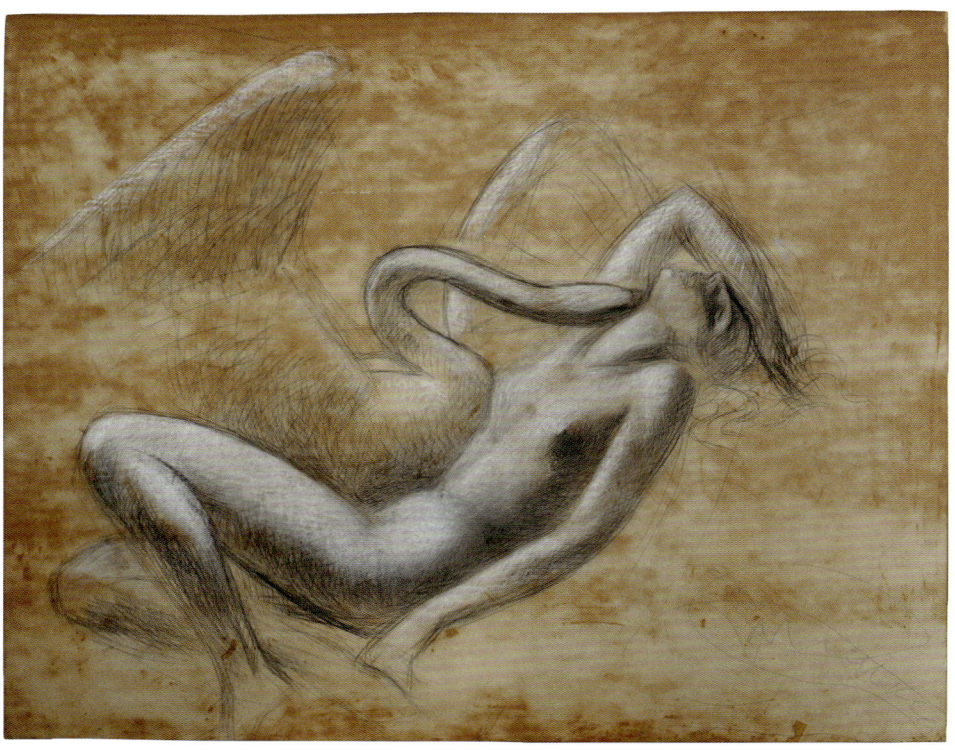

Leda and the Swan
photo by Donn Young
COURTESY OF THE COLLECTION OF TLALOC S. ALFÉREZ, MD

of his close examination of the Florence Baptistery doors, created in gilded bronze by Lorenzo Ghiberti and Andrea Pisano.

Alférez's knowledge of Italian masters can also be seen in his frequent return to the theme of Leda and the Swan, inspired by his study of Antonio Allegri da Correggio's monumental *Leda*.[11] It's likely that Alférez began exploring Leda while studying in Chicago, and he continued to return to her throughout his career; multiple extant works include a drawing in his family collection and a carved marble and concrete composite, produced in 1975, in the holdings of the New Orleans Museum of Art. These illustrate his inspirations and are examples of how his study of a particular work affected his craft. From Correggio's *Leda*, for example, Alférez learned skillful attention to chiaroscuro, a treatment of shading that reveals the volume of an object or depth in an image.[12]

Alférez was productive through his entire life, and although art trends changed around him, the figurative sculpture he created at the end of his career maintained an aesthetic consistent with some of his earliest works. He continued to borrow from his early influences: modernism, cubism, and art deco. His figures have long clean planes and lines, their bodies organized in geometric shapes, their hair often defined in clean lines or ropy, wavy. Other elements reveal the influence of cubism—high, inset eyelids and exaggerated or reduced body proportions, such as an elongated torso or a small head. In some cases, these distortions create the illusion of a proportional figure when viewed from a certain angle, revealing Alférez's appreciation for the role of depth in a viewer's interpretation of an object. Though his work continued to mature over the course of his career, he never let go of these styles. Bonner, writing in 2012, observed that even with such consistency in his art as the decades passed, "there is no sense of artistic stagnation."[13]

As Alférez's career progressed, he continued to advance in his ability to capture emotion in physical features: using the angle of a figure's head, the placement of hands, or the intensity of muscles to connote confidence or calmness. Consider, for example, the earliest extant panels of female figures whose facial features and hair—with clean lines and well-articulated topknots—are similar in concept to those that he created approximately fifty years later. Though elements remained the same, the facial features became much more expressive, giving a viewer an ability to read the emotion of a sculpture. Compare, for example, the advancement of his skill in revealing emotion in the face of the woman in Shriever Fountain (1932) with his *Pas de Deux* (ca. 1982).

Beyond his growth in his ability to represent tone and emotion, Alférez advanced in his ability to create more gravity-defying works. He saw gravity as an enemy of the sculptor, always wanting to take down that which a sculptor wanted to keep up.[14]

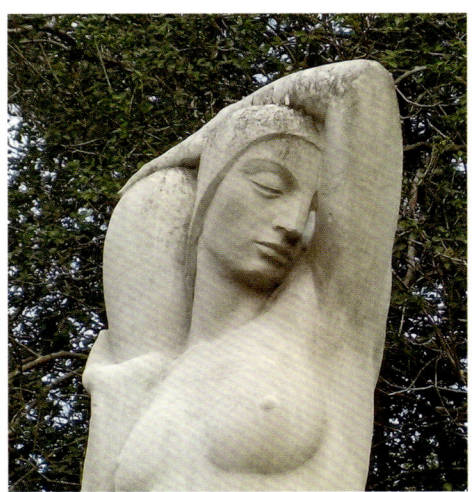

Shriever Fountain (detail) [1932]
photo by Alison Cody

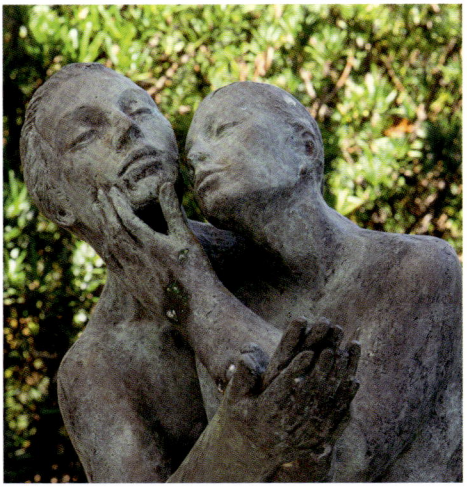

Pas de Deux in The Helis Foundation
Enrique Alférez Sculpture Garden [ca.1982]
photo by Keely Merritt, THNOC
ON LOAN FROM THE HELIS FOUNDATION

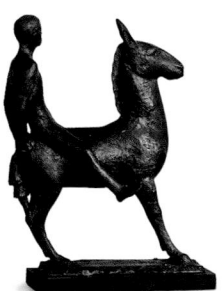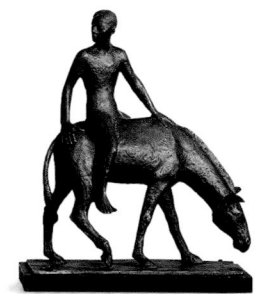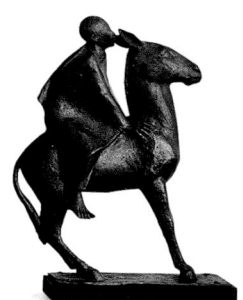

Youth on Burros [ca. 1970s]
photo by Donn Young
COURTESY OF THE COLLECTION OF TLALOC S. ALFÉREZ, MD

By the 1970s and 1980s, Alférez was modeling elegant figures of gymnasts, dancers, and bathers who seemed to defy that natural force. In some cases, a figure is balanced on a single hand.

Alférez's career can be organized into four periods, the first of which was from about 1924 until 1943, his most prolific period as a public artist. During this time, he formally studied sculpture in Chicago and began working as a professional artist, making many bas-reliefs and figurative sculptures through programs that drew support from federal, state, or municipal funds. During these years, Alférez kept a busy pace of production, creating some of his most memorable works, including the *Fountain of the Four Winds* at the New Orleans Lakefront Airport—a group of four nine-foot cast-concrete mythical figures representing the North, East, South, and West Winds—and more than twenty figures and sculptural elements at New Orleans City Park, many of which can be seen in the Botanical Garden.

The second stage of Alférez's career was from about 1943 until the early 1950s, primarily spent in New York. During this time, Alférez focused on other mediums, creating furniture, most often chairs made of wood and leather, and accessories such as women's handbags, belts, and shoes. This shift was influenced by the Second World War, with the redirection of public funds and limitations on metal. Alférez also served in the war through the US Army Transport Service. Near the end of this period, he turned back toward figurative sculpture for public installations.

Alférez experienced an abrupt shift in his career in 1951 when a commission for a public building in New Orleans soured and led to public controversy. Though he had sporadic public commissions during the decades to follow, he turned more decidedly toward creating smaller figures that have proved to be significant in his legacy as an artist. Many of these smaller figures produced during the third stage of his career—from the mid-1950s until 1981—are in private collections; there are more than sixty-five in Tlaloc Alférez's collection. These figures include bathers, lovers, and dancers, as well as two important series that reveal ties to his homeland: cast bronze youth on burros; and charros, traditional horsemen who participated in the charrería, or the rodeo, which is said to have originated in Alférez's home state of Zacatecas, Mexico.[15]

The final period of Alférez's career commenced with his return to the Botanical Garden at City Park in New Orleans in 1981; he was hired to restore art that had fallen into disrepair since he had initially created it in the 1930s, and to add new pieces to the garden as well.[16] He also had an exhibition at the New Orleans Museum of Art in 1981. In the following years, Alférez remained remarkably productive, creating some of his most iconic life-size and larger-than-life-size sculptures in public spaces, such as *David* and the *Lute Player*, on Poydras Street, and a monument to the educator and philanthropist Sophie B. Wright, on Magazine Street.

Throughout his career, Alférez's unyielding commitment to the craft of sculpture remained constant. He was usually in his studio by sunrise, working for ten to twelve hours a day, and he approached his craft with discipline, whether he was pursuing professional commissions or creating the figures that came from his heart and imagination. He saw his sculpture as his livelihood, and as what he called his "labor."[17]

José Enrique Alférez y Guzmán was born on May 4, 1903, in San Miguel del Mezquital (now Miguel Auza), in the northwestern part of Zacatecas, Mexico.[18] He was the youngest child of Longinos and Clotilde; there were nine children, six of whom survived through youth, three boys and three girls.[19] As a child, Alférez

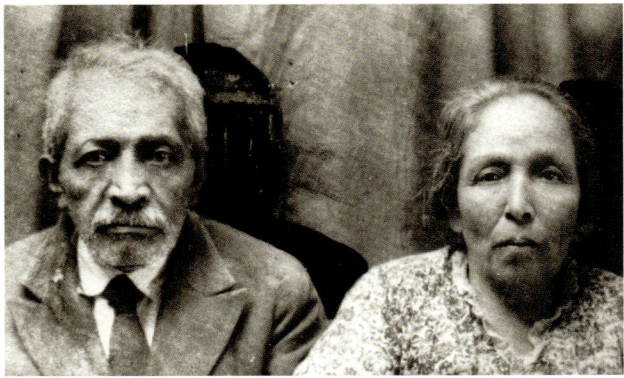

Longinos Alférez and Clotilde Guzmán
COURTESY OF THE TLALOC SELWAY ALFÉREZ PAPERS

went to school and helped care for the family livestock and tended to the crops. He also worked alongside his father, a sculptor, in his workshop. The entire family was involved in Longinos's sculpture, which was primarily focused on religious figures and carvings. From Longinos, Alférez and his siblings learned to draw, model, and carve.[20] The family also gathered materials together for Longinos's sculpture, sometimes while on picnics, seeking wood, clay, and cow dung with which to make plaster.[21]

By 1915, Alférez was swept into the Mexican Revolution, amongst the revolutionaries. Too young to be given a gun, he was assigned tasks such as giving water to the horses, drawing maps of enemy territory, and gathering wood as kindling for fires when the soldados and soldaderas stopped to make camp for the night. In his spare time, he carved small objects, such as statues of saints, and sold them to soldiers; a general observed his skills and assigned him to apprentice to the painter Mariano Hernández Arévalo, who had been hired to create a mural about the revolution. It was with Arévalo that Alférez crossed into the United States for the first time, in 1919, speaking no English. Alférez paid an eight-dollar head tax in El Paso and became a resident of the United States. This was more than twenty years before the United States issued green cards or legally defined "permanent resident" status, and it afforded him relative ease in traveling across the border for many years.[22]

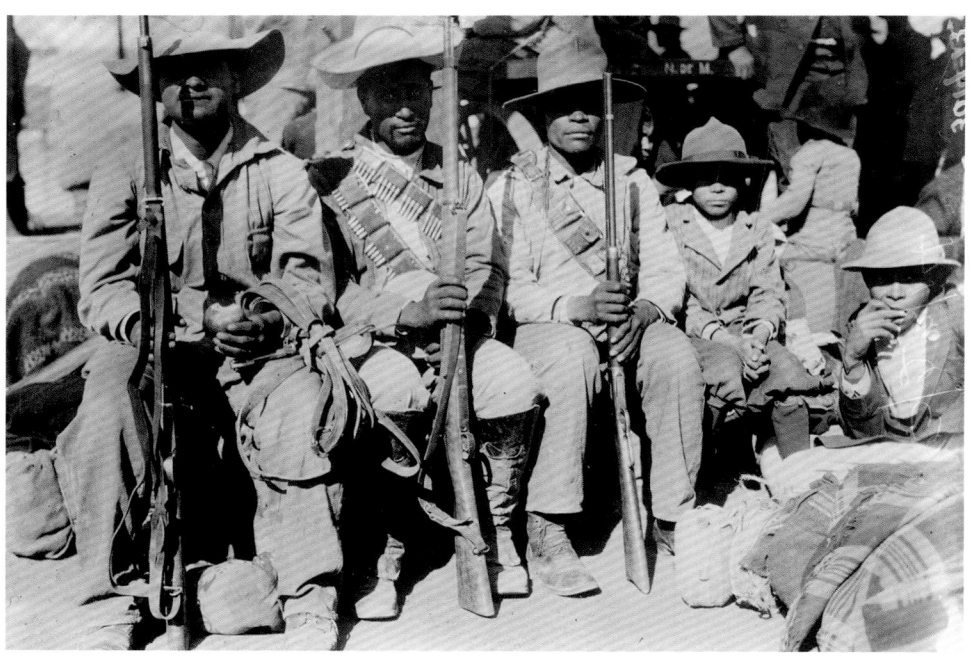

Men and boys under the command of Pancho Villa [1914]

photo by Bain News Service

COURTESY OF LIBRARY OF CONGRESS, PRINTS & PHOTOGRAPHS DIVISION, LC-DIG-GGBAIN-15727

In El Paso, Alférez became an assistant at the Fine Arts Shop and later worked as a photograph retoucher at Fred J. Feldman's photography studio. Both of these jobs introduced Alférez to artists in the community, and some of the relationships would prove supportive throughout his life. Through one such connection, Alférez received funding to study with Lorado Taft at the School of the Art Institute of Chicago. This preeminent public sculptor invited apprentices to live in his studio, where he taught them a range of skills and elements of craft. Alférez's 1924 arrival in Chicago coincided with the rise of art deco architecture in the city, and he created friezes, panels, and other decorative details in some of Chicago's prized art deco buildings, such as 333 North Michigan Avenue and the Palmolive Building.

By 1929, Alférez left Chicago for Yucatán, by way of New Orleans. He was most likely accompanied by Evelyn Kelly, a journalist whom he had met while living in Chicago. Short on funds and eager for work, Alférez delayed his departure for Mexico and was quickly absorbed into the arts community in the French Quarter. He was involved with the Arts and Crafts Club, which had been established a decade earlier to give artists a place to work, learn, and socialize. Not long after his arrival, he married Kelly, in May, and started his first job in Louisiana, a series of religious figures for Holy Name of Mary Catholic Church in Algiers.[23]

Alférez befriended Tulane University archaeologist Frans Blom, who frequently delivered talks and showed photos from his Latin American research expeditions at the Arts and Crafts Club and also lived near Alférez in the French Quarter. Blom was commissioned to create a reproduction of an important Maya site in Yucatán for the 1933–34 Century of Progress Exposition in Chicago, and he invited Alférez to join his research team. The trip was a milestone in Alférez's career, giving him a group with which to collaborate and helping him gain agency as an artist; his observations there played a key role in Blom's analysis of the site.

Before returning to New Orleans from Yucatán in 1930, Alférez sought a divorce from Kelly on the grounds that they were incompatible.[24] Ten days after the divorce was granted, Alférez married New Orleanian Rose Marie Huth. Alférez and Rose Marie had a daughter, Cloe, born in 1931. Alférez was an inattentive husband and father in these early years. It was not uncommon for him be out carousing instead of being with his family. By 1933, he and Rose Marie separated, and by 1935 Rose

FOLLOWING PAGES:
Research team posed on platform of North Building of Nunnery Quadrangle
(back row, left to right: Enrique Alférez, Frans Blom, Herndon Fair, Ciriaco Aguilar;
front row, left to right: William Hayden, Gerhard Kramer, Daniel Sweeney Leyrer,
Pablo Pantoja, Robert H. Merrill) [1930]
photo by Daniel Sweeney Leyrer
COURTESY OF THE MIDDLE AMERICAN RESEARCH INSTITUTE, TULANE UNIVERSITY

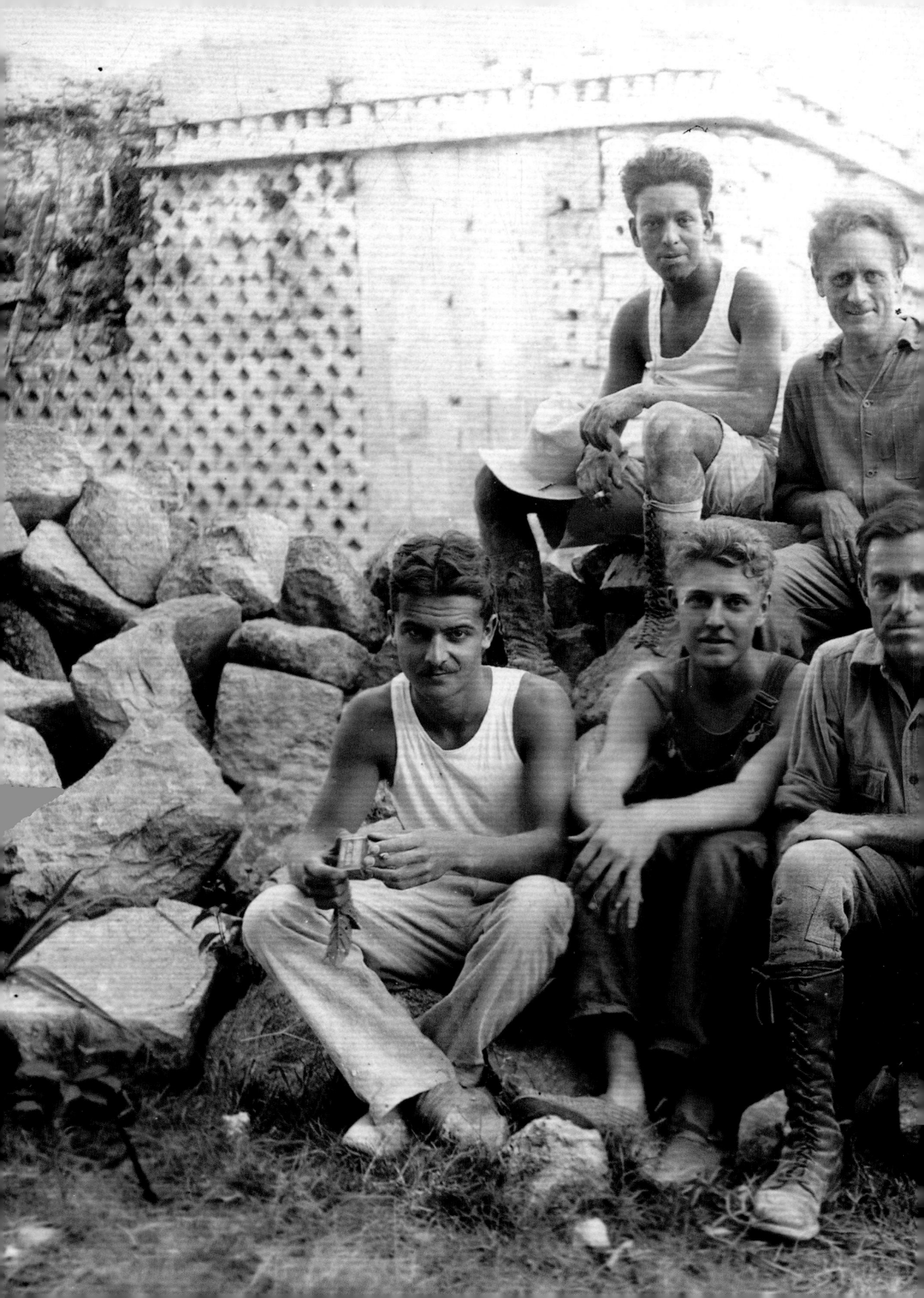

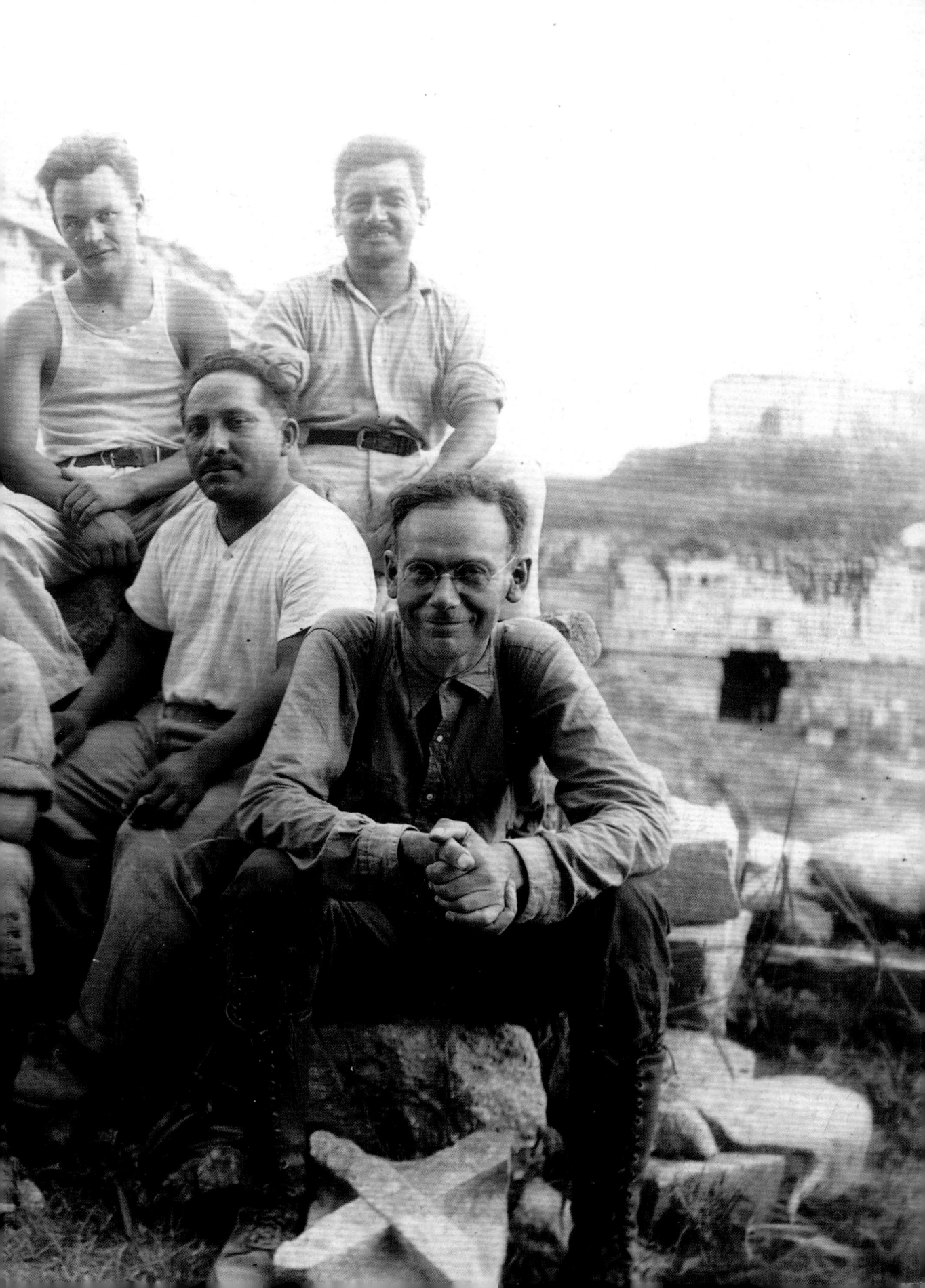

Marie was granted a divorce and custody of Cloe, who was raised by her maternal grandmother. Despite the difficulties of this early period, Alférez and Rose Marie later rekindled a friendship that came to include Alférez's fourth wife, Margaret "Peggy" Selway, and their daughter, Tlaloc. By the early 1940s, Alférez met his third wife on a visit to California, a model whom Alférez's friends knew by the name of Judy.[25] They lived together in California, in New Orleans, and likely in New York. It is unknown when their relationship ended, as there are few extant records about it. Alférez and Peggy's marriage license, issued in 1953, states that he was a widower and that the prior marriage ended in 1951; it's unclear whether the couple was still together at the time of Judy's death.

Alférez lived in Greenwich Village from about 1943 until about 1950. He served in the US Army Transport Service from 1943 until 1944, shipping out from New York to deliver tugs to the European war front.[26] He also ran a leather goods shop in the Village, turning toward women's fashion and accessories. He had a studio and apartment at 130 Christopher Street.[27] From his apartment, it was about a fifteen-minute walk to his shop at 110 Macdougal, much of it down Bleecker Street, past the pushcarts with fresh fruit and vegetables, past the carts of pastries and cheese, and past the bakeries, turning down Macdougal Street to reach a small storefront painted white, where the sidewalk provided space to spread out handmade bags, shoes, and belts to draw visitors inside.

Alférez had five assistants in his shop. They crafted accessories from cowhide, including shoulder bags, belts, and sandals, many of which were molded rather than cut and stitched into shape. Belt buckles could be spiral shaped, and were reminiscent of sculptures and jewelry by Alexander Calder, an observation noted in the fashion magazine *Junior Bazaar* in 1946.[28] The Alférez family collection contains leather goods he continued to create: canteen cases and portfolios among bags and belts.

During this period Alférez also made furniture, which was sold in New York and through magazine advertisements in publications including *Vogue*. The chairs and other pieces of furniture frequently included a blend of wood, leather, and brass fittings. Few details are available about these projects. In fact, very few personal records from the 1940s or earlier survive; Alférez burned his papers before he shipped out with the US Army Transport Service. Additionally, left to his own devices, Alférez was not a particularly good record keeper, although his fortune in this regard would change in years to come, when he married Peggy Selway, who kept prodigious records on his behalf.

Life in Greenwich Village gave Alférez an intriguing circle of artist and writer friends in the neighborhood and beyond. He befriended Patricia Blake, a model who later pursued a pioneering career in journalism and publishing, becoming a scholar of Soviet affairs and Russian literature, and the composer Nicolas Nabokov, among

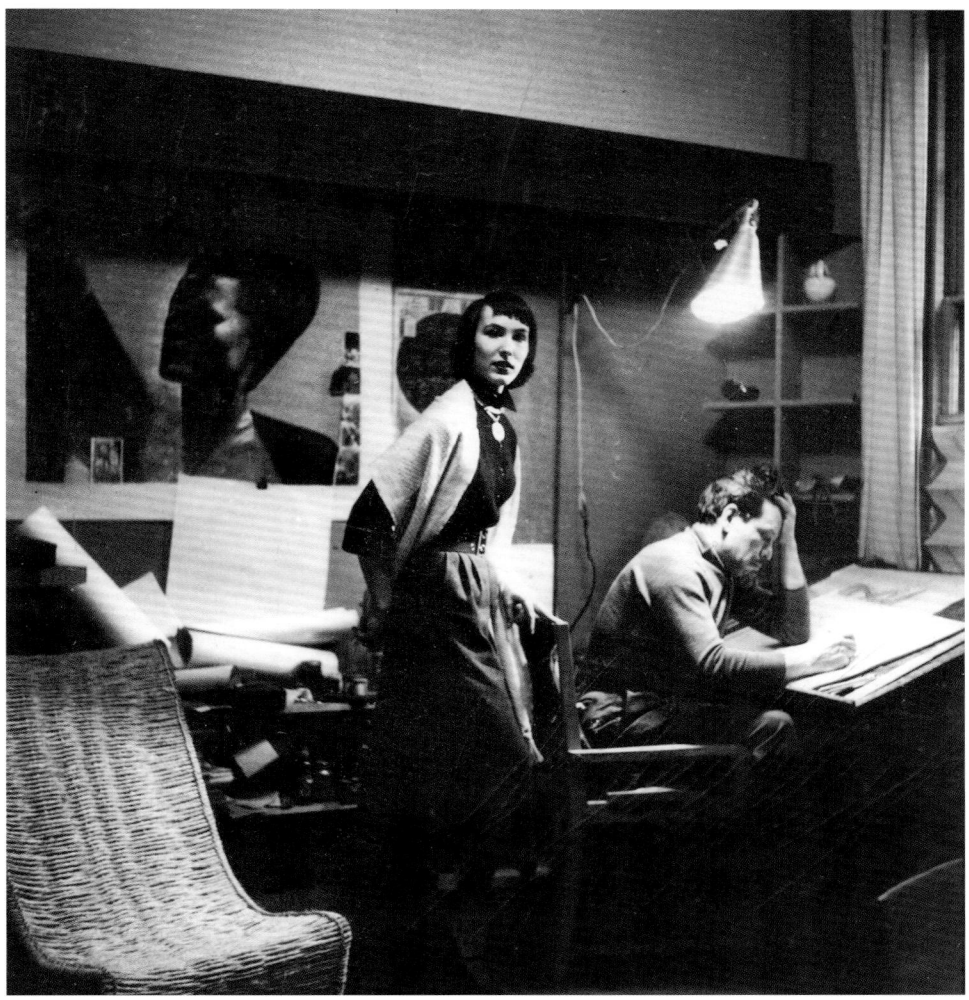

Alférez, likely in New York [1940s]
COURTESY OF THE TLALOC SELWAY ALFÉREZ PAPERS

others. In 1946, a young photographer arrived on Macdougal to photograph Alférez at the shop for a feature in *Junior Bazaar*. Photographer Arnold Newman had moved to New York the same year he met Alférez. He went on to become recognized as a paragon of environmental portraitists, creating some of the most memorable portraits of his time, with iconic images of Igor Stravinsky, Pablo Picasso, Georgia O'Keeffe, John F. Kennedy, and Berenice Abbott among them.

Alférez rarely shared details about his years in New York, likely because it was a period marked with significant personal challenges, including immigration problems. He had traveled to Mexico in 1942, and when he wanted to return to the United States in 1943, his immigration status became more complicated than it had been at any other time. He was required to submit extensive documentation and letters of support to regain entry. The process would have been an arduous one for Alférez, whose strengths did not rest in the organization of documents. And once he was able to return, he had other dilemmas: he confided to a friend in New York, for example, that he missed his daughter Cloe, who lived in New Orleans. Moreover, many years later, Alférez said that he had lost a son "during World War II." Peggy, Tlaloc, and Cloe were all aware that Alférez carried a closely held heartbreak from this period for the rest of his life, but they have been unable to provide further details about a son.[29]

It is poignant that his next major work focused on a family: a joined figure of mother, father, and child. Alférez returned to New Orleans around 1950 to work on *The Family,* which was to be installed on the exterior of a municipal building. He likely approached the job with enthusiasm, given that funds for public sculpture had dried up in the prior decade, but the experience proved deeply distressing. When *The Family* was unveiled in 1951, the figures' nudity set off a controversy that crept into newspapers across the country and in Canada, and Alférez was afraid he would never receive another commission. The fear was well founded; his commissions for public figures and architectural details remained sporadic for the next three decades.[30]

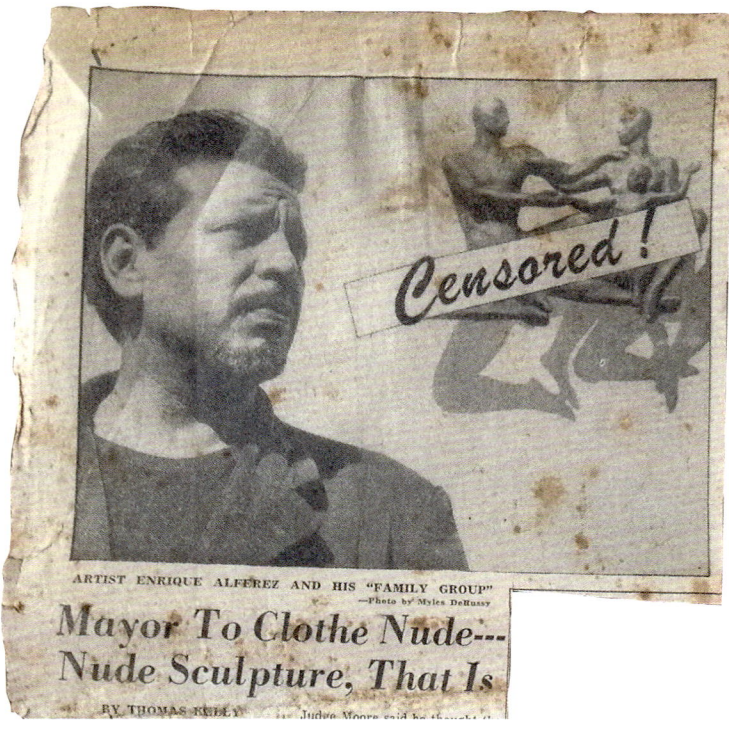

New Orleans Item article about *The Family* [1951]

IMAGE COURTESY OF THE TLALOC SELWAY ALFÉREZ PAPERS; *NEW ORLEANS ITEM*, FEBRUARY 22, 1951,
CAPITAL CITY PRESS/GEORGES MEDIA GROUP, BATON ROUGE, LA

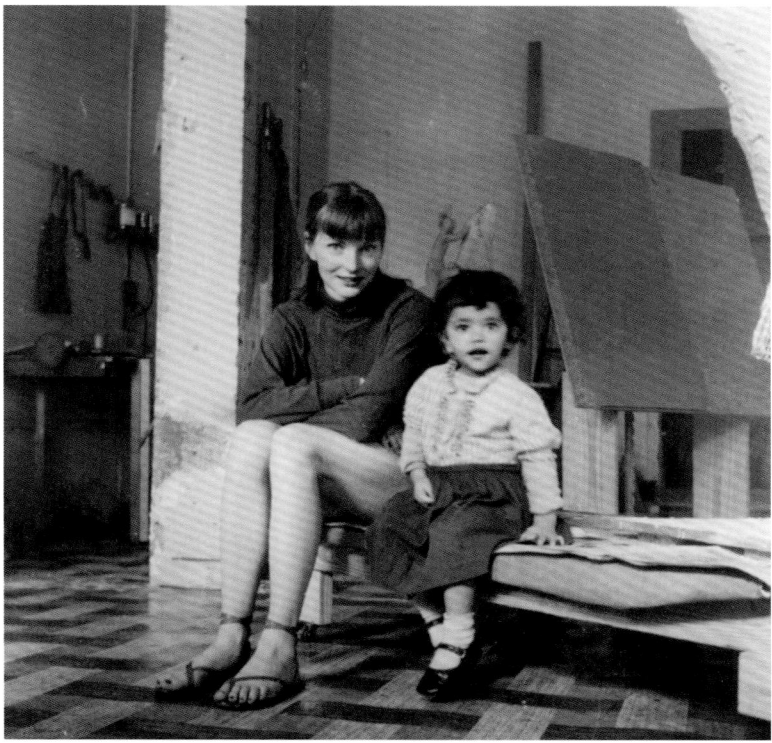

Peggy and Tlaloc Alférez [1956]
COURTESY OF THE TLALOC SELWAY ALFÉREZ PAPERS

If there was a bright spot in this dark period of Alférez's life, it was Peggy. They met in 1952 at Lafitte's Blacksmith Shop,[31] where Alférez's sculpture *Adam and Eve* depicted a couple locked in an embrace, lying in a garden. Alférez and Peggy married in 1953 and their daughter, Tlaloc, was born the next year. In Peggy, Alférez found enduring love and a lifelong companion, a best friend, a business partner, and an advocate.

Peggy was stalwart in her support of Alférez's sculpture. She researched with and for him; she made frequent trips to the library, canvassed art magazines, always looking for new methods, patinas, tools, and sources of inspiration. She read to him while he sculpted, carved, raked, and cross-hatched his textures, sometimes from weeks-old issues of the Sunday *New York Times*, and she selected music to play while Alférez built up armatures, sculpted clay, and refined his figures—filling the studio with opera and classical music, the sounds of a flute or guitar, woodwinds, chamber music, and Gregorian chants. She collected papers related to his career, such as receipts for supplies, exhibition invitations, bids, drawings, and notes from visitors, former models, and fellow artists. She kept ledgers and lists of sales and guests at openings, as well as notes about the collectors of Alférez's works.

From the early 1950s until the early 1980s, Alférez received fewer commissions than he had in the first stage of his career for large-scale public works, and he began creating small figures. During this time, he and his family also made a life across two geographies, sharing time between New Orleans and parts of Mexico including the states of Colima, San Luis Potosí, Veracruz, and Michoacán, as well as Mexico City. They established a home and studio in each destination, frequently in the capital or largest city, and alternated between destinations as called by the seasons, work, desire, or financial prospects and needs. But it was in New Orleans and Morelia that the Alférez family set their firmest roots.

Alférez continued to receive occasional commissions during these decades and worked on the pieces both at a home studio in Mexico and in New Orleans. Among

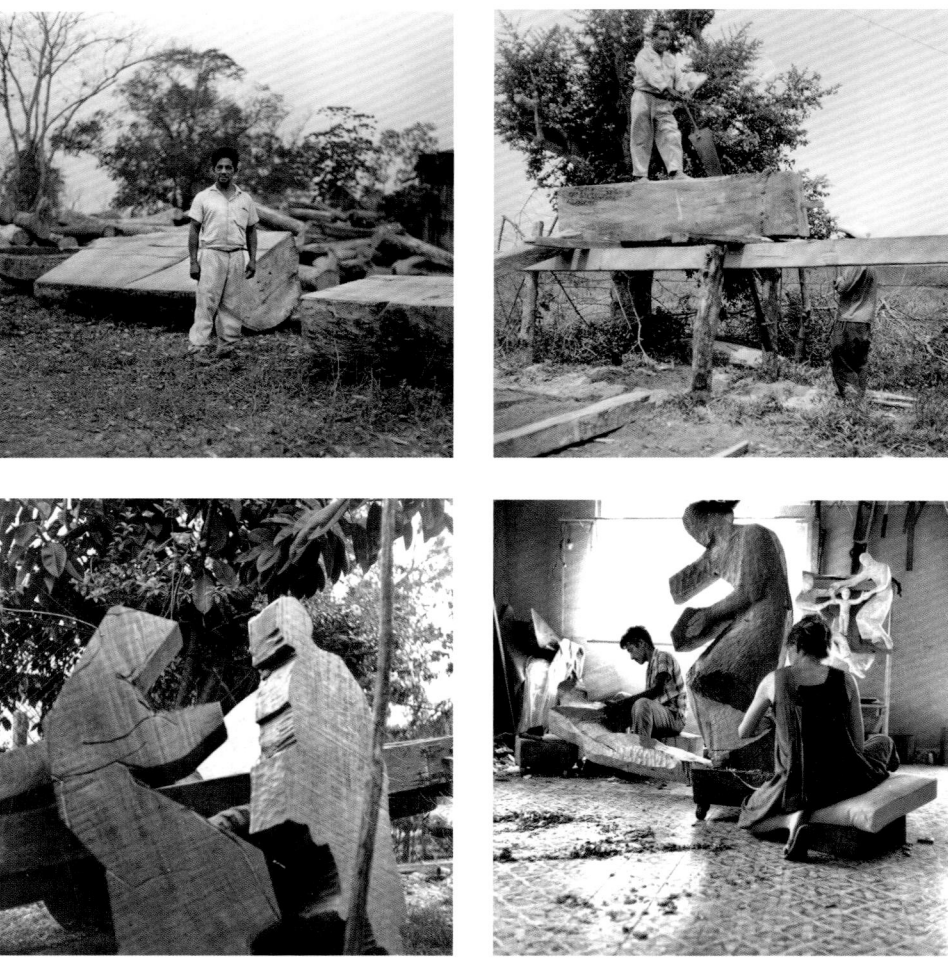

Peggy and assistants harvesting and carving mahogany
for Mobile General Hospital figures in Tuxpan, Mexico [ca. 1962]
COURTESY OF THE COLLECTION OF TLALOC S. ALFÉREZ, MD

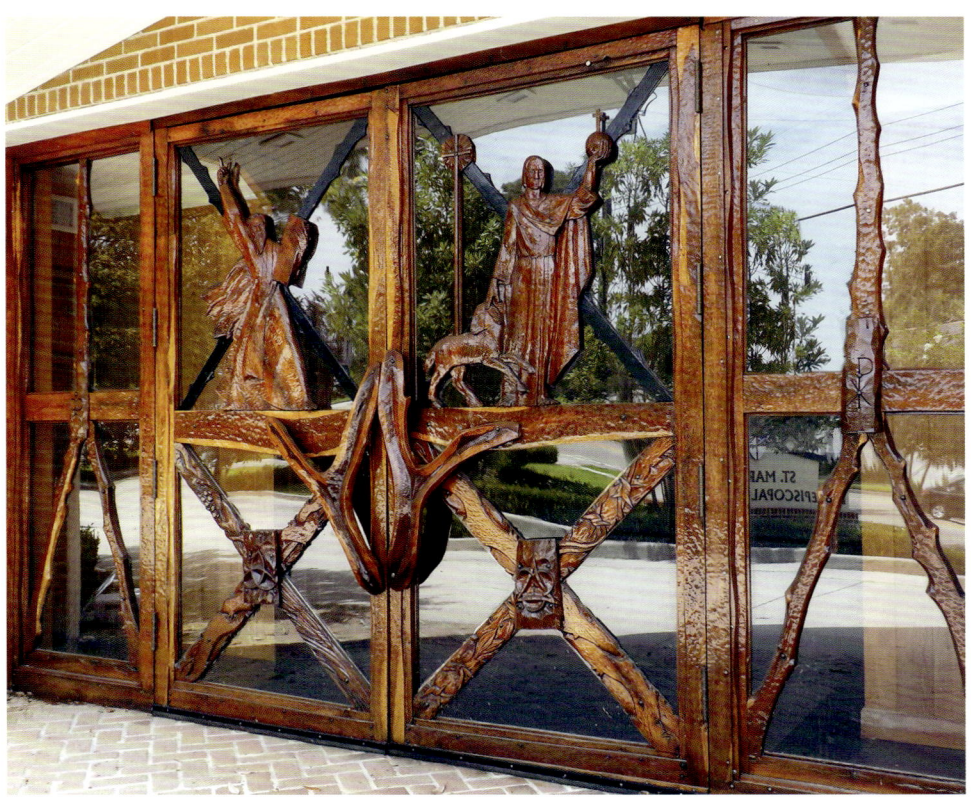

Entrance to Saint Martin's Episcopal Church [1959]
photo by Alison Cody

these projects were crosses, carved doors that feature Moses and Christ as deliverers of the Old and New Testaments, and other installations for Saint Martin's Church in Metairie, Louisiana, in 1959;[32] and six life-sized figures representing medical service and education for the Mobile General Hospital (now University Hospital) in Mobile, Alabama, in 1963. For these commissions, Alférez used mahogany, oak, and rosewood, much of which came from trees he felled himself and worked with from cut to finish.

Another significant work from this time is *Symbols of Communication*, a textured wall panel for the *Times-Picayune* newspaper's former headquarters on Howard Avenue in New Orleans, created in 1967–68. Though Alférez benefited financially from projects such as these, he became increasingly dependent on sales of smaller figures to private collectors.

World affairs of the late 1960s, including the Vietnam War, Martin Luther King Jr.'s assassination, and general unrest, prompted Alférez to return to Mexico on a more full-time basis. He was also deeply agitated by the Tlatelolco Massacre in Mexico City in 1968, a horrific event in which protestors were killed by military and police. The incident, which occurred less than two weeks prior to the 1968 Summer Olympics in Mexico City, unfolded during a period of violent government oppression of political opposition. It was a time in Mexico's history when "rumors trumped facts, propaganda masqueraded as news, and government officials were accountable to no one."[33] Alférez was also increasingly uncomfortable with US foreign policy; this, coupled with mistreatment of people of color, must have struck him at a very personal level. Despite his attempts to become a naturalized citizen, this country was not *his*, after all.

In 1969, Alférez and Peggy returned to a studio he had built with modest living amenities near a hillside in Pátzcuaro, Michoacán, only to find it burned down. They then rented a house in Pátzcuaro for a few months before finding another rental about forty miles away, on the town square in Santa María, in a hilly area in what was then the outskirts of Morelia, also in Michoacán. Here, in 1971, Alférez had a life-altering experience.

He and Peggy had arrived home with a packed trailer attached to their International Harvester Scout; Alférez pushed the trailer away from the Scout and into the yard, and though typically an immediate and thorough unpacker, he delayed, feeling a bit unsteady. He thought his uneasy feeling was due to the long drive, and he told Peggy that rather than unloading, they should run an errand and make a deposit at the bank.

When they arrived at the bank, Alférez sat down in the lobby to endorse a check. He held a pen in his hand and turned over the check, trying to place his signature on the line. The line was visible, but he failed to transfer the idea of his name from his brain to his hand. He later said that at that moment, he felt like the ground was coming to meet him. Instead of revealing his distress, he turned to Peggy and asked her to sign the check.

Peggy, who had been a nurse at Columbia-Presbyterian Medical Center in New York City, immediately recognized that Alférez was having a stroke. She rushed him home and tried to stabilize him. Health care options in Morelia were limited at the time, and she knew she needed to find a doctor. Peggy went to the nearby home of family friends, the Shoemakers, who had the largest business in town, manufacturing furniture. She knew they had a telephone. Before leaving home, though, Peggy began monitoring Alférez's blood pressure and trying to get it under control.

At the Shoemakers', she called New Orleans–based sculptor Arthur Silverman, whom Alférez had befriended and mentored. Silverman was also a urologist, and through professional medical connections he was able to identify a neurologist in Guadalajara. In the meantime, Alférez's blood pressure began stabilizing, but he could no longer speak and was paralyzed on the right side of his body.

Over the following twelve hours, Peggy continued efforts to lower Alférez's blood pressure. She fed him soups without salt and gave him papaya.

The next day, she and Alférez traveled nearly two hundred miles by bus to Guadalajara to see the neurologist. By this point, his speech was coming back, but he was weak, and he still had limited use of the right side of his body. At the doctor's office, he was given medication to continue lowering his blood pressure.

Without question, Alférez's life's work was a labor of the hand. He had disciplined his hands to instruct the textures of wood, clay, plaster, and leather, and he had fine motor skills that allowed him to carve and shape with chisels, rasps, and other tools, some of which he had made with his own hands as well. He had worked his hands to the point that he wore his fingerprints down beyond recognition.[34] But suddenly, the ends of his arms had unfamiliar appendages that he couldn't command into action.

Alférez improved in the following months. Peggy, still a nurse at heart, organized his physical therapy regimen. Much of his retraining occurred in domestic household chores, such as hemming Tlaloc's school skirts.[35]

Alférez never fully recovered. The stroke continued to prevent him from regaining a full range of motion in his right arm. Despite this, he taught himself to draw again, beginning with his left hand before moving on to his right, and his family papers include sketches that demonstrate the process of relearning a skill that had come so easily to him for many decades. Despite this setback, Alférez went on to create some of the most memorable figures and statues in his career, such as the *Flute Player*, now in the Botanical Garden at City Park, and series of gymnasts and bathers.

As his recovery continued, Alférez and Peggy began searching for a home of their own and found one within a year. Just a few blocks from the square in Santa María where their rental house was located, on a narrow street called Antonio Plaza, Alférez found an old house that had been long neglected. The first time he took Peggy and Tlaloc to see it, he placed a ladder on one side of the property's wall so they could climb over and into the brush and thick vegetation that he had begun cutting back earlier with a machete and which he cleared further as they walked together through the yard, toward the house. The vegetation was so thick that they rarely knew what was just a few feet ahead of them. In the days to follow, the family cleared more, and echoed one another's surprise when, through a break in the overgrowth, they came face to face with a stone dragon nearly twice their height.

The dragon was a cistern and watering system. Rainwater collected in an open barrel—the body of the dragon—then drained through waterspouts that led to different parts of the garden. According to a neighbor, the dragon had possibly been a water source for the community many years earlier.[36] By the time the Alférezes lived in the house, a public water spigot at Templo de Santa María de Guido,

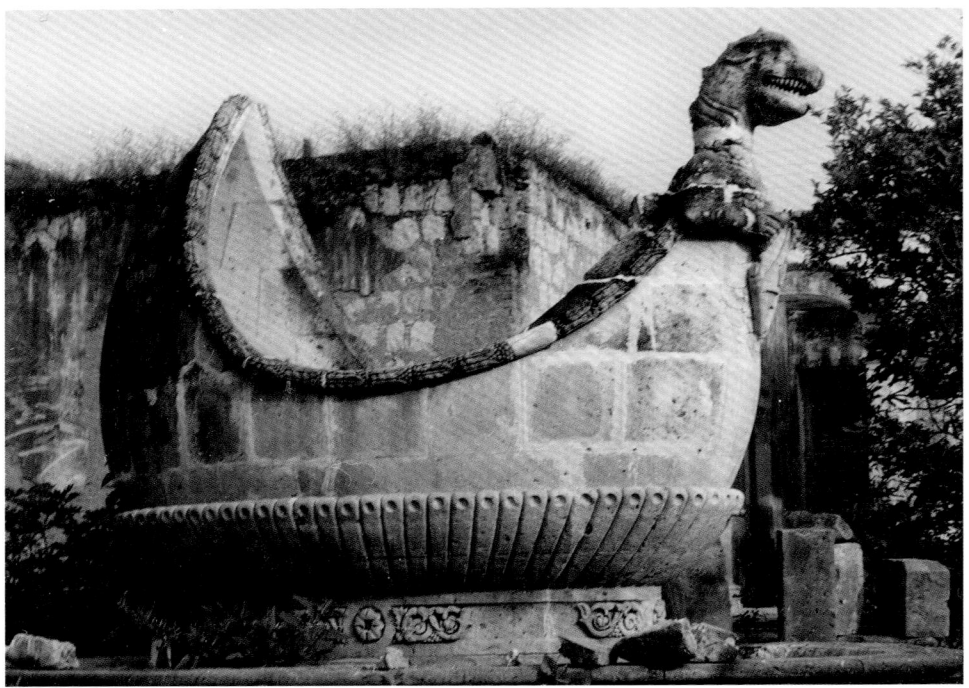

Dragon cistern at the Alférez home in Santa María de Guido, Morelia [1970]
COURTESY OF THE TLALOC SELWAY ALFÉREZ PAPERS

just a block away, served the community—and during their first year in residence, the Alférezes, too, gathered buckets of water from the church while renovating their home.

Alférez worked by hand on the house and yard and hired laborers from the area as well. He established a home, studio, and foundry, and he had ample space in which to live and work. He and Peggy cultivated the land, filling the yard with trees and plants: lime, avocado, coffee, persimmon, pear, and pomegranate among them. Sheaths of bamboo clapped and rattled with the wind while Alférez toiled in his studio, beginning early as morning light crept through the windows. He carved doors and architectural details and restored the home with elements reminiscent of his mentor Lorado Taft's studio, such as filtered skylights, which brought in so much sun that visitors often thought they needed to turn off lights before they left a room.

The Alférezes filled the home with guests—friends who traveled from the United States to visit, others from the local community or expats living nearby, and some of the area's prominent left-leaning politicians. They often hosted Cuauhtémoc Cárdenas, a Mexican senator, who would later serve as governor of the state of Michoacán and as head of the government of Mexico City and who ran unsuccessfully for president of the country.[37] On occasion, after public events, he would retire in the evening, along with his family, to enjoy a drink with the Alférezes at their home, surrounded by plaster models, carved figures, and the evening sounds of Santa María.[38] Beyond the wall of the Alférezes' home stood a neighborhood with adoquín streets, with houses and small shops such as a bakery and market, food stalls with roasted corn, tortilla makers working on outdoor comals, and fruit stands with produce from nearby farms. In short, Alférez and his family felt at home.

Between 1971 and 1984, when the Alférezes bought a house of their own in New Orleans, they returned to the city periodically, renting a series of houses on Saint Peter Street in the French Quarter. The neighborhood shared similarities with Santa María, where houses stood shoulder to shoulder with small markets and shops, and with comparably textured soundscapes, even if altogether different worlds: the distinguished bells of hallowed churches in New Orleans, which stood in contrast to the unpretentious banging of the bell at Templo de Santa María de Guido. There were other contrasting sounds too: the clack of mules and buggies in the Quarter, the loudspeakers of gas delivery trucks announcing the day's prices in Santa María;

Night at the Alférez home, Santa María de Guido, Morelia
photo by Donn Young

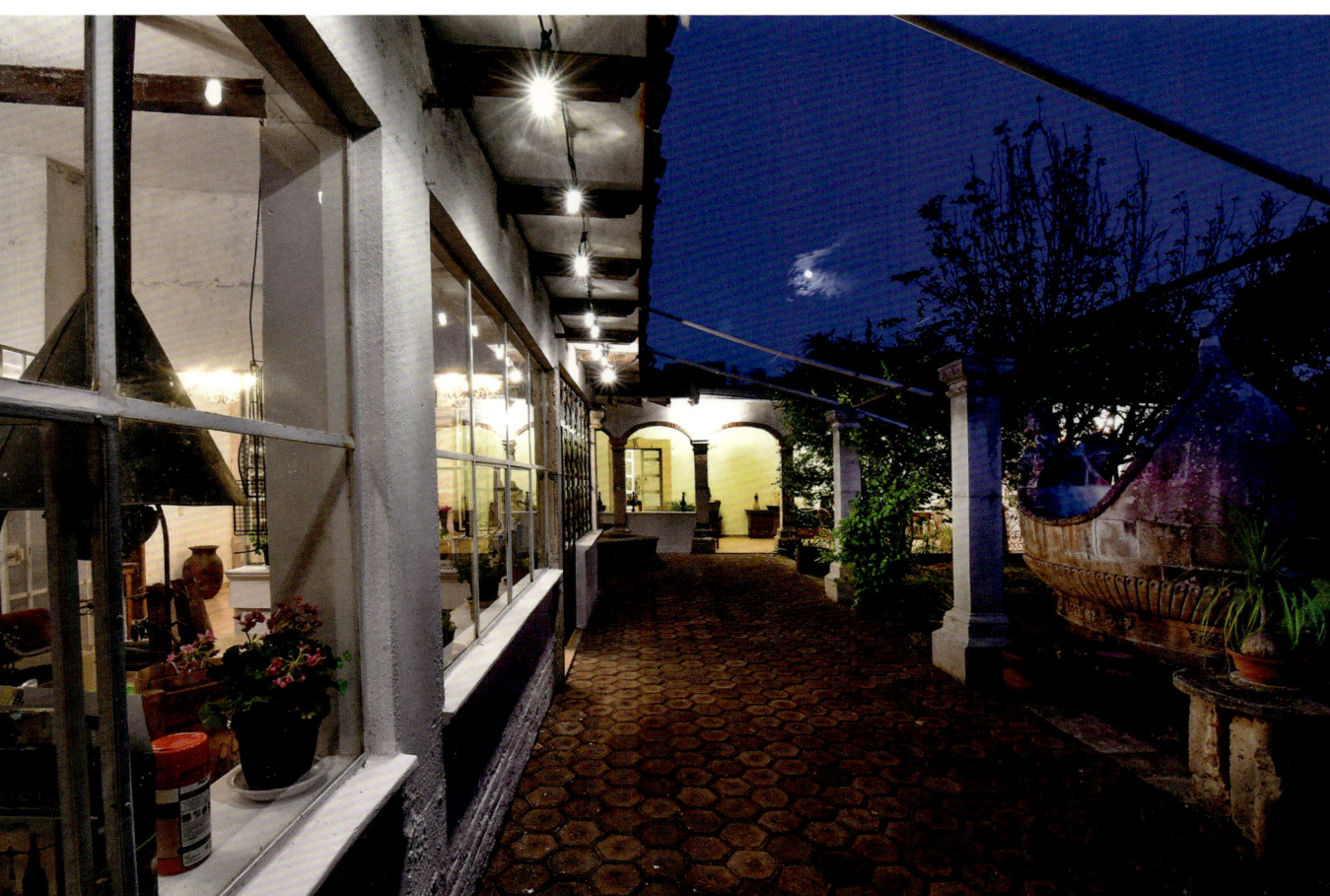

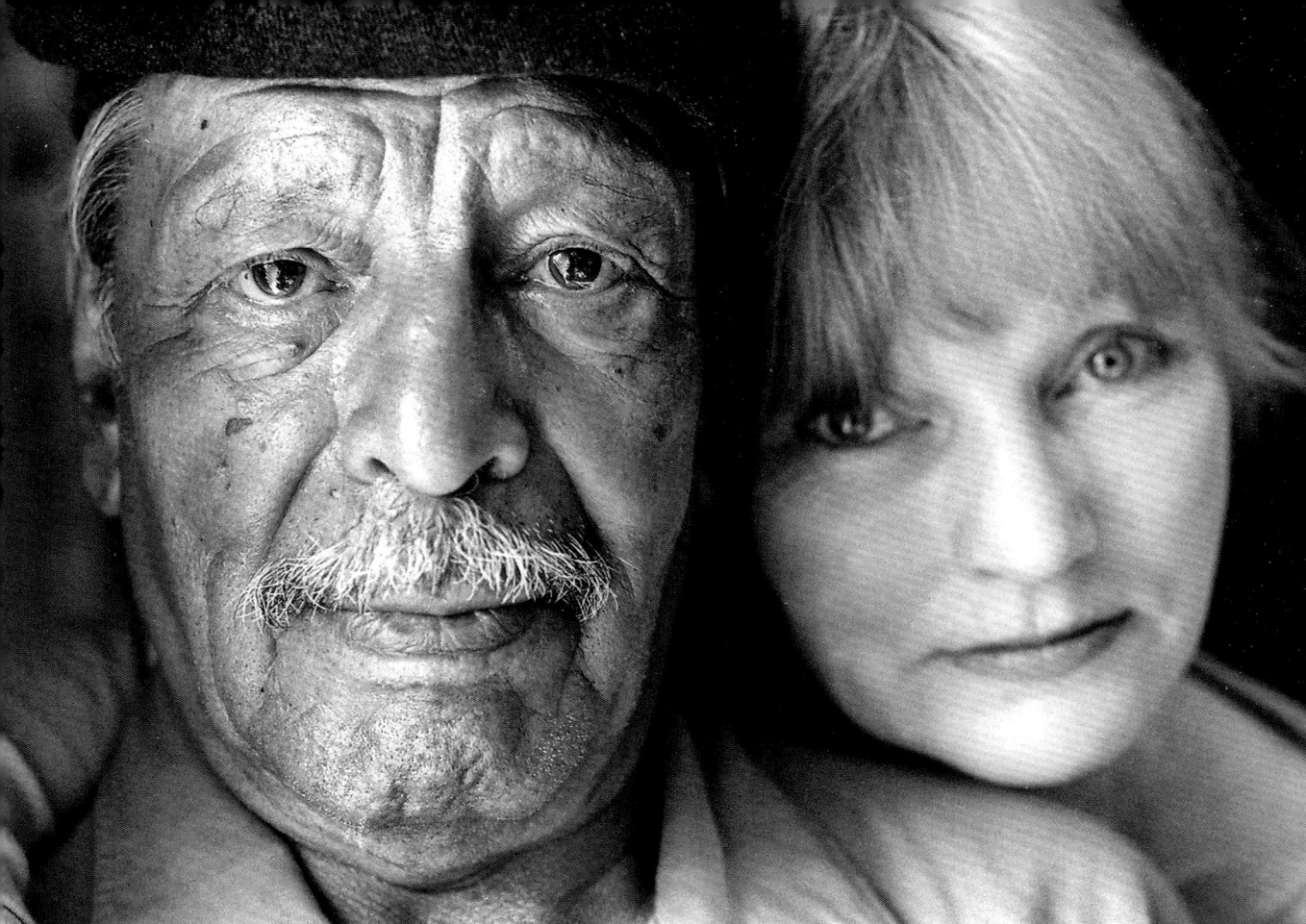

Enrique and Peggy Alférez [ca. 1980]
photo by Donn Young

the calliope of a New Orleans steamboat, the crowing of roosters long after dawn in Santa María. Alférez and his family lived between these two worlds, their frequent moves prompted by economics: one destination offering income, the other a less expensive lifestyle and raw materials.

Before returning to Mexico for longer periods of residence, Alférez had to decide what to do with the art he produced in New Orleans, since the family didn't have a permanent place to live or store belongings until 1984. Tlaloc noted that the family lacked resources to rent sufficient secure storage space. Sometimes he would give works away to friends or sell them below cost, but he and Peggy recognized that both steps could flood the market and diminish values.[39] Other times he destroyed his work with his own hands, causing Peggy much distress.

One evening in 1973, New Orleanians Willa and Timothy Slater were leaving the symphony and ran into an agitated Peggy walking the family dog on the edges of the French Quarter, where the Alférezes were living at the time. When asked what was wrong, Peggy said that she and Alférez would be returning to Morelia soon. The Slaters were perplexed by the response, given the frequency with which the Alférezes returned to Mexico and their impression that Peggy liked going. She acknowledged that the move itself wasn't the source of her concern; instead, she was worried that Alférez would do what he had done on their last return to Mexico: destroy his artwork and then take discards and debris to the dump.

This wasn't unusual; Alférez had been destroying his own work for many years, and in a sense had been trained to do so. Taft, his mentor in Chicago, taught his students by having them build up a clay piece in a day and then take it down, not an uncommon approach to teaching sculpture. But destroying completed works of art is quite different from pedagogical process.

Peggy's agitation likely stemmed from multiple sources: the loss of potential income had the pieces been sold, plus the loss of time and resources that had already

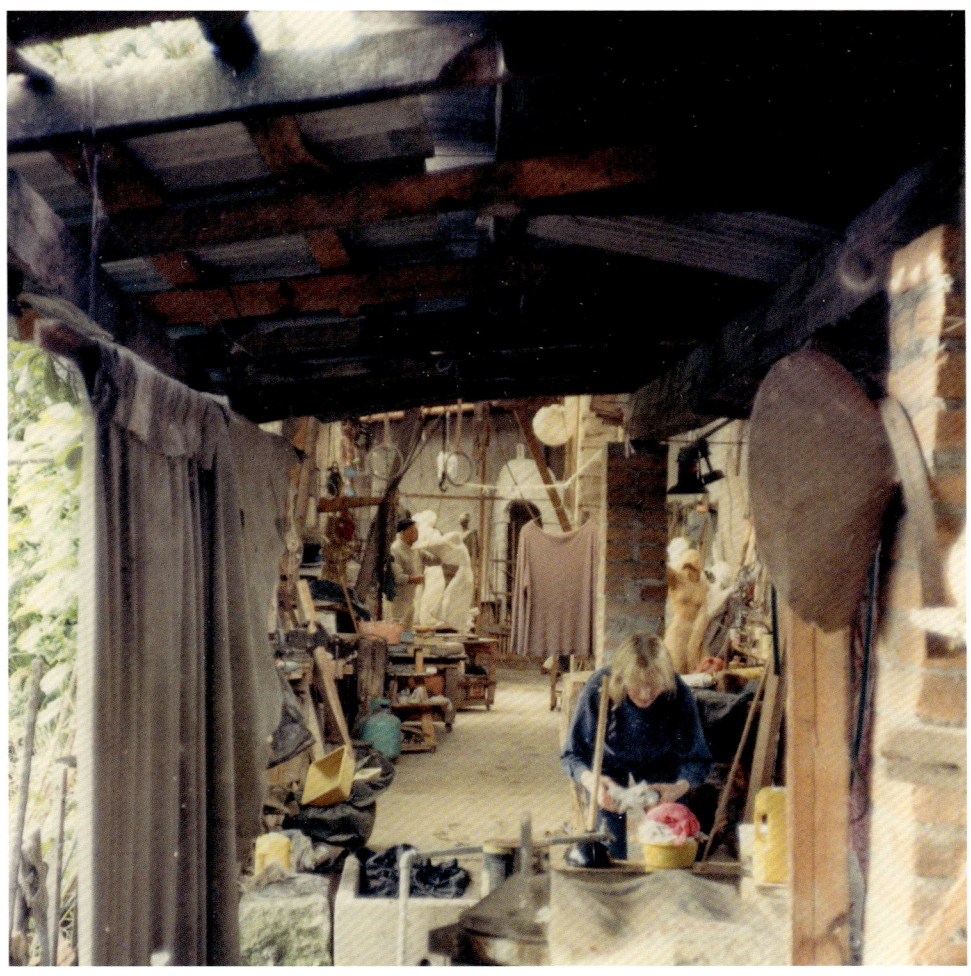

Enrique and Peggy at work in Morelia studio [1986]
photo by Jack Kerrigan
COURTESY OF THE FAMILY OF JACK KERRIGAN

been invested in the materials and production. Peggy was steadfast, if not hawkish, in her management of Alférez's business, and at a more emotional level, she was inextricably tied to his creative process.

That evening after the symphony, the Slaters offered to store figures at their house and sell them during gatherings they hosted; Willa, a corporate art buyer, frequently entertained in their Garden District house. Peggy and Alférez left twenty-seven figures at the Slaters' home, some of which were sold. What began as a storage solution became a new pattern in which Willa facilitated sales. Sometimes, the Alférezes would haul a trailer full of new works from Mexico and leave pieces with the Slaters, and many of their guests became buyers of Alférez's figures.[40] Alférez and Peggy subsequently took similar steps with other friends and "agents," returning from Mexico with his works and, on occasion, other traditional crafts from Mexico to sell, trunk-style, in the homes of friends.[41]

Alférez returned to New Orleans on a more permanent basis when he was invited to revisit some of his earliest pieces in the Botanical Garden at City Park in the early 1980s. Many of the works he had created in the 1930s had deteriorated,

Terra Cotta Head
COURTESY OF AN ANONYMOUS COLLECTOR

and the garden was undergoing a revitalization in advance of the 1984 world's fair in New Orleans. The commission to repair old works and create new ones rekindled his connection to the city, and in 1984, his family bought their first home in New Orleans, a former church on Eighth Street.

When Alférez lived in the house, it had the decided feel of a garage or workshop, with supplies, experimental casts, maquettes, tools—anvils, mallets, calipers, chisels, saws, drills, wire-end modeling tools, oversized scissors, and other shaping tools, many of them handmade or restored by Alférez—and dusty remnants of plaster interspersed throughout living spaces. Today, the only evidence of the workshop days is in the collection of Alférez's clean tools and papers.

Alférez's return to the city in the early 1980s marked a turning point in his life; though he was aging, he was still producing some of his most memorable large figures. He would go on to create the iconic *David* and the *Lute Player* on Poydras Street and the *Flute Player* in the Botanical Garden. He increasingly needed greater assistance in his studio, seeking support from assistants who could help move his figures or who could offer extra hands.[42] Since some of his statues are one-and-a-half to two times life-size, Alférez often used a ladder, scaffolding, or a lift to reach the top of a figure. He also made use of a post, to which a winch was attached, to move large, heavy parts of a figure.

Late in life, Alférez began earning greater external recognition for his art. He received a special lifetime achievement award in conjunction with the New Orleans Mayor's Arts Award in 1993; the Meritorious Public Service Medal, presented by Brigadier General Jon A. Gallinetti of the Marine Forces Reserve, in 1999; and one of his highest honors, the Palacio de Bellas Artes Medal, posthumously presented to Peggy by Gerardo Estrada Rodríguez, the director general of Mexico's Instituto Nacional de Bellas Artes y Literatura. One of his works in Morelia, a monument to Benito Juárez, was unveiled in a public ceremony presided over by Mexican President Miguel de la Madrid in 1984.[43] There were other markers of acclaim and honor in New Orleans: in 1991 Mayor Sidney J. Barthelemy proclaimed his birthday, May 4, "Enrique Alférez Day." In 1993, a street on the northeast side of the New Orleans Museum of Art was named Enrique Alférez Drive. There's also the Enrique Alférez Oak in the Botanical Garden; according to Tlaloc, the named oak was a particular thrill to this master carver.

Alférez's last stay at his home in Morelia was in 1998. When he and Peggy packed for the long journey back to the United States, he told his property caretaker, Antonio García, that he would not be returning to Santa María; his health was deteriorating, so this would be his final journey to New Orleans. But before he left, he told García something else: a secret that the caretaker would not divulge until more than fifteen years after Alférez's death; in the ground beneath the foundry, Alférez had buried works of art. As of the publication of this book, these works have not been exhumed.

In 1999, Alférez was exposed to cold weather during the long hours he spent outdoors to restore his monument *Molly Marine*. He contracted pneumonia, and his health weakened in the months to follow. Though he was able to return to his sculpture for a few months, he came down with pneumonia again around August and never fully recovered; just a few weeks before his death, he was diagnosed with lung cancer. Alférez died on September 13, 1999, at home with Peggy and Tlaloc by his side.[44]

Since his passing, the city of New Orleans has continued to celebrate his influence. In 2001, the New Orleans City Council proclaimed the month of May "Enrique Alférez Month." A float in the 2006 parade of the Carnival krewe Rex paid visual tribute to him, with papier-mâché replicas of iconic works. The Ogden Museum of Southern Art hosted two posthumous exhibitions, in 2002 and 2012. The nonprofit organization Sculpture for New Orleans, which installs sculptures in public spaces in New Orleans, included Alférez's *Gymnast* on Poydras Street in 2013. And in 2015 The Helis Foundation Enrique Alférez Sculpture Garden in the Botanical Garden at City Park opened. The 8,000-square-foot garden features figures and bas-reliefs reproduced or relocated from elsewhere within City Park, and others donated by people in the community. Public programming in the garden, including music performances, honors Alférez and the link he fostered between New Orleans and Mexico. In short, the city continues to celebrate Alférez as "the premier New Orleans sculptor."

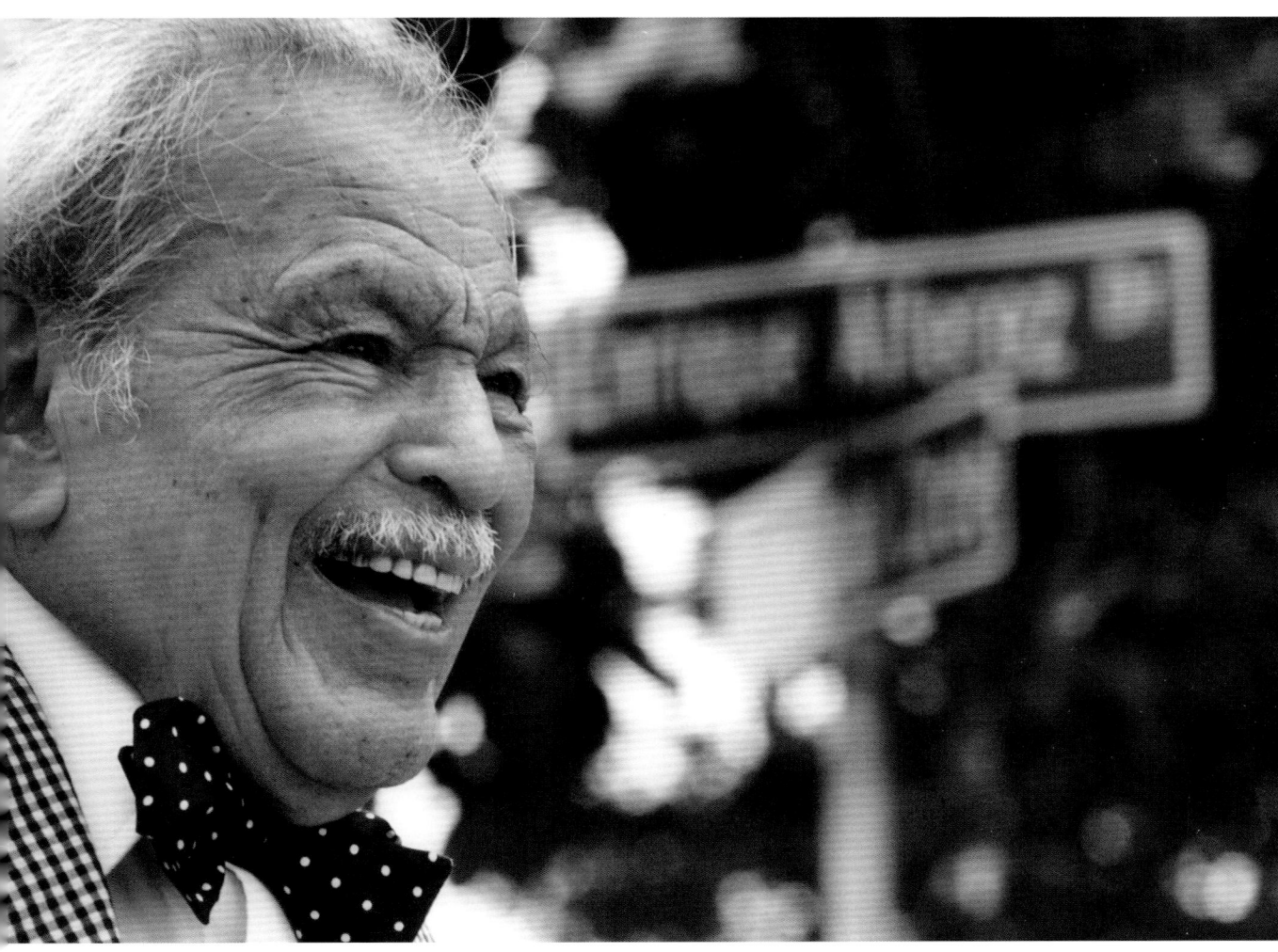

Alférez reacts to having a street in City Park named in his honor [1993]

photo by Ellis Lucia

NEW ORLEANS ADVOCATE, MARCH 17, 2018, CAPITAL CITY PRESS/GEORGES MEDIA GROUP, BATON ROUGE, LA

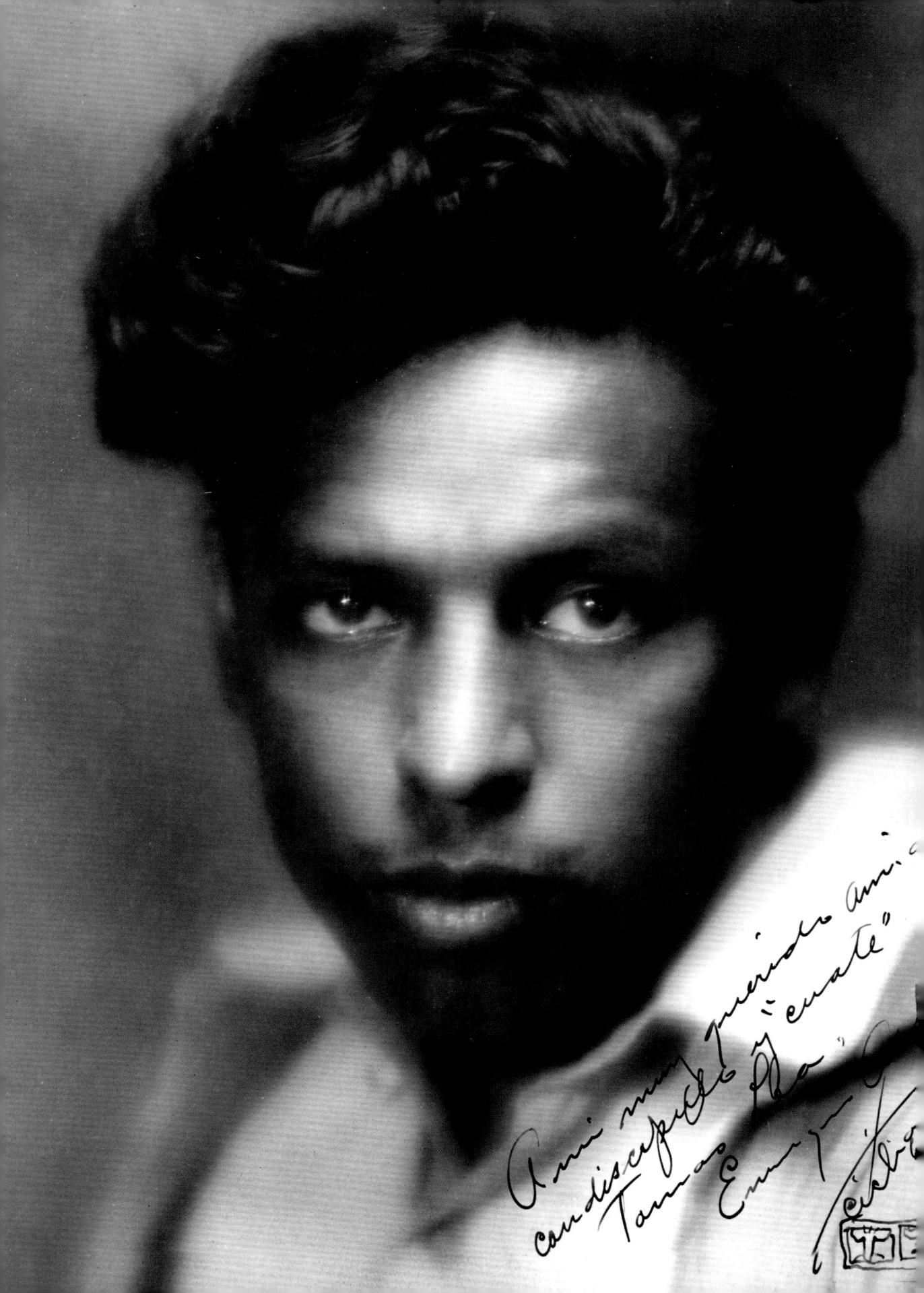

CHAPTER TWO

Culture and Belonging

ENRIQUE ALFÉREZ HAD ORIGINS in the small town of what was then San Miguel del Mezquital, and from a very early age he had a curiosity for the world. Most of his life stretched across geographies and cultures, and the degree to which he was accepted and understood varied by location. Duality was at the core of his identity, his lineage bearing both European and Indigenous Nahua origins. He identified as Aztec, and his first language was a variety of Nahuatl, followed by Spanish, and then English. Although for his sculpture he drew on art and folklore prevalent in Mexico, he didn't consider his art to be Mexican and he didn't identify as a nationalist—"because it limits you," as he said to writer Gina Cortez in 1996.[45]

The social constructs through which people defined one another in the United States changed over the course of the century in which Alférez lived. There were vast shifts in attitudes, everyday language, and law. Alférez was classified and categorized by employers, journalists, the public, and the US government, with their changing nomenclature in regard to ethnic and racial terminology. Immigration, census, and other official records, going through their own transitions in language, indicate he was of the "Mexican" race, "Indian," and "white." One journalist referred to him as a "poor Mexican boy," and an illustrator drew an exaggerated image of him engaged in a goofy motion, accentuated with a large nose and ears in a manner that would be considered racially insensitive in the US today.

Likely influenced by his own treatment, Alférez remained concerned about how people were treated throughout his life and was skeptical of the exclusion he saw in more elite social circles—despite being hired by those within them and gradually moving toward a higher position in society himself. His projects were frequently

Portrait of Enrique Alférez, inscribed "A mi muy querido amigo condiscípulo y 'cuate' Tomas Lea"/ "To my very beloved friend, fellow student, and 'twin' Tom Lea" [ca. 1920s]
COURTESY OF TOM LEA PAPERS, C. L. SONNICHSEN SPECIAL COLLECTIONS DEPARTMENT, UNIVERSITY OF TEXAS AT EL PASO

commissioned by those who had accumulated a wealth Alférez could not have imagined attaining in his lifetime. His politics were leftist, born from his identification with the working class, and he enjoyed close relations with leftist leaders and artists in Mexico and the avant-garde in the United States. Some of his artworks express his pluralist beliefs—for example, through ethnically and racially diverse representations of the human figure. Sometimes public acceptance of these displays was rather limited. His politics, when expressed through his art, occasionally led to tension with his employers too.

In 1941, for example, Alférez was hired by Richard Koch to create interior details during a renovation of the Chapel at Christ Church Cathedral on Saint Charles Avenue.[46] Two parts of the project illustrate Alférez's sociopolitical views, and at least one of these strained his relationship with Koch. The church's altar features a central triptych with paintings by Matthew William Boyhan enclosed in a monumental, intricate frame carved by Alférez and finished in gold leaf. Incorporated into the frame, to the left of the central panel, is Alférez's carved portrait of Bishop Leonidas Polk standing above the church he built in Thibodaux, Louisiana; on the right side, Saint George slays a dragon. From nearly any perspective in the chapel, the frame is a stunning example of the long-lasting influence of the years Alférez spent in his father's workshop, where objects of religious faith were always at the forefront. From a modest distance, a viewer can see Saint George and the dragon, and upon close inspection, more detail emerges: a series of swastikas on the dragon's hide, symbolizing the Nazi rise to power and the ensuing Second World War. Alférez was giving Saint George an additional responsibility at a time when neither the United States nor Mexico was engaged in the war. And although Alférez said Koch wasn't pleased with their inclusion, the swastikas remain.

Alférez also created an oak tabernacle with silver medallions, a credence table, and a white oak reredos, or ornamental screen, covering the back wall of the chapel. The second element of Christ Church that illustrates Alférez's pluralistic world view can be seen in the putti he incorporated into the reredos. These round chubby faces are often seen in religious iconography, sometimes appearing with wings as angels. In the US, they are almost always Caucasian faces. At Christ Church, the small faces that adorn the reredos are ethnically and racially diverse, bearing African, Asian, Inuit, and Indian features among them.[47]

Chapel at Christ Church Cathedral (details) [ca. 1941]

photos by Donn Young

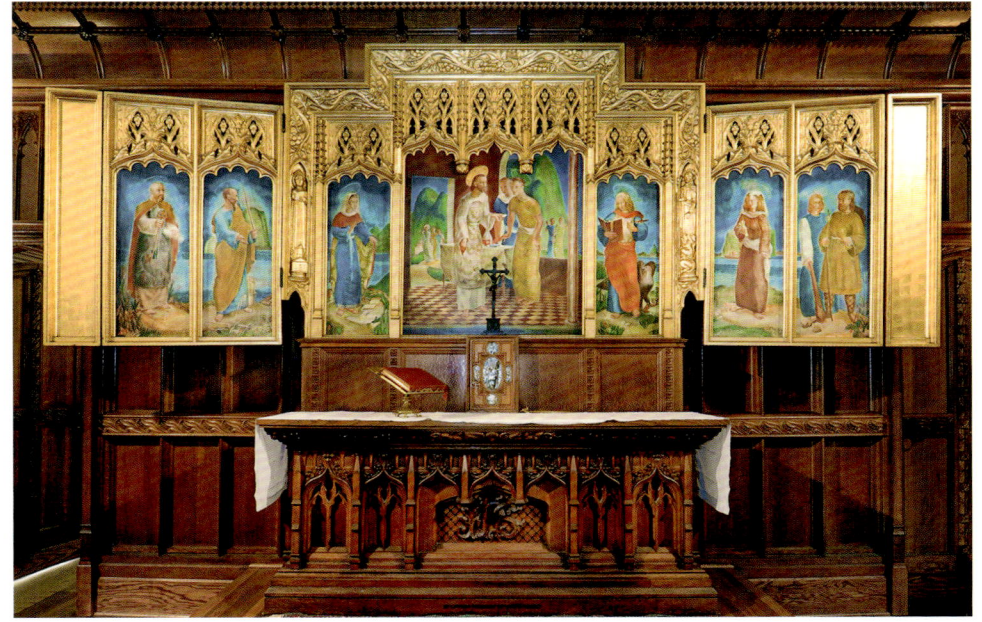

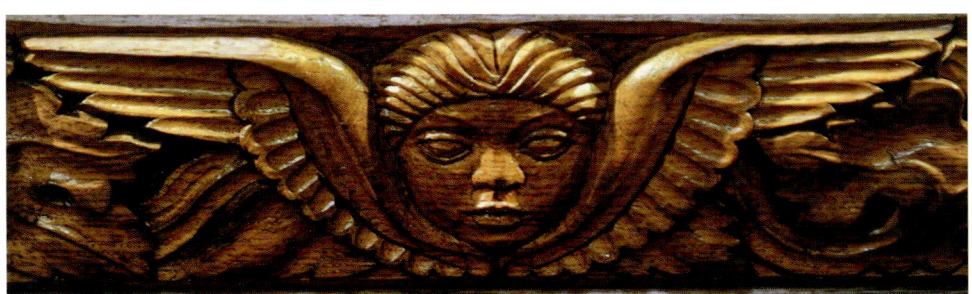

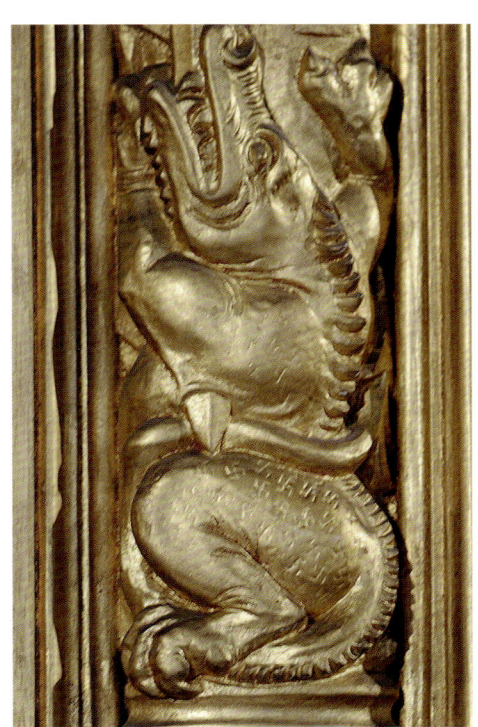

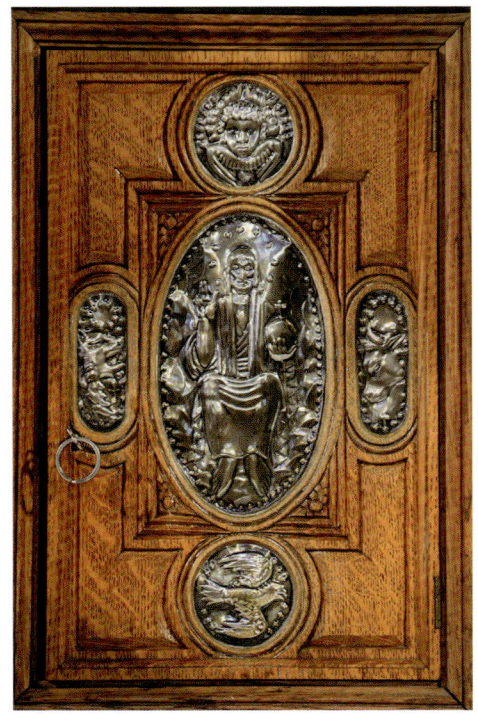

◈

Enrique Alférez's immigration status presented periodic challenges. He arrived to the United States in 1919, paying an eight-dollar head tax at the border in El Paso. He made a new home in Texas, and in the decades to follow, had a fluidity of movement across the border that would be virtually impossible today. Permanent resident status came into being with the Alien Registration Act of 1940; Alférez then had to register with the US government and ultimately became a permanent resident, though never a naturalized US citizen. As immigration policies shifted, he increasingly faced difficulties, and he also ran into personal problems, including losing his documentation.

In interviews, Alférez stated that he tried only once to become a naturalized US citizen. In truth, he made multiple attempts, though none of his closest living family members or friends appear to have been aware of these efforts. His attempts were fruitless; his immigration record suggests various reasons for the denial of his application. In one undated note, likely written prior to 1940, an immigration officer observed that Alférez spoke "vehemently in disrespect of the United States and its government and lauds the [communist] principles." Another note indicated that immigration officials had received a number of complaints about him, although Alférez's immigration record doesn't contain the complaints themselves.[48]

In what must have been the most stinging rejection, Alférez was denied citizenship in 1934 on the basis of his ethnicity. He met with an immigration examiner in New Orleans who made it clear that though he could apply for naturalization, his application would be rejected. The examiner's report notes that Alférez "took cognizance of the prima facie ineligibility of [his application] from a racial standpoint under Sec. 2169 of the US Revised Statutes as said applicant's color, features, general contour, etc very obviously reflected a preponderance of Indian blood." The 1870 law he referenced gave naturalization eligibility to "aliens of African nativity and to persons of African descent" as well as to white applicants and set a precedent for exclusion based on physical differences, without always clarifying whether the exclusion was based on race, nationality, or ethnicity. The officer noted that although there were "racial limitations with reference to naturalization," Alférez still "had the right to make and submit" the application, which he did. His application was rejected.[49]

Alférez also faced challenges in his regular travel between the United States and Mexico. Over the course of eighty years of crossing the border, he saw changes in modes of transportation and highway conditions. In 1934, Alférez, journalist and author Natalie Scott, and *New Orleans Item* reporter Austin Boyle traveled together by horseback from Brownsville, Texas, to Ciudad Victoria, Tamaulipas.[50] Alférez's journeys to Mexico got easier as highways improved, but he still faced challenges that were all the more painful for their mundane nature. He and Peggy regularly took long trips between New Orleans and the cities in which they lived in Mexico—Colima, Tuxpan, San Luis Potosí, Pátzcuaro, Morelia, among others. The drive required an overnight stay along the way, and when they stopped in Texas, the fair-skinned, blonde, and blue-eyed Peggy would often need to check in at the hotel and then sneak Alférez and their daughter through a back entrance.

Other times, Alférez's travel was initiated by changing geopolitical circumstances. Mexico declared war against the Axis powers in May 1942, and although Alférez had been a resident of the United States for more than twenty years, he left New Orleans in June 1942 in anticipation of serving in the Mexican Army.[51] He likely left on his own accord in response to requests for volunteers in Mexico. While he may have initially expected to serve, he was not called into service.[52] When he attempted to return to the United States, less than a year after his departure, he had significant difficulty gaining reentry. It didn't help that he didn't have his alien registration card.

In April 1942, just a couple of months before he departed New Orleans, Alférez left his registration card in a coat pocket, and the coat was stolen from a car. The replacement card was mailed to him at 923 Chartres Street in August—after he had already left the city—and subsequently returned to the Immigration and Naturalization Service. Since he was lacking the card, the US immigration office required him to provide letters of support from colleagues and friends in the United States before granting him reentry. A number of people wrote to the immigration office on his behalf, including Mary Rose Bradford, a friend of Alférez's and the spouse of author Roark Bradford; architect, preservationist, and his former client, Richard Koch; and coffee importer George G. Westfeldt, then treasurer of the Arts and Crafts Club. Each of them reaffirmed Alférez's long-standing intent to return to the United States or offered support for his value as a craftsman, attesting to his employability.[53] Alférez was granted a visa to return in early 1943, and he eventually got his permanent resident card. Also in 1943, Alférez fulfilled his wish to serve in the war with the US Army Transport Service.

Alférez faced other difficulties in social and professional situations, with notable experiences while living and training as a sculptor in Chicago between 1924 and 1929. There, he formed enduring friendships with other artists, writers, and intellectuals and began working as a professional sculptor. But in addition to making lifelong friendships, he also found a rival in Fred Torrey, whom Alférez referred to as "a bad sculptor."[54] Alférez didn't miss an opportunity to find fault with Torrey's creative work, and his sour perspective likely hinged on business matters. Alférez lost a job to Torrey and was not credited for projects they worked on together. Alférez saw issues of discrimination as possible factors in at least one of these instances; he believed that his ethnicity and accent prevented him from being taken seriously as a professional sculptor.

More than a decade after Alférez's death, a contemporary referred to him in a manner that reveals the engrained nature of stereotype. The friend described Alférez as sharp and emotionally intelligent, with an insightful perception of people; this was an instinct, the friend said, "that you find with Third World people," a backhanded compliment and generalization that rings close to the reference to Alférez as a "poor Mexican boy."[55]

How did Alférez manage his relationships with people who put him "in check"? And what role did his race, ethnicity, English language skills, and immigration status have in shaping his career and his art? These are questions I consider when examining his body of work, and when seeing how his figures fit into the landscape of a city that celebrates its multiculturalism.

Bas-relief decoration on bridge in New Orleans City Park [ca. 1936]

photo by Alison Cody

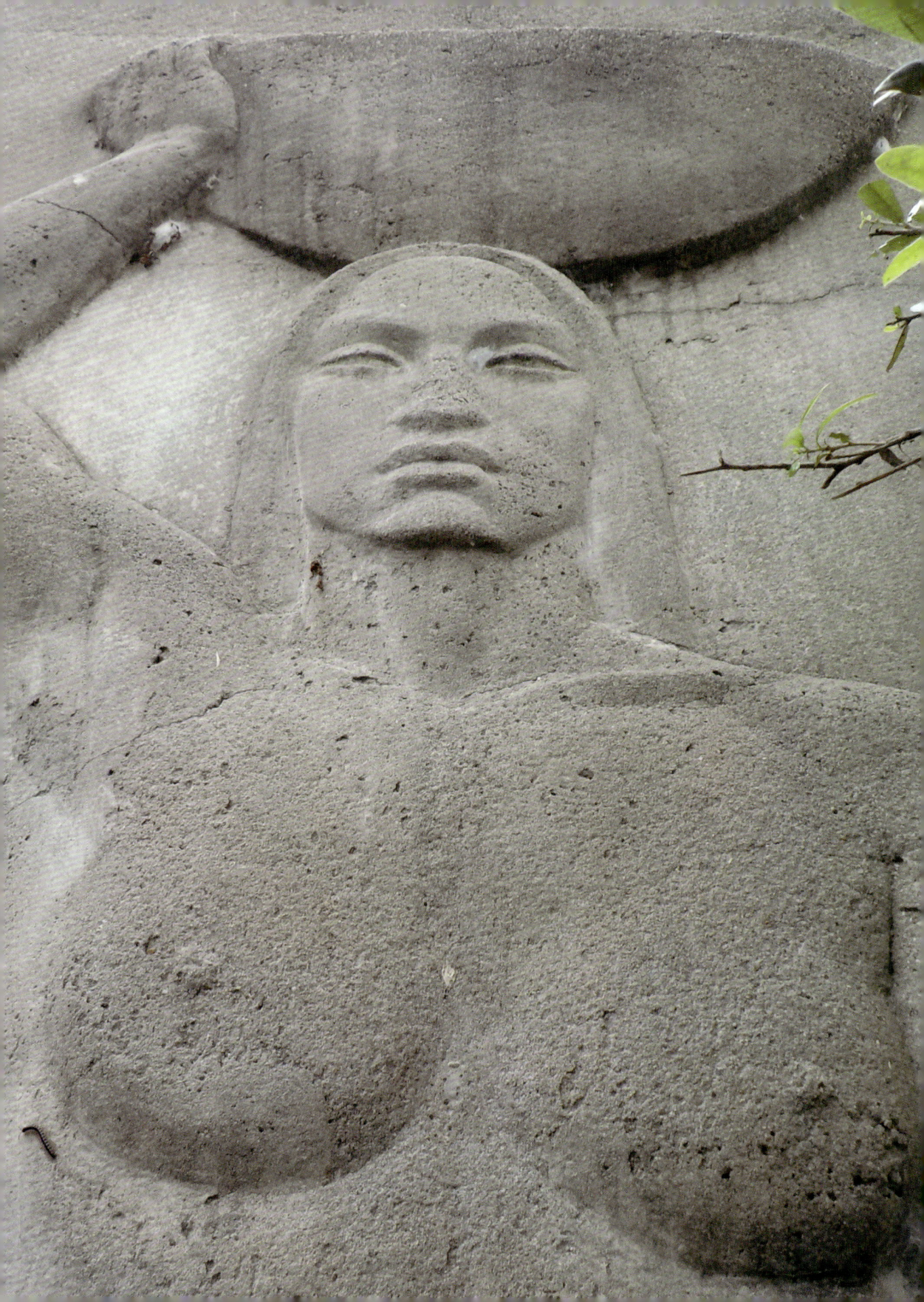

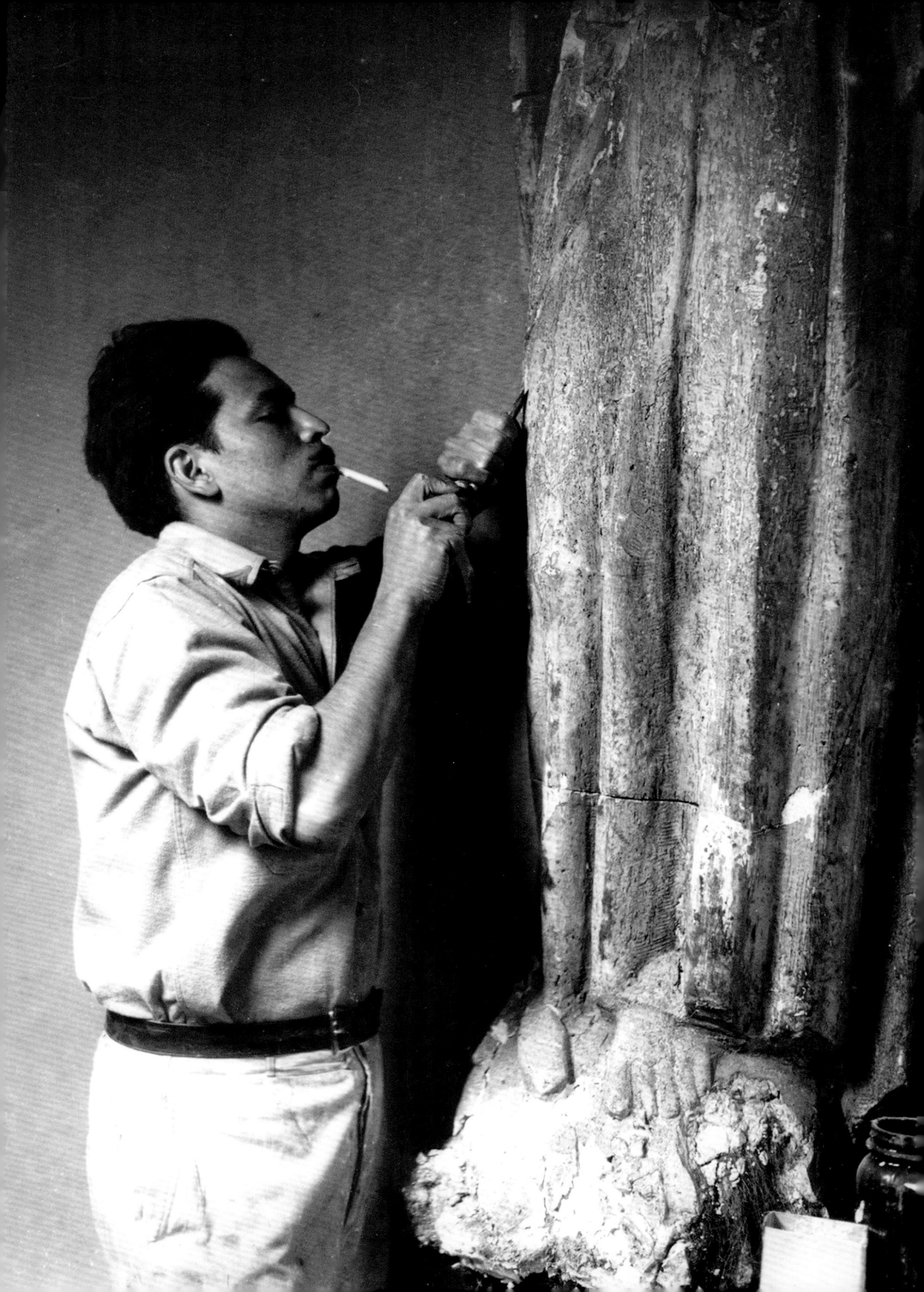

CHAPTER THREE

Craft and Process

LONG BEFORE ENRIQUE ALFÉREZ began his formal study at the School of the Art Institute of Chicago, his father, Longinos, taught him carving and sculpture techniques that had been handed down through the centuries. According to a family story, Longinos had trained for eight years in classical sculpture in Rome and Paris in the nineteenth century, having been afforded this opportunity by the Mexican government's reparations to his family, which lost all of its sons but Longinos in one day during the Franco-Mexican War of the 1860s.[56] After studying in Europe, Longinos returned home to Mexico.

In his workshop in San Miguel, he created religious sculptures and sold these to neighbors, sometimes trading for livestock, including cows and pigs, which he raised on the family's land.[57] He also carved altars; images of Christ, the Virgin Mary, and saints; and the reredos for the Iglésia de San Miguel. Alférez and his siblings worked alongside their father, learning to draw, model, and carve.[58] Among the children, two were particularly drawn to the craft. Alférez's brother Juan also became a sculptor and painter; he taught for many years at a school he started in Gómez Palacio, a city in the northeastern part of the state of Durango and a few hours away from the city of Durango, where the family lived when the brothers were boys.[59]

A number of artists who would later know and learn from Alférez noted that many of his skills originated in lessons from his father, who taught him to carve and build up a model, as well as how to use additives that could make plaster more durable, especially for outdoor use. In his father's workshop, he learned how to mix gauging plaster, molding plaster, marble dust, and other organic materials to create his medium.[60]

Alférez working on a figure for Holy Name of Mary Catholic Church [ca. 1929–31]
photo by Daniel Sweeney Leyrer
THNOC, GIFT OF ALLAN PHILLIP JAFFE, 1981.324.2.403

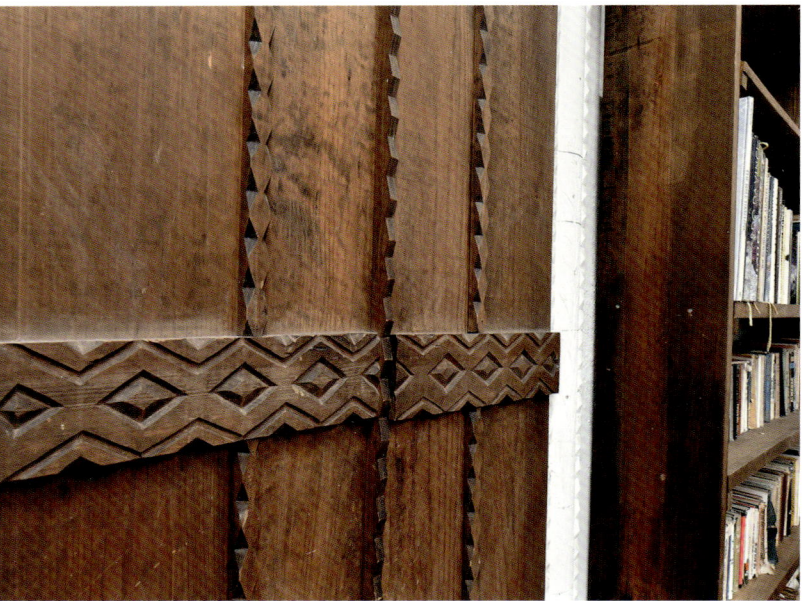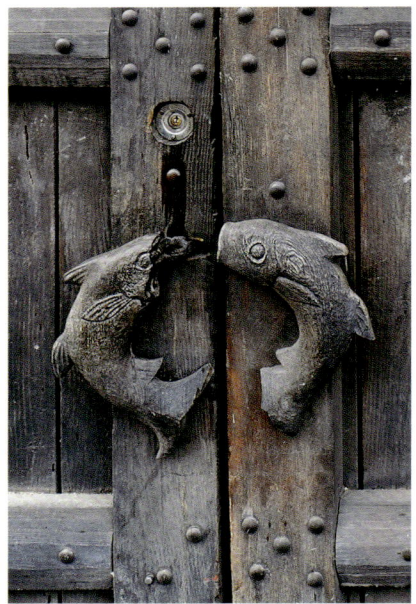

Bedroom door (left) and hand-carved door handle (right) at the Alférez home
in Santa María de Guido, Morelia

photos by Donn Young

Throughout his life, Alférez carried with him a level of inventiveness and an ability to draw materials from the relatively scant resources around him. He became a high-functioning problem solver and an inventor. In addition to possessing creative skills and an ability to improvise and make the tools of his craft, he also regularly made objects for his house, including intricate locks for interior and exterior doors, a copper bathtub, a wall fountain, and a small sliding door in a kitchen wall to allow for a phone to be passed from room to room with ease. He made furniture that was as useful upside-down as right-side-up.[61] He built bookcases and doors, and he carved details into them—rosettes, zigzags, and animals, including two fish used as handles for the doors to his home. In these ways and more, Alférez was nearly always creating and revising the world around him.

Casting

Enrique Alférez worked in many mediums: clay, stone, leather, wood, papier-mâché, plaster, bronze, lead, concrete, steel, gold, and silver. Some of these, such as wood and papier-mâché, resulted in a single final figure, which Alférez carved or built up. He intended for many of his figures to be cast, whether in bronze, concrete, or another medium, knowing from the outset that a model was an early step in his process toward a final sculpture.

Whether his intent was to create a fountain, piece of furniture, or cast bronze figure, Alférez's figures nearly always began as drawings. He drew on anything he could find, from sketchbooks to brown butcher paper. Most drawings were made with graphite, charcoal, carbon pencil, or Conté crayon. Alférez was color-blind; there are very few extant works with details in color. Many drawings were explorations of an idea to see whether it might become a sculpture, after which he would begin defining a final form. Even his roughest sketches reveal a strong awareness of three-dimensionality, an ability to see depth from multiple angles.

He most frequently modeled works based on the human form, and the female form in particular. Alférez typically based his drawings upon models: his friends, family members, and strangers. Early in his career, it wasn't uncommon for him to place want ads in classified sections of newspapers, seeking an "American girl" or announcing that "Enrique Alférez needs a model for his sculpturing and, as usual, informs the artistic world of this fact by a want ad."[62] At other times, he found models through word of mouth, and later in life, his wife Peggy helped him seek them out. When his models posed, Alférez typically drew them from multiple perspectives and in various positions.

After he had sketched out his idea on paper, the next step was to begin working on a clay or plaster model. At times, he kept his drawings clipped or hanging nearby during this process. When modeling, Alférez began by creating the armature, or skeleton around which a sculpture is formed. The armature was usually created from wood and metal, and he used anything from fittings purchased at a hardware store to repurposed scraps of metal and wood that he picked up from nearby companies.

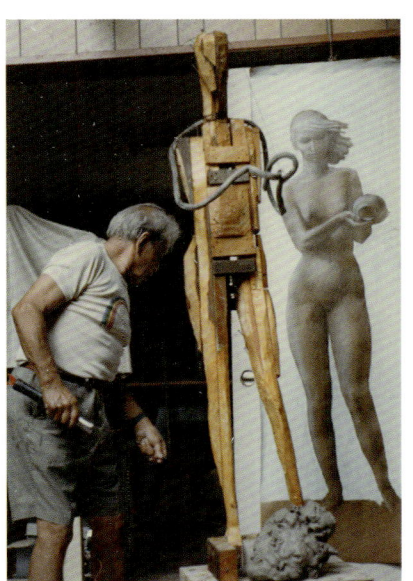
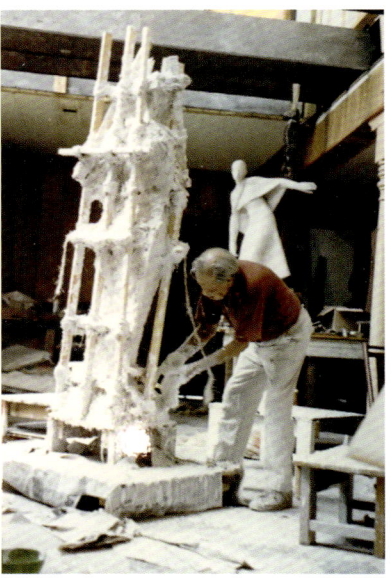
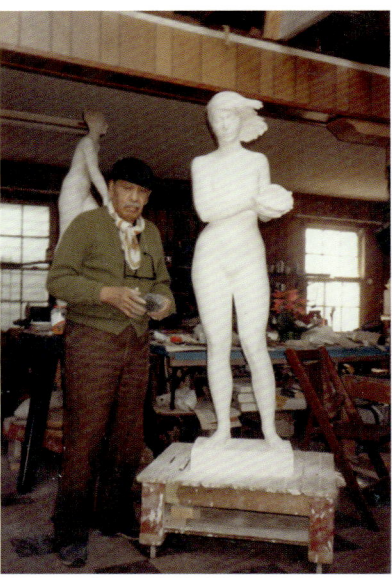

Alférez working on *Woman with Shell* for Windsor Court Hotel, New Orleans
COURTESY OF THE TLALOC SELWAY ALFÉREZ PAPERS

He was friends with business owners who saved such materials that might otherwise have been discarded.[63]

Once his armature was finished, Alférez added clay or plaster, shaping it into the figure he had imagined and drawn. The form and its texture were further defined by hand and tools including rasps, rifflers, and calipers, which he used to shape, smooth, and add texture to a clay or plaster model. Many of Alférez's works gained subtle cross-hatched texture during this stage. He was careful to apply his textures evenly, avoiding spending an unbalanced amount of time and attention on one part of a figure. He incorporated elements of modernism, art deco, and cubism. By the time a figure was lifted from the page to become a figure in clay or plaster, Alférez had often blended features from multiple individuals, both models and people he knew.

Early in his career, and in keeping with trends of the time, Alférez cast many works in concrete. In a 1936 interview about City Park projects, he reflected on its use, noting that "in the old romantic tradition, there could be no fine statuary that was not cut by hand from Carrara marble or expensive granite." Such materials had been used for works including Michelangelo's *David* and the *Venus de Milo*. "In this way," said Alférez, "we were taught to admire the sculptor's strength and become awed with the hardship of cutting, as much as by the quality of his art." In contrast, he observed, "Liquid concrete could hardly be more pliable. . . . It is inexpensive, and in keeping with my idea that the media an artist uses has nothing to do with the quality of his art."[64]

While cast concrete did prove economical, as his work matured he began casting more in bronze, often using the lost-wax casting, or investment casting, process. In this method, a clay or plaster model became the first "positive." The next step was to create the first "negative." A plaster mold was created around the positive, dried either by time or in a kiln, and then removed from the positive to create the negative space into which heated liquid wax was poured. Wax was poured through a small opening and spread throughout the empty space to create a hollow replica of the original model—a wax positive. Next, the mold was carefully removed, and Alférez or foundry professionals inspected the wax positive. At this stage, minor imperfections could be tended to: seams chased, texture reapplied in an area where it may not have fully taken in the wax, and so on.

Bronze sculpture of a charro [1977]
THNOC, 1981.215

Wax rods, or sprues, were then attached to the wax piece for two purposes: to create tubes through which melted metal, such as bronze, could later be poured, and also to create gaps through which gases could escape when the bronze was poured in. Once the sprues were added, another shell or mold—typically made of layers of ceramic and plaster—was formed around the wax figure. Then the piece was fired in a kiln, hardening the shell and melting the wax, which would be poured back out. The result was a strong, durable mold that could withstand the heat and pressure of molten bronze being poured in.

Separately, bronze was melted in a crucible, allowing impurities to rise to the top and the metal to heat evenly. When Alférez was in his own foundry, he would occasionally throw a glass bottle into the liquid bronze to force impurities to rise, which he subsequently scraped away. Using tongs, foundry professionals lifted the crucible full of bronze to pour it into the mold. After the bronze cooled, the mold was removed and the sprues cut off. Imperfections were sanded or welded, and special attention was given to the areas where the sprues had been, as well as other seams. Some pieces were also welded together at this stage; a large figure, for example, might have endured this process in three sections, with the head, torso with arms, and legs cast separately and then assembled and welded together to create a single figure.

Alférez had control over this process at his home foundry, where he often cast smaller works. Peggy or an assistant typically worked with him on many of the stages at home, given that, even with the smallest figures, the effort often required more than one person at a time. In many cases, he had support from assistants he was mentoring. In 1971, for example, New Orleans–based artist Ersy Schwartz was an apprentice in his studio in Morelia, and she would have worked with him through many stages, from modeling to casting.

When casting with a foundry, Alférez typically visited to inspect the cast bronze piece. He might ask for minor changes, looking for details that needed additional finishing or spots where there was a slight warpage in the texture of a seam that had been welded. He looked for dimples or areas where the chasing may not have been fine enough, and he carefully inspected distinctive details such as a figure's eyes, nose, hands, and feet.

The next step, applying the patina, created a protective covering while also contributing to his aesthetic. A patina is a crucial element in controlling tone—not just the visual style and range of color, but a figure's emotional character—and it

FOLLOWING PAGES:

Alférez foundry, Santa María de Guido, Morelia
photo by Donn Young

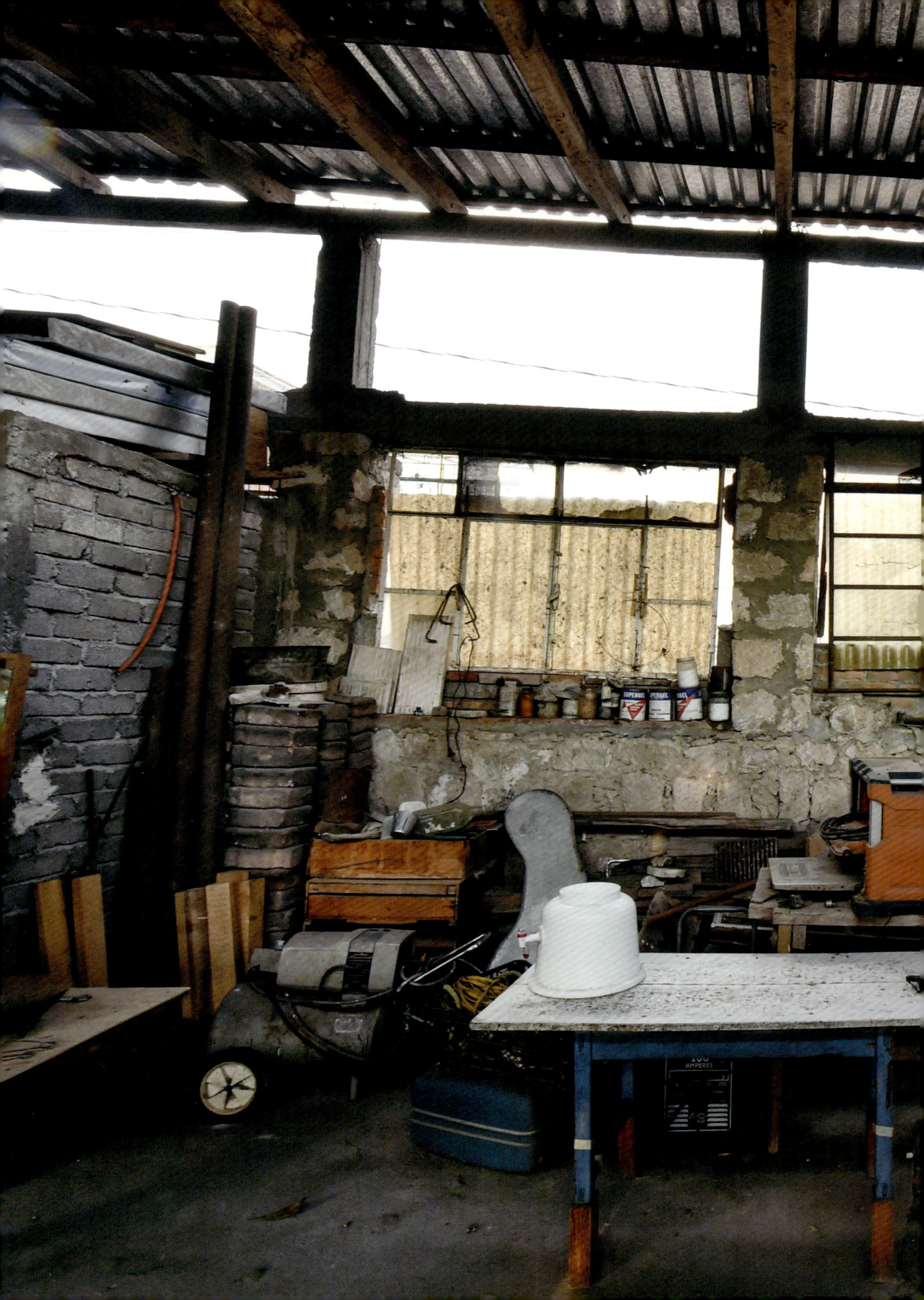

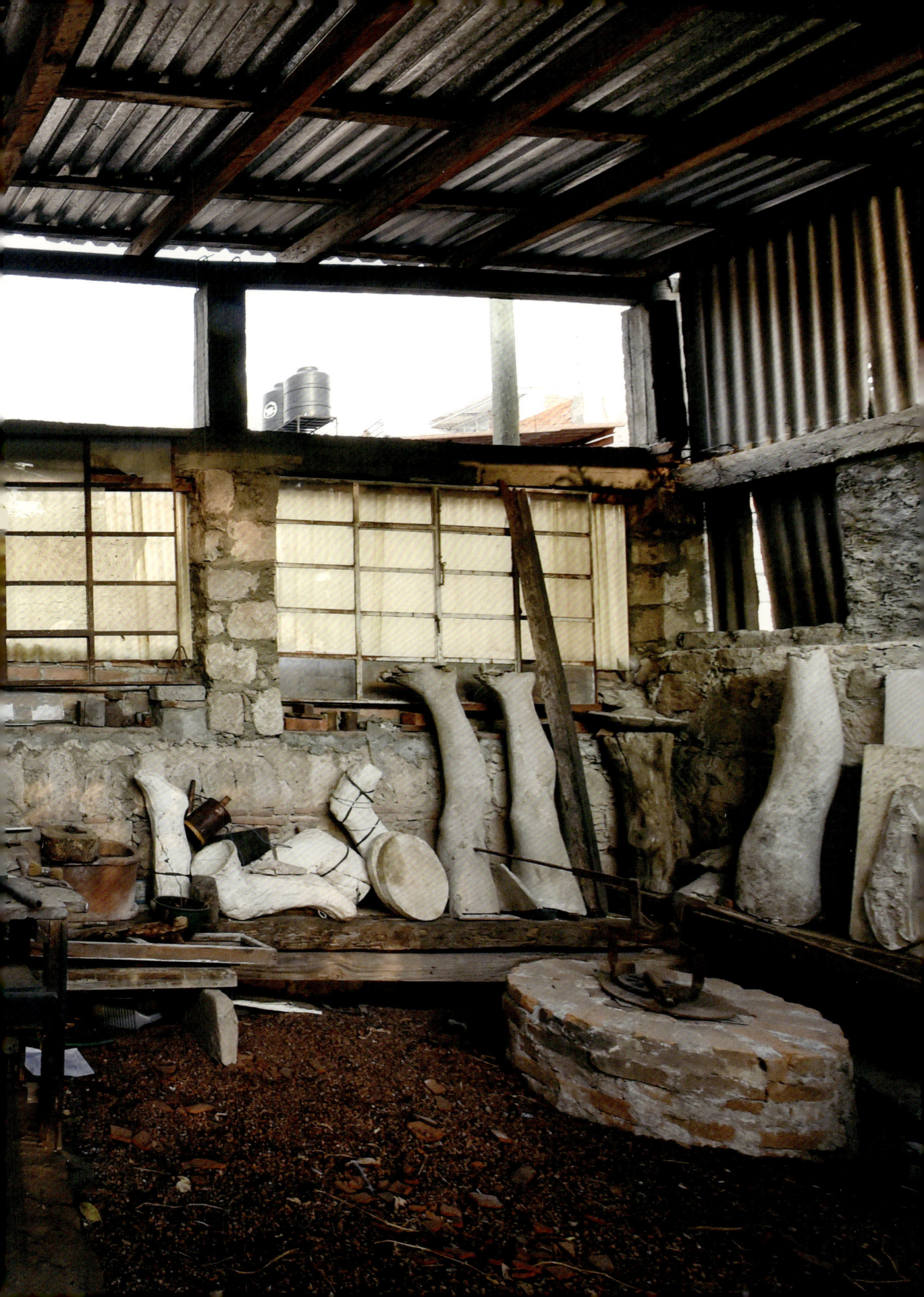

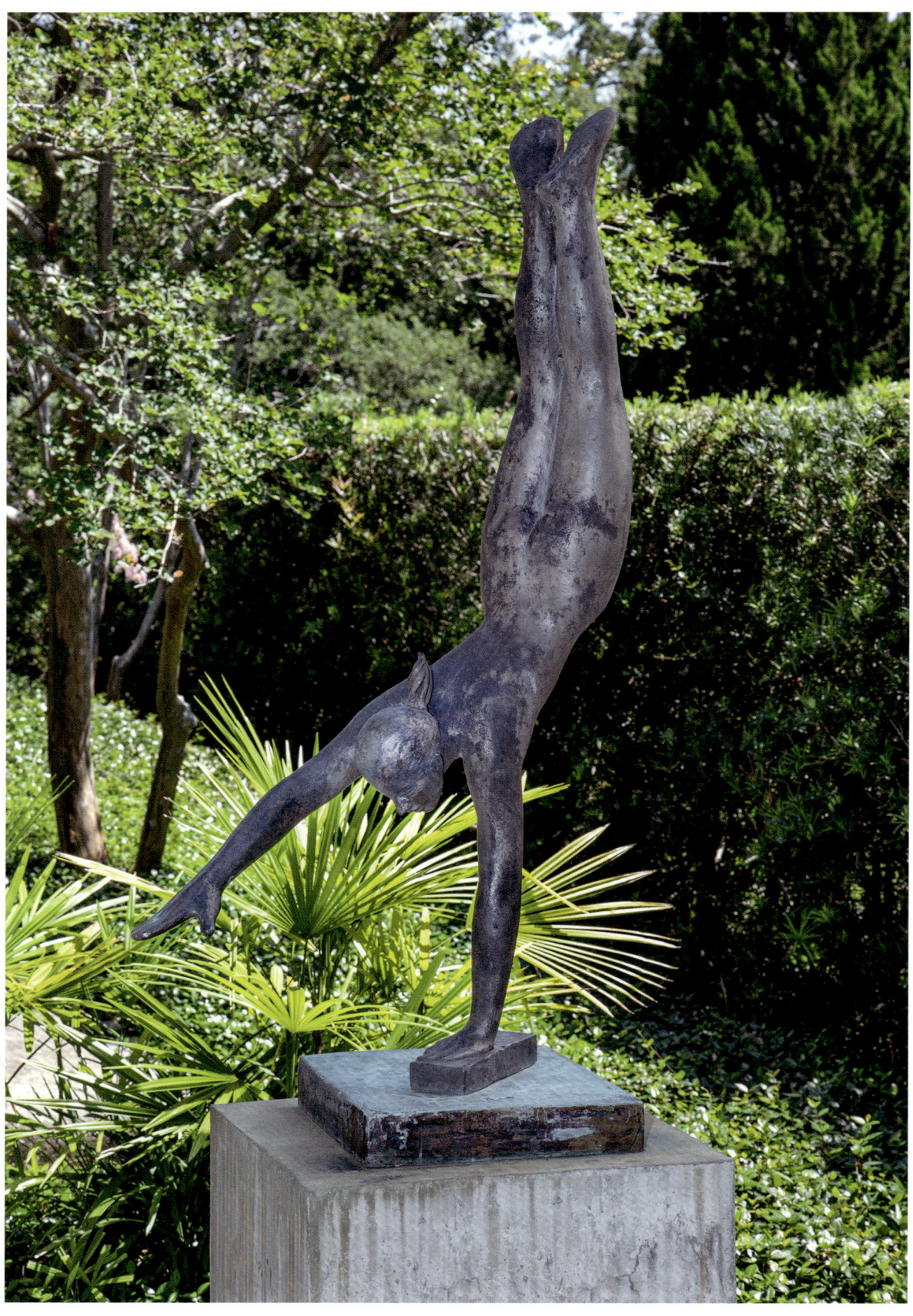

deepens the artist's control of how shadow shapes a figure and allows it to be seen in varied light.

Patinas are categorized as hot or cold, depending on whether the figure needs to be heated for the patina to adhere, and they produce a range of colors, from green to reddish-bronze. Hot patinas require the bronze to be heated to about three hundred degrees Fahrenheit. Alférez used a number of patinas and had a strong preference for hot silver nitrate because he could control its brightness and adjust for expectations about the figure's lighting. Silver nitrate appealed to Alférez because of its dark, classical coloring and because it allowed him to finish a piece in a range of colors from soft gray to moderately bright silver, by applying it hot and then burnishing it off until he achieved his desired color. If Alférez found a disadvantage to silver nitrate, it was that it tends to be among the most expensive patinas.[65]

In many cases, Alférez applied the patina himself. Though he was skilled at this, later in life he began more routinely working with a foundry for this final stage of completing a figure. His allegiance to a foundry was solidified when he found his "patina man," Karl Reichley, in the late 1980s. Reichley, who grew up in Lake Charles, Louisiana, was employed by Piero Mussi's Artworks Foundry in California when he traveled to deliver a talk and demonstration at the New Orleans Academy of Fine Art. Alférez and Peggy attended the talk, and Alférez was taken with Reichley's process. Their discussion after Reichley's lecture turned into a cooperative partnership. Alférez came to rely on Reichley's expertise, and, in turn, developed an enduring relationship with the California foundry where Reichley worked.

The casting process Alférez undertook required significant time and financial investment: drawing and building armatures, clay models, and plaster models, as well as carving and casting. And there were other steps too: negotiating the scope of a project, finding a model, reimagining a theme or image, sometimes on paper, other times in clay or plaster, relying on his carving skills as he sorted out details for a piece. The casting process, from model to finished cast bronze, could take weeks to many months, depending on the size of the final cast work. By the time he was finished, more than a dozen people could have been involved in the effort: assistants, models, professionals at the foundry who poured the hot bronze, who removed molds or welded seams and applied a patina. Was a final figure worth all of that time and effort? "Sometimes," Alférez said in a 1941 interview, and perhaps with a wink, "[a sculptor] should stop with the armature."[66]

Silver nitrate patina applied to *Gymnast* in
The Helis Foundation Enrique Alférez Sculpture Garden [ca. 1990]
photo by Keely Merritt, THNOC
ON LOAN FROM THE HELIS FOUNDATION

Revising a Figure

Over his long career, it wasn't uncommon for Alférez to revise a figure multiple times to reach the version that pleased him; in some cases, he did so as many as a dozen times. Some of his iconic pieces were cast and then reenvisioned with modest changes to alter the tone and emotional impact. As he took these steps to revisit figures he had previously cast, he gave careful attention to planes and to nuanced details that enabled him to capture human emotion as honestly as he could. Two key examples of this continuous reworking of a sculpture include *La Soldadera* and *Woman in a Huipil*.

The strength and fortitude of the soldaderas in the Mexican Revolution settled on Alférez in his youth and took many years to result in one of his signature sculptural figures. The oldest evidence of him experimenting with depictions of a soldadera is from the early 1930s: in 1932, he created drawings for a potential statue near the US-Mexico border.[67] That project was never executed, but his drawings became the foundation for the piece created decades later. One version of *La Soldadera* is a sixty-nine-inch sculpture modeled in 1970 and cast in bronze in 1989–90 that can be seen today in The Helis Foundation Enrique Alférez Sculpture Garden. The soldadera holds her nursing infant close to her chest, her head turned and an intensity to her eyes, as though she is assessing a potential threat.

One way that Alférez revised *La Soldadera* was to increase the tension between the mother's and infant's perspectives, an effect he achieved by altering the infant's feet. As he remodeled the figure, he put the infant's feet in a loose position that conveyed ease, comfort, and a lack of awareness of the possibility of a threat. In this way, Alférez was illustrating a mother's ability to protect and comfort her infant, even in a moment of potential danger.

In this portrait, Alférez also incorporated aspects of his mother's facial features. The gesture is symbolic rather than literal, for there is no evidence that Alférez's mother was a soldadera in the revolution. At least two additional soldadera sculptures exist: a second bronze in Tlaloc Alférez's collection, and a cast stone *La Soldadera* Alférez gave to his hometown, Miguel Auza, in the early 1980s, which eventually went missing. While rumors have indicated it might be on view in a restaurant in Morelia, its location has not been identified.

Although it is unlikely that Alférez began experimenting with the idea of *Woman in a Huipil* quite so early in his career, he continued to refine the figure over the course of more than twenty years. From at least 1960 until the 1980s, he modeled and revisited the subject in plaster, concrete, and bronze. It was common for him to create a small maquette as a study for a larger figure, and thus for a number of his sculptures there are smaller earlier renditions; in the case of *Woman in a Huipil*,

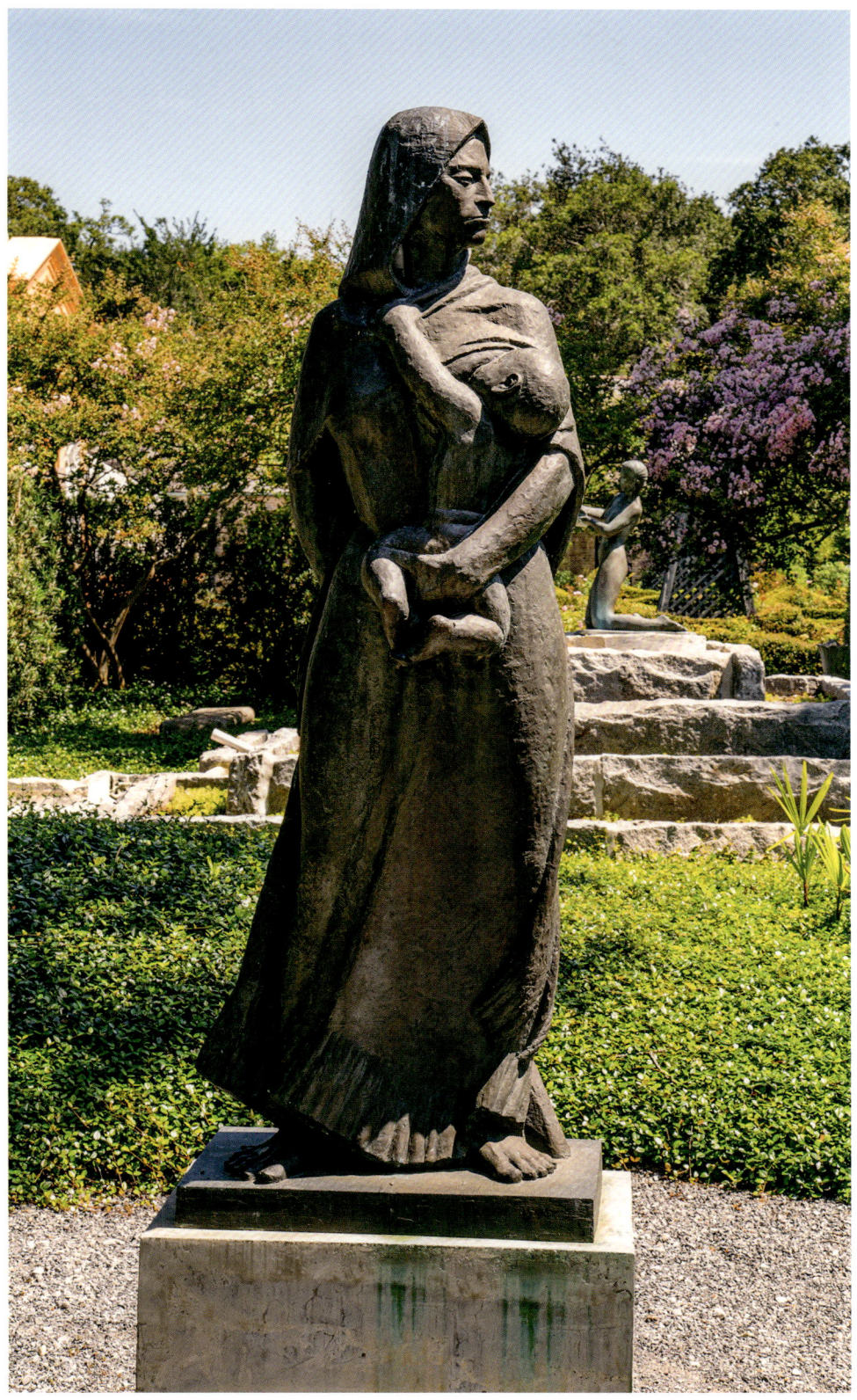

La Soldadera in The Helis Foundation Enrique Alférez Sculpture Garden [ca. 1970; cast 1989–90]

photo by Keely Merritt, THNOC

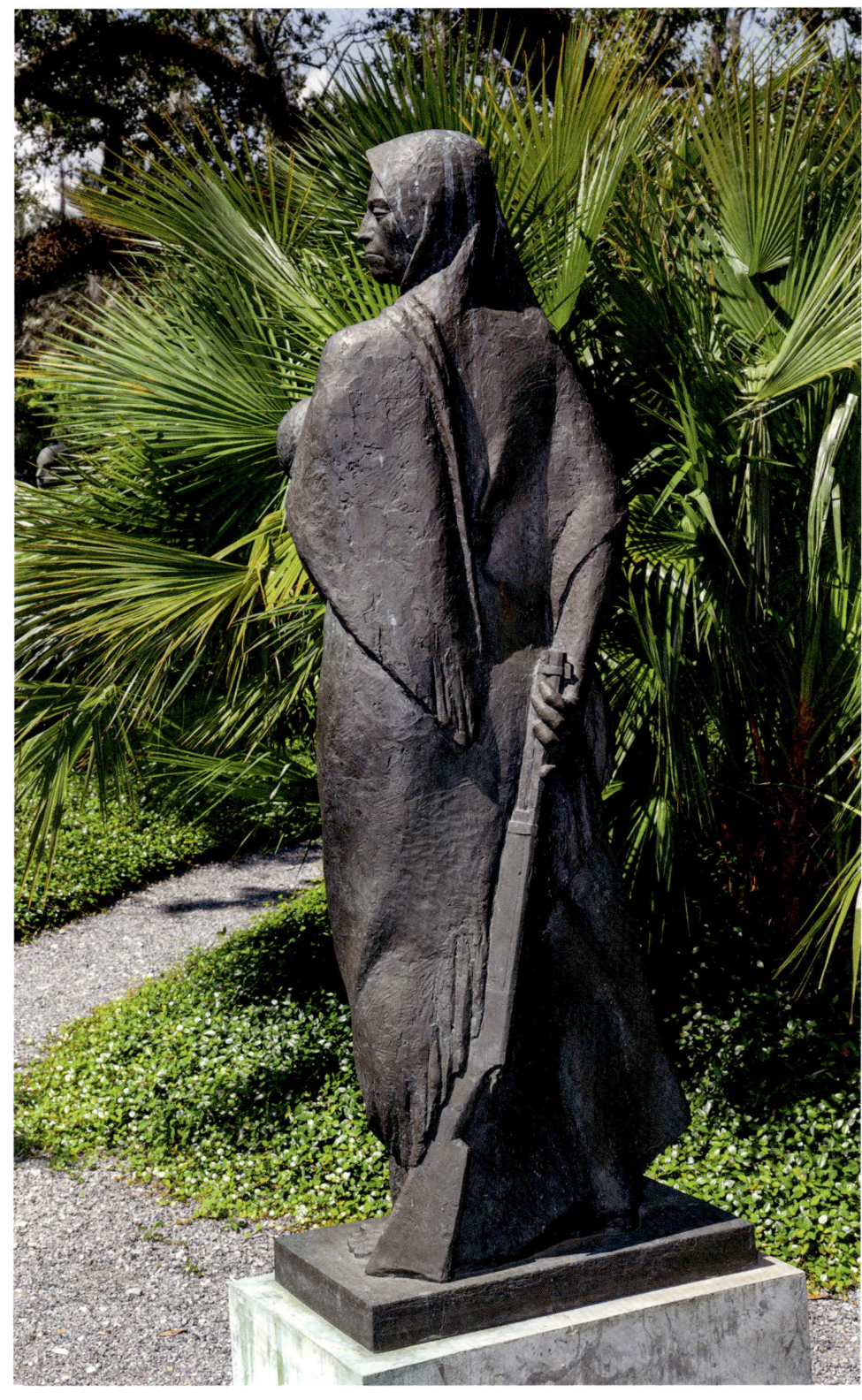

La Soldadera in The Helis Foundation Enrique Alférez Sculpture Garden [ca. 1970; cast 1989–90]

photo by Keely Merritt, THNOC

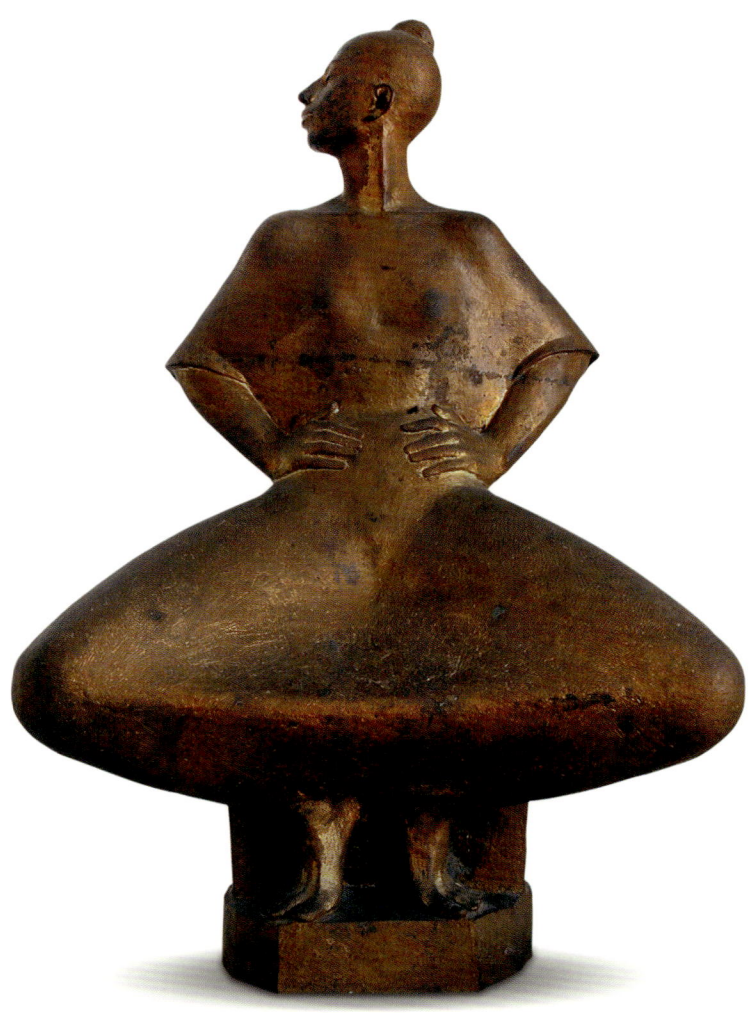

Woman in a Huipil
photo by Donn Young
COURTESY OF THE COLLECTION OF TLALOC S. ALFÉREZ, MD

Alférez modeled and executed bronzes in multiple sizes, with revisions, until he came to terms with the scale that produced his desired effect in its planes, which are more pronounced in her larger renditions. While there were multiple revisions, the figure is always on her toes with her hands at her waist; he made changes to how her hands are folded or placed and to the direction of her head, with the final iteration connoting the greatest sense of power and confidence. Close examination of the variations of *Huipil* provide insight into Alférez's goal of controlling emotion "more honestly."

Part Two

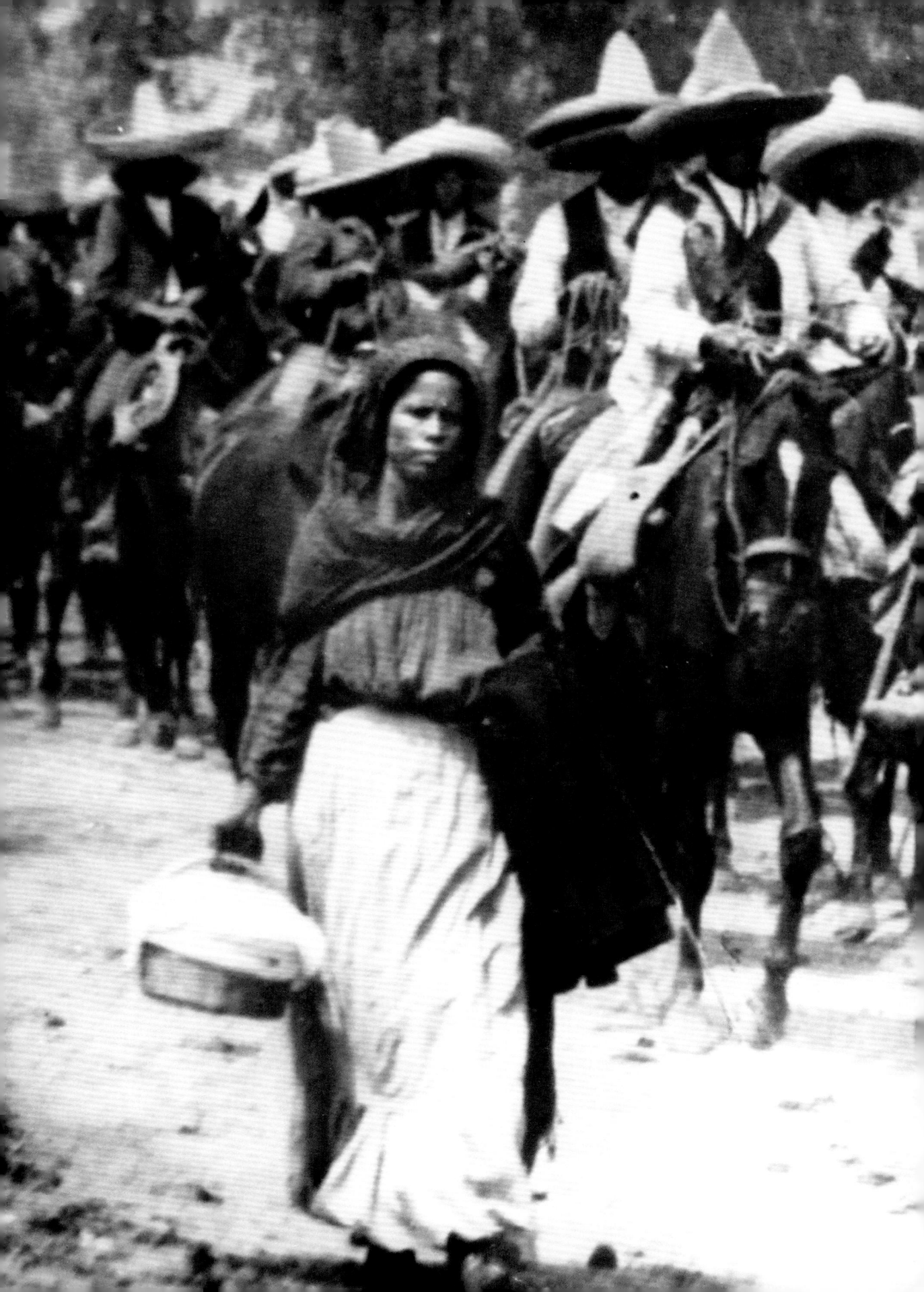

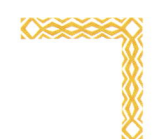

CHAPTER FOUR

From the Mexican Revolution to the Arts Community in El Paso

BY THE TIME THE ALFÉREZ FAMILY moved to Durango, about a hundred miles west-southwest of San Miguel del Mezquital, in 1909, Mexico had been approaching the likelihood of revolution for years. As a young boy, Alférez may not have understood circumstances pushing his country toward war, but decades later, he reflected on its origins: issues around land ownership, poverty, and lack of freedoms. He remarked that, from cradle to grave, lives were controlled by the owners of haciendas: the owners grew richer, he said, while the workers only grew in debt. "You were born poor, you died poor. There was no way for you to get anywhere."[68]

Mexico was feeling the effects of the decades-long, dictatorship-like presidency of Porfirio Díaz, who abdicated under pressure in 1911. And beyond a need for land reform, the country had also been facing an increase in industrialization, a change that came fast but did not bring increases in income.[69] There was also persistent interference by the US government, coupled with issues related to foreign investment. In short, across the country, people were experiencing a lower standard of living, a reality that gave rise to revolutionaries—among them Pancho Villa in the north and Emiliano Zapata in the south. Facing their own difficult economic realities during this time, Alférez's family sought opportunities in the city of Durango, which, as a regional center for commerce and industry, offered a better economy.

While much of the violence of the Mexican Revolution eased by 1917, some armed conflict continued until 1920. Alférez was most likely involved in the war beginning around 1915, when he was about twelve years old. The revolution was the backdrop of Alférez's youth, and just as it cast a long shadow over the country, it also cast a long shadow over his life and art. The revolution was marked by

Anonymous soldadera of the Mexican Revolution [1910-14]
photo by Agustín Casasola
IMAGE COURTESY OF SECRETARIA DE CULTURA.-INAH.-SINAFO.F.N.-MEX.
REPRODUCTION AUTHORIZED BY INSTITUTO NACIONAL DE ANTROPOLOGÍA E HISTORIA

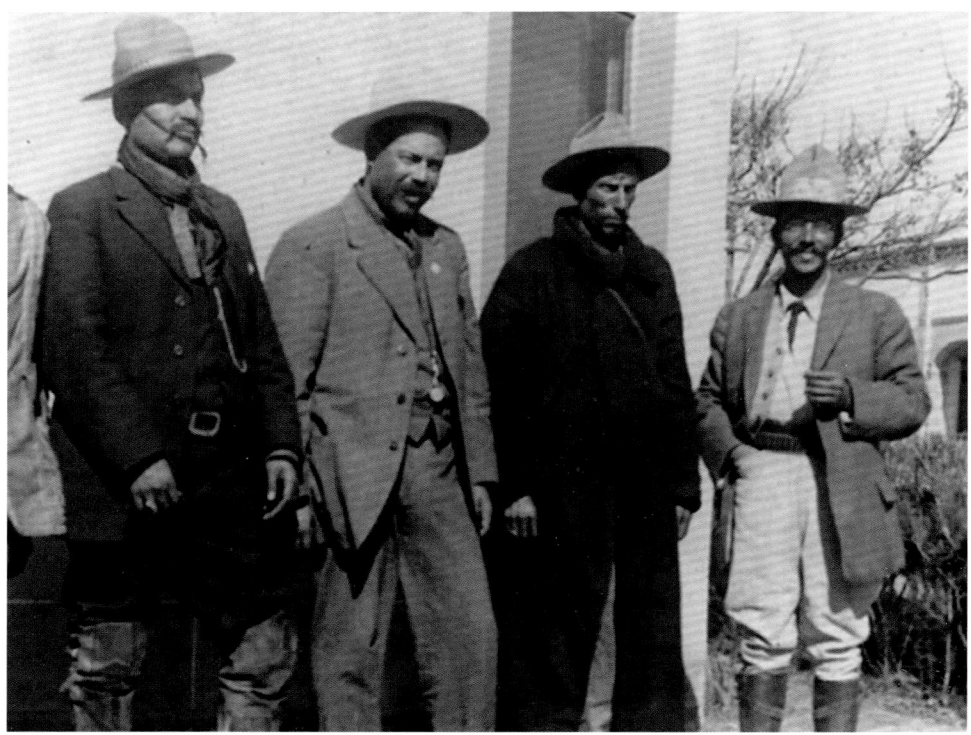

Officers of the Mexican Revolution (left to right: General Rodolfo Fierro,
General Pancho Villa, General Toribio Ortega, Colonel Juan Medina) [ca. 1913]
COURTESY OF NATIONAL ARCHIVES AND RECORDS ADMINISTRATION, 533444

political, social, and cultural resistance, with "a renaissance of national conscious-ness" expressed through many artistic movements, including muralism.[70] And while Alférez's work was distinct from that of many of his Mexican contemporaries, the revolution influenced his choices as an artist—namely, his preference for common people as subject matter—and it opened up paths for him to pursue his art.

Alférez told a well-repeated story, perhaps embellished over the years and punctuated with interesting turns of adventure, about how he went from being a schoolboy to being a child amongst revolutionaries, or a revolutionary himself. At school one day in Durango, he said, he broke a glass siphon; glass was expensive at the time and Alférez perceived it to be valuable. It's unclear whether he was more afraid of the financial consequences for his family due to the breakage or the punish-ment his father would have doled out for such an offense.[71] But as a youth, the solu-tion to the problem must have seemed simple: he ran away with a classmate.

In an interview in December 1975, Alférez recounted the incident: "We got past the line of federal troops and fell into the hands of the rebels. They thought we were federal spies and some of them wanted to shoot us. But the leader gave us a choice—either join them or be shot. We joined up! So I became a revolutionary."[72]

The forces that Alférez and his friend found themselves among were led by Pancho Villa, known as a guerrilla revolutionary, cold-blooded bandit, and, ultimately, hero. Alférez was still too young, with weapons too scarce, to be given a gun of his own. He could draw, and thus received cartography assignments, entering enemy territory to draw maps of battle terrain. He was given other tasks, too: he gathered water and kindling for fires tended by the soldaderas, the women who joined their husbands and men, who made camp at night for the soldiers, and who sometimes fought as well. Alférez spent significant time with the soldaderas, and the experience had a profound effect on him. In his own words, he "grew up in the revolution."[73] He was moved by the role of these women, and he was drawn to them both to help them with chores and also out of necessity, for they helped him too.[74] While some of the soldaderas took on roles as combatants and officers, Alférez came to know others in a more maternal role. They provided him with food, such as beans and tortillas cooked over the fires for which he had gathered kindling, and he witnessed the challenges they faced, caring for families in the midst of war. It was a "hell of a life for the women," he said.[75]

Alférez's own description of a soldadera appears in an interview from the early 1930s: "An infant was strapped to her back or straddled her hip, and she led another child by the hand. A goat was tethered to her waist, and from her belt there hung a bag of provisions—corn and beans.... With this entourage, she moved along with the regiment to which her soldado belonged, and without her, the Mexican soldier would have been helpless. If he fell in battle, she picked up his rifle and fought in his place."[76]

Even if the description was somewhat romanticized, it was rooted in the reality of what women faced and accomplished during the war. Stories that Alférez told to friends of his family about this period sometimes have an absurd lightheartedness that defied the reality of the effects of the war on children and child-soldiers. In articles written for Mexican publications, historical details about his life in the war tend to be more matter-of-fact. Those related in American publications are, unsurprisingly, often presented with more of a sense of adventure.

Two men, Brigadier General Gabriel Gavira and artist and teacher Mariano Hernández Arévalo, played important early roles in Alférez's transition from the revolution into the arts, and in his move to the United States. They appear regularly in his reflections on this period, though he sometimes seems to have conflated the two in his storytelling, merging them into a single character.

Numerous accounts and family narratives have established that, during his time with the revolutionaries, Alférez carved small religious objects and sold them to soldiers and made paintings of saints using a limited palette of brown, black, and white. Across multiple sources, Alférez stated that Gavira saw his artwork and responded well to it, and then placed Alférez under the tutelage of Arévalo, an artist who had been commissioned by the governor of Durango to paint a mural of the history of the revolution.[77] Alférez was known to recount stories about this period of his life with typical dramatic flair. But in a 1975 interview, and in personal accounts retold by family and friends, he appears to have conflated details about Gavira and Arévalo. It is possible that the stories were misunderstood or transcribed inaccurately, or that Alférez was just slippery with the historical facts. For example, Alférez describes details about the artist Arévalo that are more consistent with Gavira, such as referring to him as a military judge.

At different times, Gavira had been a military commander of Durango and Juárez, and he served as a military judge in Juárez, where he purportedly oversaw more executions than any other military leader. He was said to have a band play military music while he oversaw executions.[78] Arévalo was an artist and teacher, not a military judge, and his relationship with Gavira remains unclear. Any circumstance that allowed Gavira to place a child in an artist's care is perplexing.

Arévalo had studied at the oldest art academy in the Americas, the Academia de San Carlos, and at least as early as 1917, he was living and working as an artist in El Paso, just across the border from Juárez.[79] He taught art and painted portraits of many prominent figures of El Paso and Juárez, as well as the bishop of the Roman Catholic Archdiocese of Chihuahua, Antonio Guízar y Valencia.

It was with Arévalo, his wife, and his two children that Alférez first crossed from Mexico into the United States at El Paso, in 1919. When Alférez shared stories of the painter later in life, he had few kind words. He lived with Arévalo and his family between 1919 and 1921 and was even declared Arévalo's adopted child in the 1920 census.[80] In an oral history, Alférez said Arévalo was always "chasing women" and that he would "corner the rough characters" in Juárez to kill them, even ordering Alférez—at the time "a scared, skinny boy"—to draw floor plans of saloons, gambling houses, and brothels so they could more easily trap victims.

Arévalo was shot in a barroom altercation in Juárez in the summer of 1921. At least one newspaper report indicates that Arévalo was intervening in a fight between others.[81] Alférez visited Arévalo's corpse at the hospital at the request of his wife, who wanted him to make a death mask. "I was so happy to be free of him that I would have done anything," Alférez said. At the hospital, he began his task with a fear that Arévalo was not actually dead. "Suddenly I was so sure that I saw his eye move," he said, "and I was terrified that somehow he was still alive." Alférez picked up a mallet he had brought, and just as he was about to finish, a fly zoomed from Arévalo's eye. Alférez, in a sweat by the time he left, wondered what he would have said to authorities if he had actually hit Arévalo's dead body.[82]

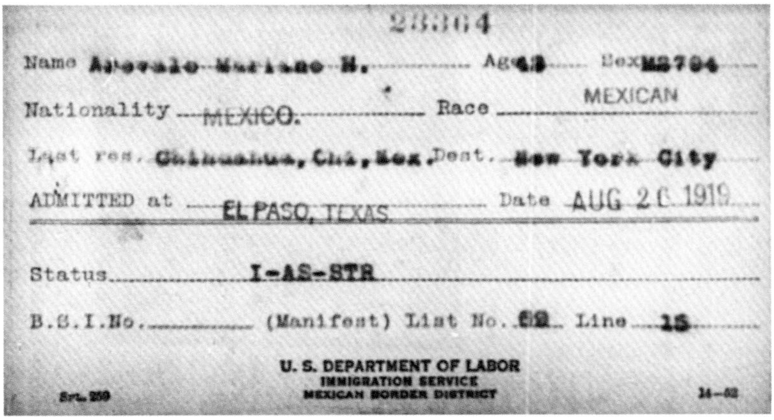

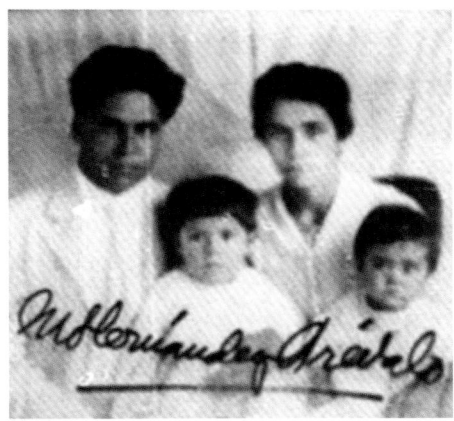

Mariano H. Arévalo immigration documents

NATIONAL ARCHIVES AND RECORDS ADMINISTRATION; IMAGES COURTESY FAMILYSEARCH.ORG

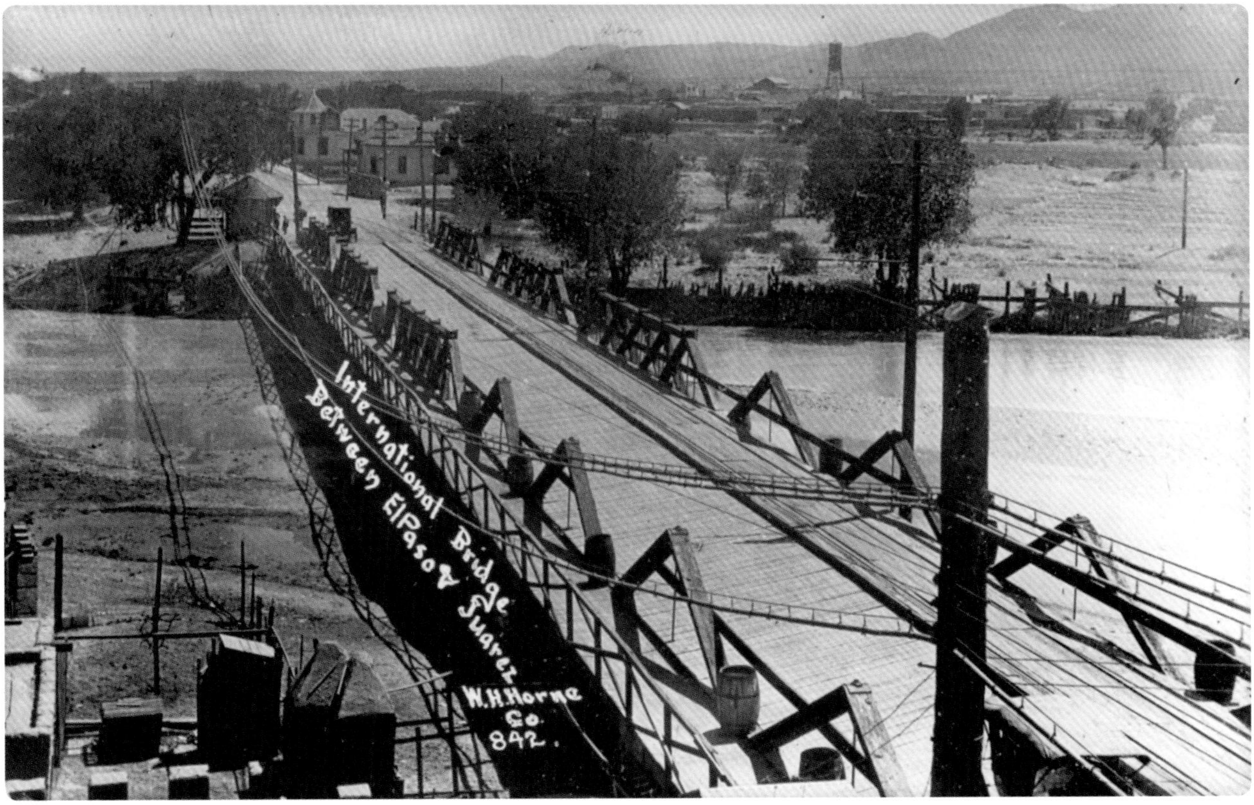

Postcard showing bridge between El Paso and Juárez [1915]

by W. H. Horne Co., publisher

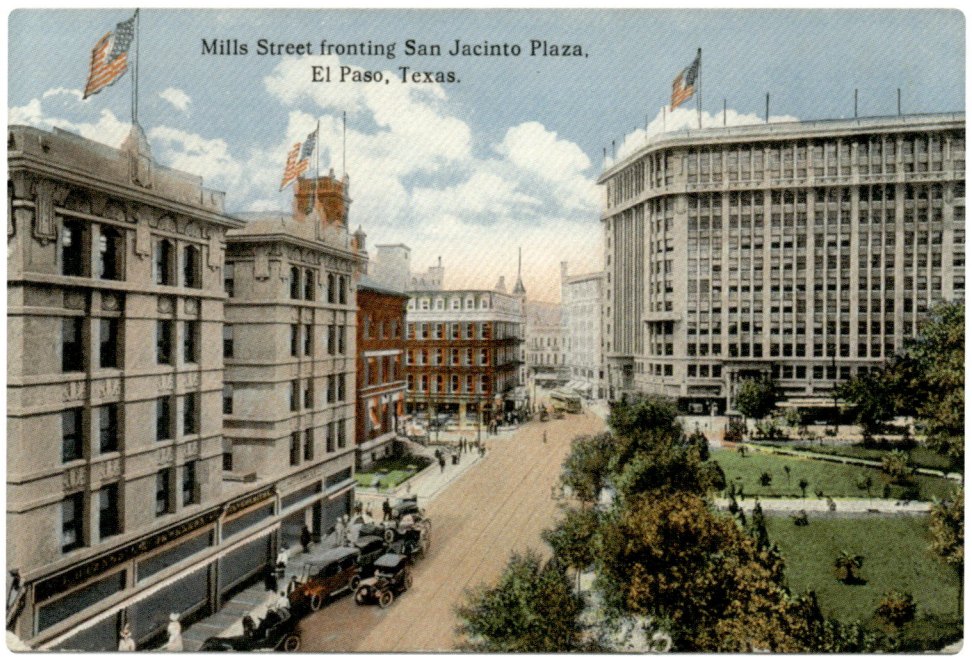

Postcard of downtown El Paso, with Roberts–Banner Building
(location of Fine Arts Shop) at left [ca. 1903–13]
by Curt Teich Postcards, publisher

Making a New Life in El Paso

Enrique Alférez lived with the Arévalo family for some time, likely from 1919 until the artist's death, in 1921. Between 1921 and his departure for Chicago in 1924, Alférez resided in at least four different places in El Paso, sometimes living with an employer and other times taking a room in a hotel.[83]

He found a position at the Fine Arts Shop, which had opened in 1918 in the Roberts-Banner Building in downtown El Paso.[84] Alférez worked as a janitor, framer, and assistant, and he performed a number of tasks, from mopping floors and washing windows to antiquing frames and novelties.[85] The Fine Arts Shop was run by Harry B. Wagoner, a painter who had previously lived in Chicago and who moved from Chicago to El Paso in search of a climate that was better suited for his health, given his history of tuberculosis.

Wagoner's shop sold artwork, etchings, and other knickknacks. A motto for the shop was, "You can live without art, but not so well."[86] Alférez later said that there seemed to be less fine art in the shop and more mottos in frames, "all those clichés people live by."[87] While that may have been true to some extent, the Fine Arts Shop provided custom framing and represented artists from El Paso, Santa Fe, and Taos, setting itself at the forefront of the burgeoning art scene in El Paso.

Alférez said he was paid four dollars a week at the Fine Arts Shop. Wagoner's interpretation of his compensation was slightly different, although it added up to about the same in pocket money. Wagoner said he paid Alférez thirty dollars a month and that he had written to the youth's father to ask for permission to start a bank account for him; half the wages were granted in cash, the other half deposited.[88] Wagoner proved helpful to Alférez in other ways too. He encouraged Alférez to take English and penmanship classes. "Why penmanship, I don't know, because I never had any use for it," Alférez later said, despite acquiring an elegant handwriting.[89]

Wagoner's extensive connections in Chicago likely influenced the young sculptor's ideas about studying art there. Wagoner also organized what was likely Alférez's first exhibition, a group show of thirty-three artists in a chamber of commerce building in El Paso in February 1922.[90]

Wagoner's Fine Arts Shop was also frequented by some of El Paso's prominent residents, and it was through Wagoner's relationship with Tom Lea II, a former mayor of El Paso, that Alférez met Lea's son Tom. The younger Tom was an artist and writer who later wrote the Southwestern classic *The Brave Bulls*, and he is recognized as a renowned painter of the US Southwest. The two became friends and attended the School of the Art Institute of Chicago together, and Lea was a lifelong friend and supporter of Alférez's.

When they met, Alférez was living in a small room at the Hotel Alamo on El Paso Street, and Lea thought of Alférez as "very, very poor."[91] Alférez became close with Lea's family; even after moving to Chicago, he returned to El Paso periodically to visit with the Leas. Much later in life, he occasionally made journeys longer than necessary when traveling between New Orleans and Mexico, making El Paso an intermediate stop so he could spend time with Lea.[92] The two continued to correspond throughout their lives, and decades later Lea was instrumental in facilitating introductions that led to one of Alférez's two major exhibitions outside the city of New Orleans.

The Fine Arts Shop was a vibrant but short-lived part of the El Paso community. It closed after only a few years in business. Wagoner moved to California and Arizona, where he accrued significant respect as a landscape painter of deserts.[93] Before he left the area, he was asked by the local paper what advice he would give to a young man about to go into business. Wagoner thought a young man should "travel two years representing the business he has in mind."[94] This life advice would have resonated with Alférez.

After working at the Fine Arts Shop, Alférez became a retoucher for the portrait photographer Fred J. Feldman. Feldman photographed a number of El Paso's community leaders including bankers, mayors, and judges. Feldman's studio had a large staff, more than a dozen at a time, including women and Latinos—unusual for the time.[95] Feldman offered to leave Alférez his studio after his death.[96] But Alférez was not interested in a career in photography, and, by 1923, he had already settled on his next step.

There had been a defining moment early that year: on a fair Monday evening, March 26, 1923, a slight chill setting in after sunset and frost in the valleys of El Paso, Alférez went to Liberty Hall to attend a lecture by Lorado Zadoc Taft, the dean of public sculpture in the United States. The artist had studied at the École nationale supérieure des Beaux-Arts in Paris from 1880 until 1883 and was well known for his large Beaux-Arts–style public fountains and monuments. When Taft visited El Paso that March, he had already spent more than thirty years in affiliation with the Art Institute of Chicago, where he taught clay, plaster, and marble carving. He delivered lectures at the University of Chicago and the University of Illinois, inspiring thousands of students and members of the community.[97] Taft toured regularly, delivering hundreds of lectures on sculpture around the United States, and in 1924 he published

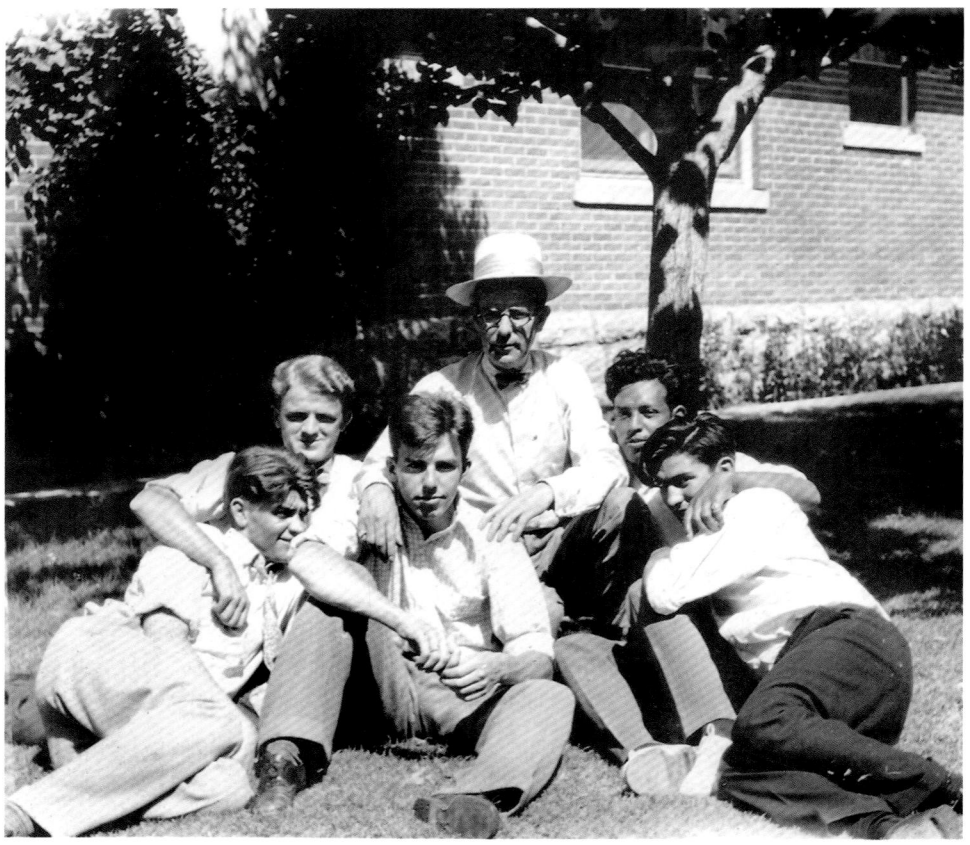

All-summer house party bunch at the Leas (left to right: Scott Wilkey, Oscar Will, Tom Lea III, Tom Lea II, Enrique Alférez, Dave Lacy) [ca. 1919–24]

COURTESY OF THE TOM LEA INSTITUTE

A History of American Sculpture, the first survey of the subject. He advocated for realism in representation of the human figure and criticized the growing movement toward modern, abstract work.[98]

The year before Alférez saw Taft in El Paso, Taft had overseen the installation and dedication of his *Fountain of Time* on the south side of Chicago. Featuring more than a hundred figures on a single platform and extending more than 126 feet in length, the massive sculpture rises "like an apparition" on the west end of the Midway Plaisance in Washington Park. Taft used steel-reinforced cast concrete to create the work. The material was thought to be less expensive and more durable than alternative mediums for such an enormous piece.[99]

For the *Fountain of Time,* Taft utilized the Earley method, patented by John Joseph Earley in 1922, in which aggregate, such as small quartz pebbles, was mixed with cement and sand; once set, the surface of the cast cement was scrubbed to create a finish that, viewed from a distance, appeared smooth and consistent. Earley initially used the process for architectural purposes, and he and Taft experimented together to cast the *Fountain of Time.*[100] Their success led to a new stage of cast concrete in art and design, and Alférez would ultimately use the process as well.

Taft frequently delivered "clay talks," lectures illustrated by his on-stage modeling of clay or by a presentation of slides.[101] In El Paso, Taft's stage was set with a table topped with clay and other tools and equipment. He also had a papier-mâché replica of a bust by Michelangelo. Standing before the audience, he shaped clay into the face of Marie Antoinette, adding and removing material, giving attention to facial muscles and wrinkles, until he had transformed the young Antoinette into an aged woman. Throughout the demonstration, he spoke to the audience about his process, and sculpture more broadly, earning "constant ripples of laughter" in response to his "homely philosophy and dry wit." That night, Taft also talked about the state of US sculpture, saying that the country had not yet learned to express itself in art. "We leave it for the foreigner who comes to this country to lead the way," he said.[102]

The evening resonated with Alférez. Even more than sixty years later, Alférez said watching Taft on stage that night was "like seeing magic."[103]

After the talk, Alférez and a few of his friends, including Tom Lea, went backstage to talk with Taft. Taft asked the boys, "Who's the genius here?"—and Lea pushed Alférez forward.[104]

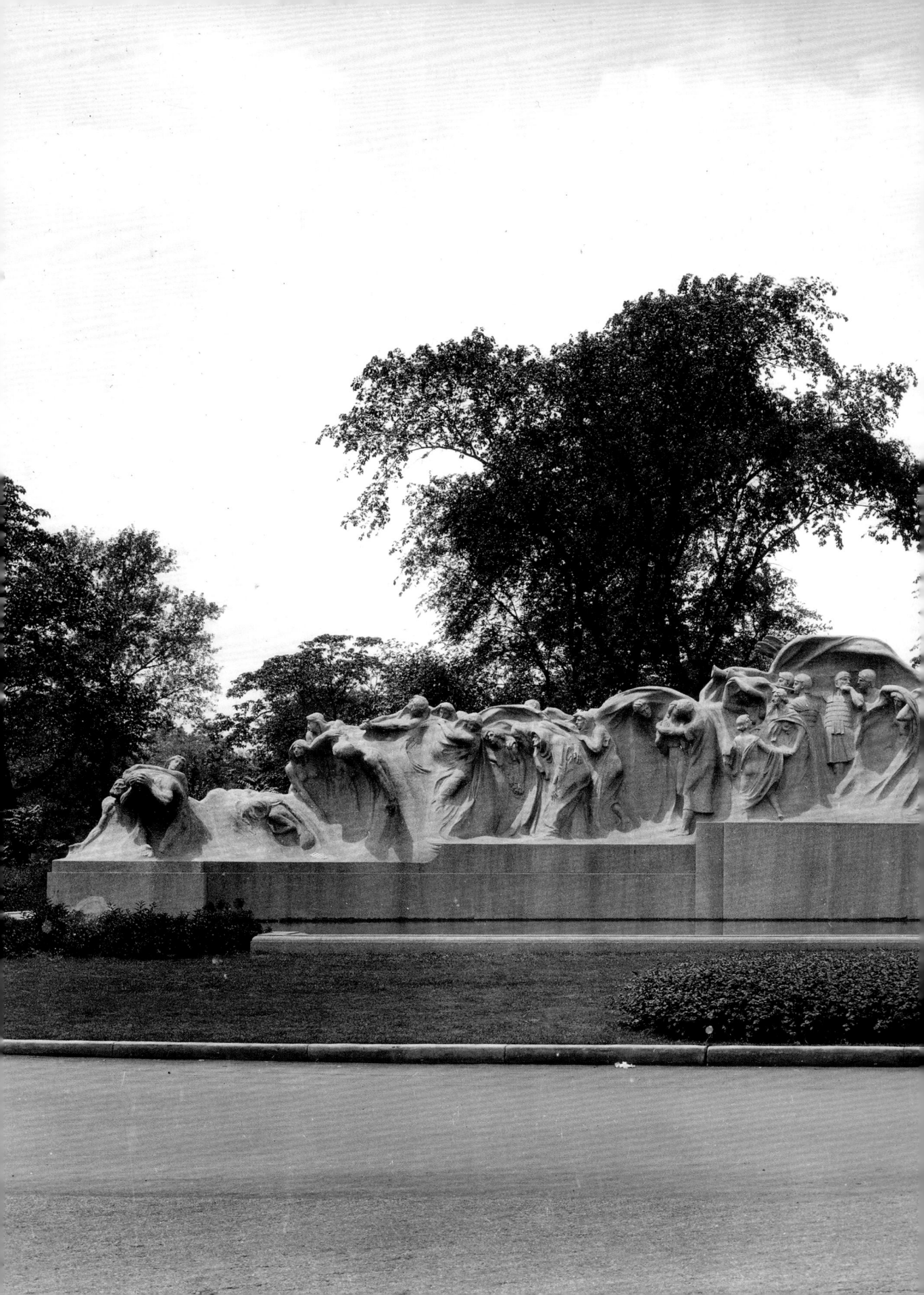

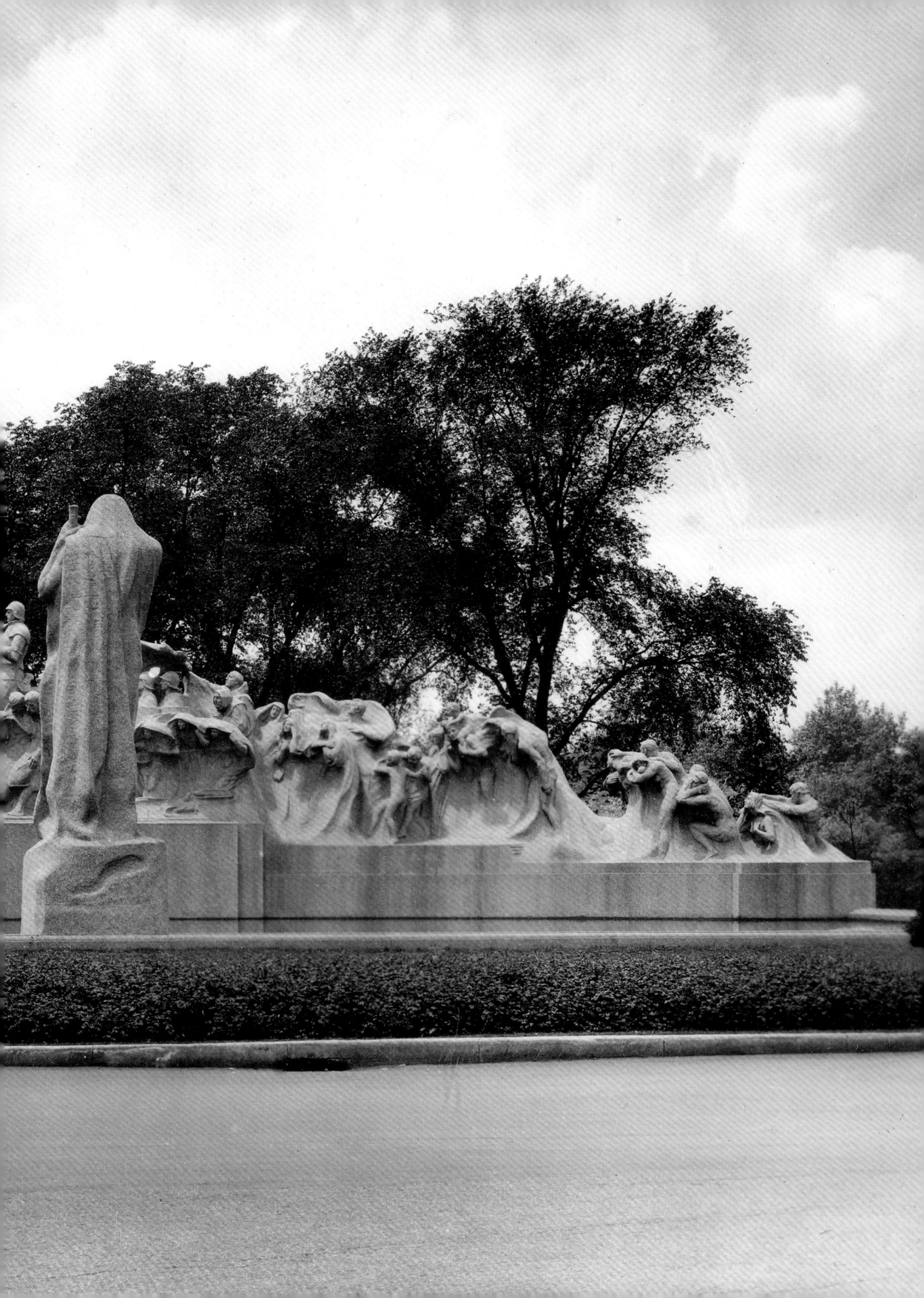

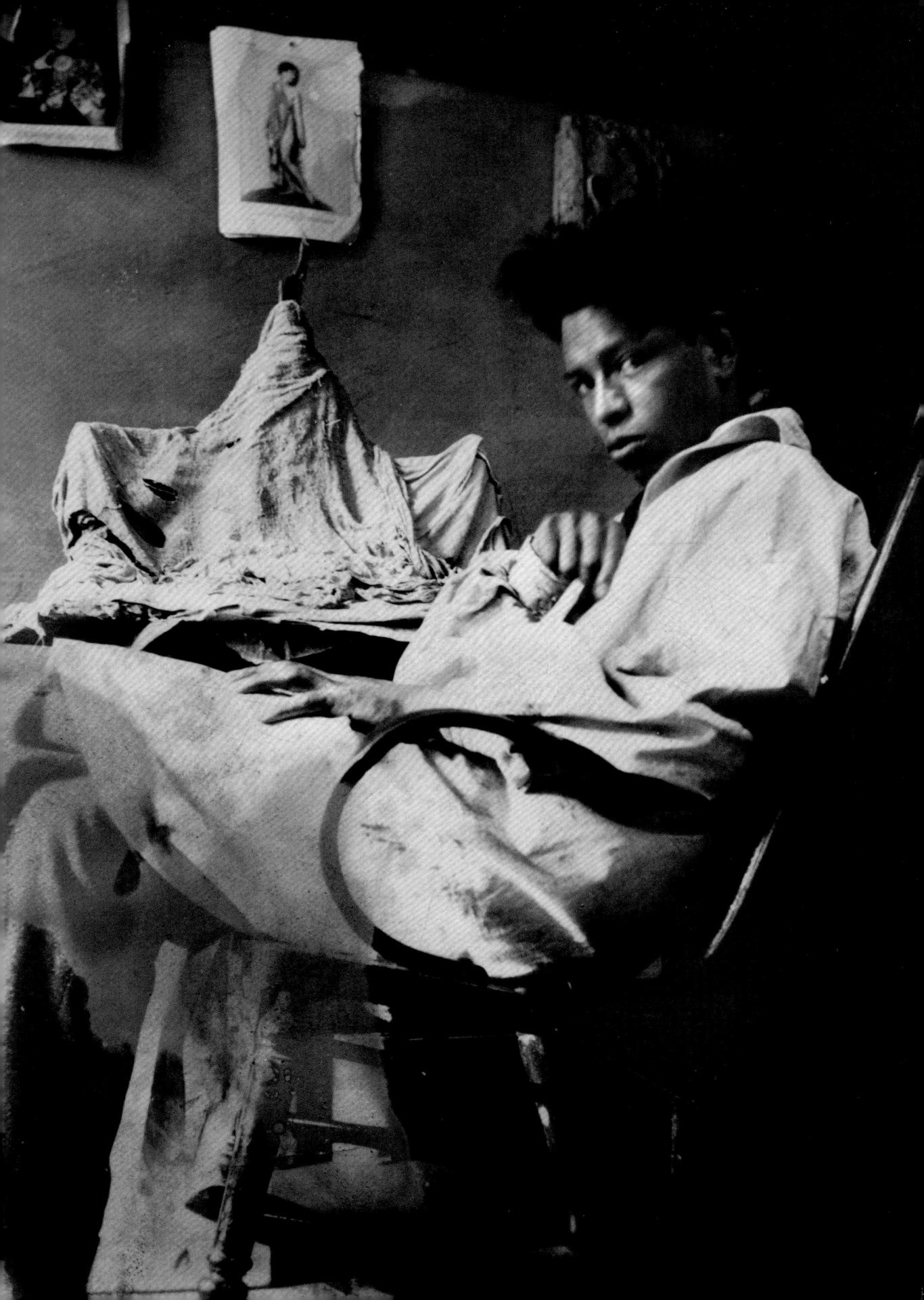

CHAPTER FIVE

The Chicago Years

WHEN ENRIQUE ALFÉREZ ARRIVED in Chicago, in 1924, he had with him two suitcases and fifteen dollars.[105] He stayed at the YMCA on South Wabash Avenue for a few days, for a dollar a night, before moving into Lorado Taft's Midway Studios.[106]

His travel to Chicago had been supported by the El Paso Kiwanis Club, members of which raised the funds to send him to the Institute after a prompt by Bertha Wuehrmann, a benefactor of Alférez's in El Paso. In a 1935 interview, Wuehrmann offered insight about why she decided to help the young sculptor get to Chicago. She visited him one night, finding him in a "cheap south El Paso hotel working away at his sculpture with a picture of Taft, cut from a magazine, in a carved frame of his own making, setting before him."[107] She said that the scene she encountered "was too much" for her.

She wrote to Taft to ask if he would accept Alférez at the Midway Studios. Taft agreed to accept him if he was willing to do chores to support his room and board, a common arrangement he offered his residents. Alférez agreed to this requirement, and he took on responsibilities such as helping in the studio's kitchen before meals. Wuehrmann wanted to make the transition as easy as possible on both mentor and student, and the *El Paso Herald Post* later reported that she even arranged to have Alférez's tonsils removed to minimize the chances of him "getting ill."[108]

By the time Alférez arrived in Chicago, the Midway Studios had been located for nearly twenty years on University of Chicago property adjacent to the Midway Plaisance, home to Taft's *Fountain of Time*. Two large barns were converted into studio space, with separate residence halls for men and women.[109] Taft biographer Allen Stuart Weller called the Midway Studios "a unique contribution to American

Alférez in an early work space
COURTESY OF THE TLALOC SELWAY ALFÉREZ PAPERS

sculpture," noting that nothing like it had been previously created in the United States. He described Taft's studio as a "rather democratic and Beaux Arts conception of an Italian Renaissance *bottega* reborn in Chicago."[110]

In a bottega, students assist the artist, apprentice-style, to learn a range of skills. At the Midway Studios, residents worked alongside Taft on his large-scale commissions, and approximately twenty of them lived on-site at a time.[111] Alférez had arranged for Tom Lea, also studying at the Institute, to live at Midway Studios; his friend once commented that the students would do "some of the sort of peon work" for Taft.[112] In fact, residents gained many skills, and Taft supported his students in obtaining their own commissions. He supported the development of a number of professional sculptors, many of whom Alférez met and worked with at the studios, including Leonard Crunelle, Nellie Walker, and Fred and Mabel Torrey.

When Alférez lived at the Midway Studios, it had more than a dozen rooms. In addition to studio space, it included a small stage, kitchen, and community room. The main entrance led to a large room filled with plaster models, and at the center of the room there was a small pool filled with goldfish. Vines partially covered the buildings, and a number of skylights offered natural light.[113] By night, the skylights brought in moonlight and the "reflected glow of South Chicago steel furnaces . . . [making] the tall plaster figures seem ghostly among the shadows," according to Ruth Helming Mose, who was a resident at Midway Studios and whose husband, sculptor Carl Mose, studied and worked with Taft for many years.[114]

By the time Alférez arrived on the scene, Taft's career was well established, and he was recognized for his advocacy of a public role for the arts, a commitment infused into daily activity at the Midway Studios. Taft was designing—on paper, if never in reality—a dream museum with a great hall filled with skylights and galleries of art from around the world, with rooms dedicated to England, Germany, Italy, and Scandinavia, as well as Egyptian, Islamic, and Asian art. Taft kept an open studio, inviting in students and guests to introduce them to art in a variety of ways. He produced "peep shows"—diorama-like miniature scenes of the studios of Renaissance artists—as a way of enlivening art history; he had students dress up in costume as master artists; and he was continually discussing the value of making art accessible to more people.

To achieve his dream of making art more accessible, Taft proposed that secondary schools develop small galleries with reproductions of work by sculptors such as Praxiteles, Edvard Eriksen, and Augustus Saint-Gaudens. "Do you know that there is hardly a school-child in Chicago who has ever been privileged to see reproductions, even, of the masterpieces of ancient art?" asked Taft. "How can Chicago—or America—be expected to produce a surpassing art if these same young people, among whom are future artists, have no foundation on which to build?"[115] Questions

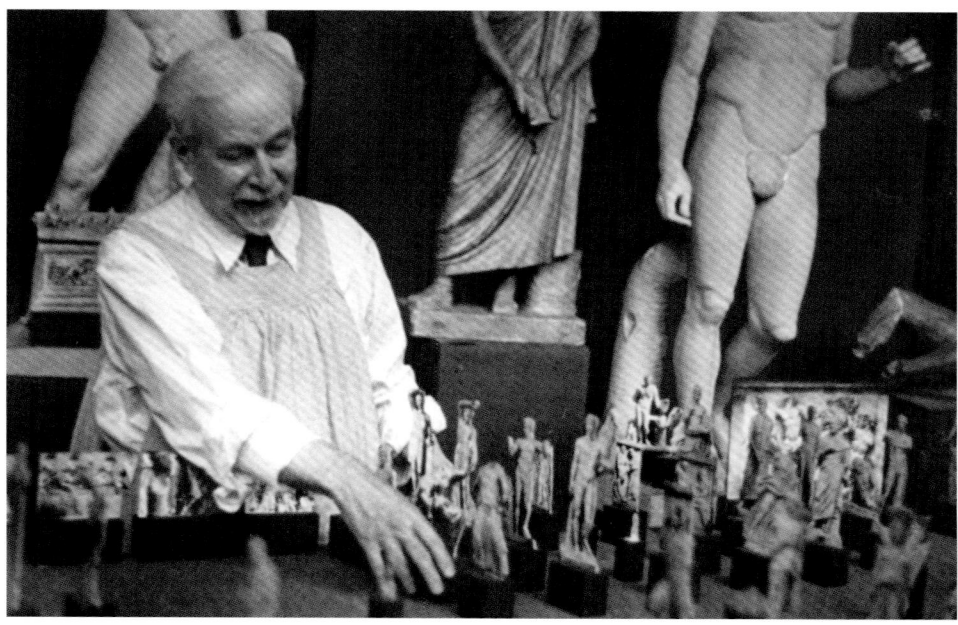

Lorado Taft at Midway Studios
COURTESY OF THE UNIVERSITY OF ILLINOIS AT URBANA-CHAMPAIGN ARCHIVES, IMAGE 0006294

and concerns such as these underpinned Taft's lifelong commitment to supporting the role of the arts in education and installations in public spaces.

In addition to writing and lecturing, Taft remained focused on his own art and his students. His obituary in *Art Thoughts* in 1936 estimated that he had spent a quarter of a million dollars, a vast sum for the time, supporting his students and the young sculptors who lived at the Midway Studios, many of whom lived there expense-free. Taft's obituary also dedicated three paragraphs to Alférez as a star student, celebrating their relationship as an example of Taft's success as "a molder of men as well as of clay."[116]

Diversity was a hallmark of the Midway Studios and the School of the Art Institute. Taft included women, immigrant, and African American students in his studio at a time when this wasn't the norm.[117] The School of the Art Institute was one of the few art schools in the United States that enrolled African American students, and students and faculty increasingly embraced "socially concerned art."[118] While Alférez experienced aspects of discrimination throughout his life, he was generally welcomed and accepted in Chicago, befriending leading intellectuals, writers, and artists.

Alférez stayed in Chicago for about three years, taking the Chicago "L" from the Midway Studios to campus for his classes at the School of the Art Institute, where he took a night course on modeling in the fall and winter of 1924–25 and a figure

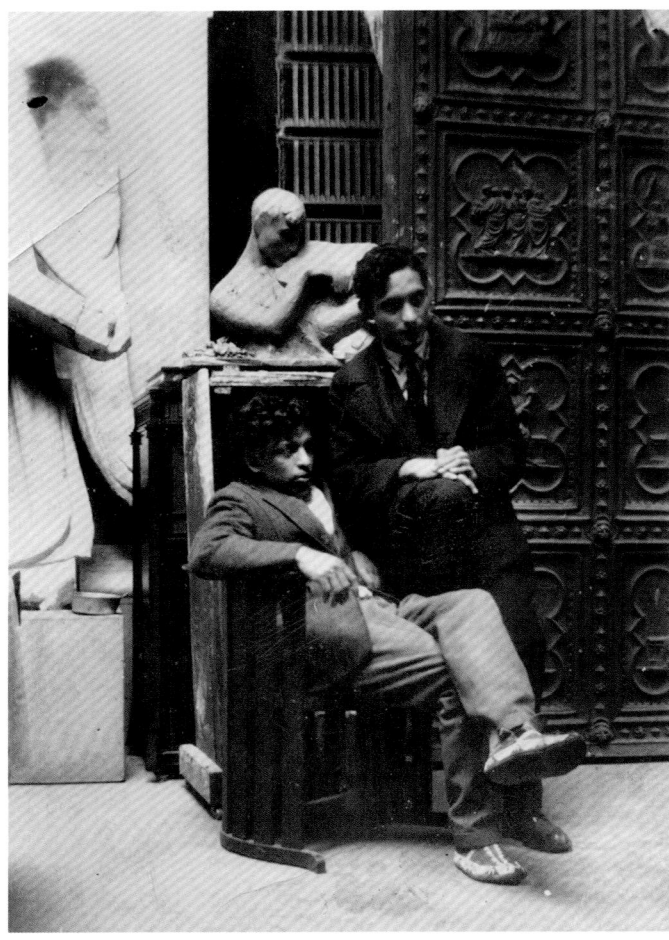

Alférez (seated) **and unknown man in front of a replica of Andrea Pisano's**
Florence Baptistery doors at Midway Studios, Chicago [ca. 1924–25]
COURTESY OF THE TLALOC SELWAY ALFÉREZ PAPERS

modeling course in the fall of 1925.[119] These early years of Alférez's formal training in art coincided with a period when aesthetics were becoming streamlined, emphasizing long horizontal lines, geometric motifs and curved forms, symmetrical patterns, and shapes such as zigzags and chevrons. This transition was underway in many areas of art and design, from architecture and interior design to furniture and fashion. There was also a blending of contemporary and ancient visual elements of Maya, Egyptian, and Asian cultures. Other early twentieth-century art movements, such as cubism, Russian constructivism, and futurism, influenced art deco and modern aesthetics.[120]

While Alférez's skill continued to mature throughout his career, he held onto many of the early influences of art deco and modernism, as well as technical and philosophical approaches to sculpture that he learned from Taft. He was persistent in his appreciation for the axes and planes of classical sculpture, and he saw public sculpture as a medium through which to influence and portray the character of a place.

Residents of the Midway Studios contributed to Taft's large sculptures and also had the opportunity to learn how a working artist received, negotiated, and executed public commissions. Many of the figures Alférez created throughout his career originated in his artistic imagination, but others, such as portraits or bas-reliefs in architectural details, were conceived by those who commissioned him or hired him on a project. At Taft's studio Alférez learned how to implement the vision of architects who provided the basic structure, theme, and medium. He also learned about a sculptor's capacity to influence the content of architectural details. Working as a professional sculptor, Alférez would typically be given a synopsis or narrative of the project he needed to model in clay; he would subsequently prepare drawings and submit them to the architect for approval or modification. Taft's mentorship provided Alférez with experience in these areas.

Taft and his family lived in an apartment near the Midway Studios. He walked to the studio each day; at midday, lunch was served from a small kitchen. Twelve to twenty-five people typically convened for this meal—Sundays were particularly lively—and guests included the young artists who lived and worked in his studio, as well as their friends and Taft's. They gathered at a long dining table in a community room situated between replicas of the large bronze Baptistery Doors at Florence, Andrea Pisano's on one side and Lorenzo Ghiberti's on the other. One constant for students in the studio was the presence of plaster figures in their midst. For some of the time that Alférez lived there, a plaster model for *Recording Angel,* cast in bronze as a memorial in 1923, watched over the lunch table. During meals, conversations drifted from personal lives and romances of those in the studio to exhibitions in Chicago to Taft's relentless plans for educating the public and youth in particular about art.[121]

It must have been a remarkable transition for Alférez, from the death and destruction of the Mexican Revolution, where soldaderas cooked evening meals over campfires, to the white-clothed table of one of Chicago's greatest studios and its bevy of artists and intellectuals, talking of art exhibitions and romance.

Alférez's financial situation didn't improve significantly while he lived in Chicago. He got by on little, frequently stopping at a bakery to buy day-old cinnamon rolls, and he found work and odd jobs to help cover expenses.[122] Tom Lea recalled that

ON THE FOLLOWING PAGES:
Lunch at Midway Studios, with Alférez at far right [between 1924 and 1928]
COURTESY OF THE UNIVERSITY OF ILLINOIS AT URBANA-CHAMPAIGN ARCHIVES, IMAGE 0006285

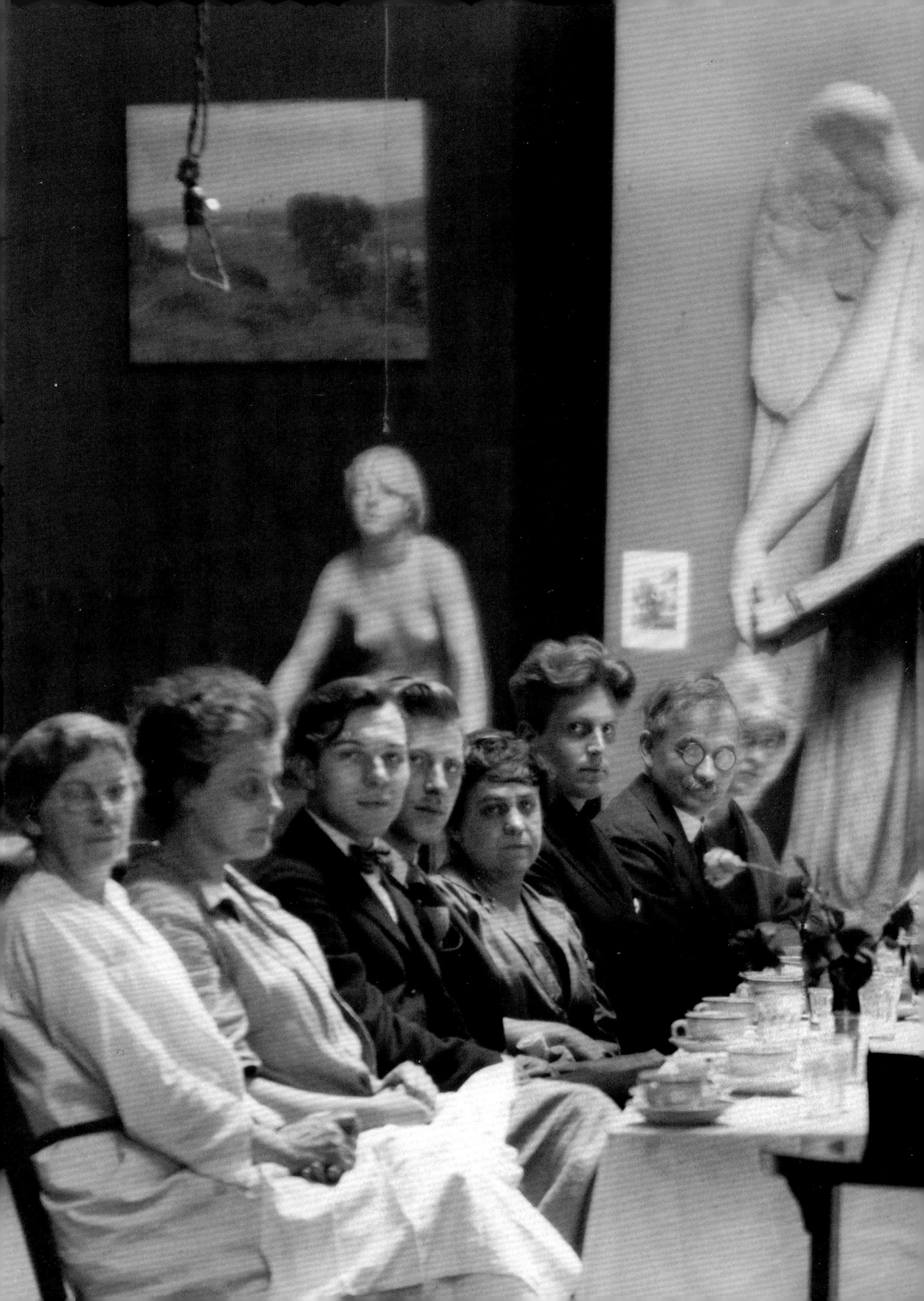

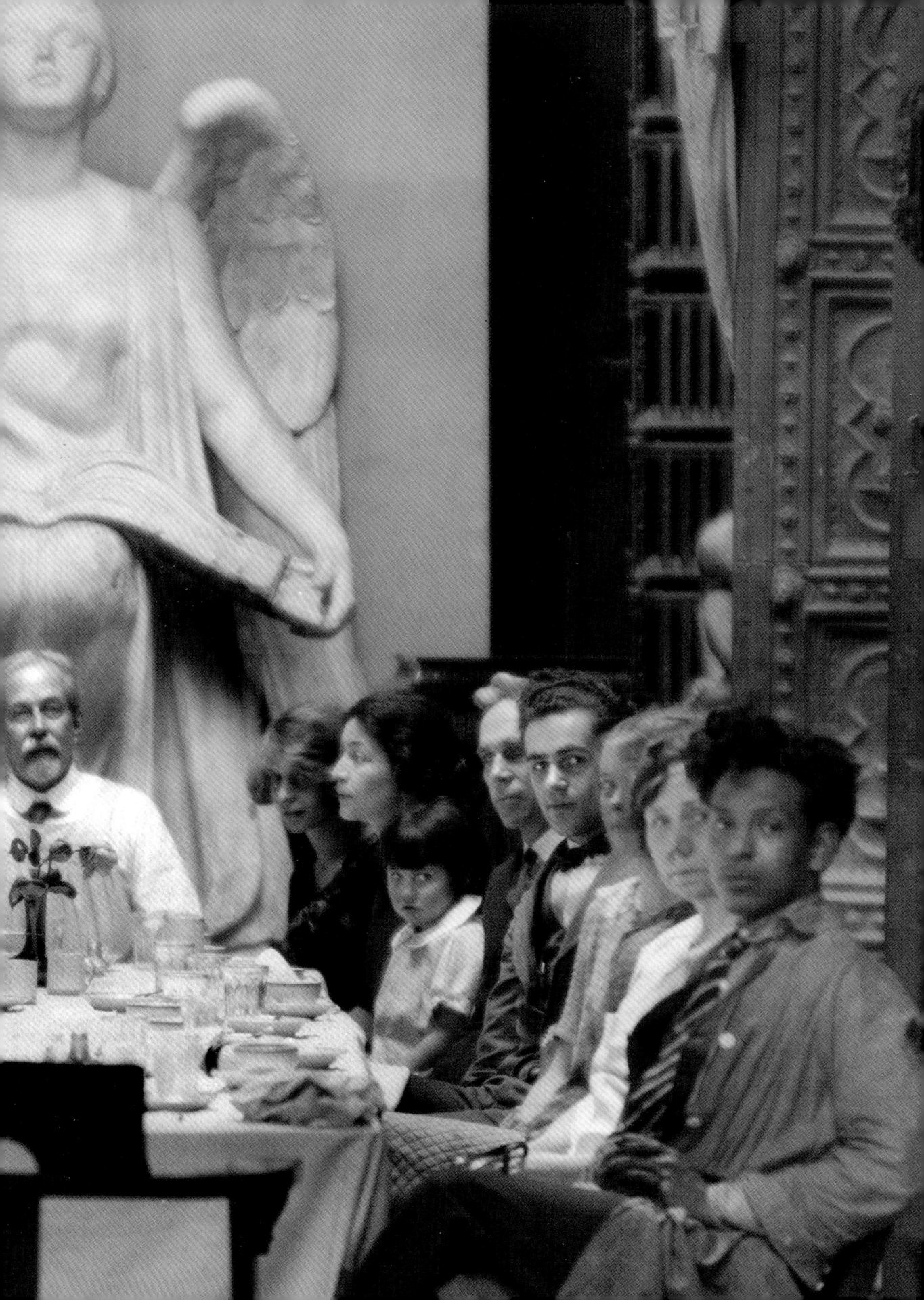

Alférez washed dishes in one of Chicago's oldest cafeterias, the Glen Inn, just a block away from the school on South Wabash Avenue. Alférez also worked as a model, earning a dollar a day and typically posing for twenty-five minutes, followed by twenty-five minutes of rest, repeating this pattern for three hours at a time. When modeling, Alférez posed as a Mexican caballero, wearing a borrowed sombrero and wrapping himself in a silk sash that had belonged to Victoriano Huerta, a military officer and president of Mexico from 1913 to 1914. The sash too had been borrowed—from Lea's father. Alférez added to this costume a serape and a short jacket, onto which he sewed coins.[123]

Alférez seems to have moved out of Taft's studio months before leaving Chicago for New Orleans in 1929. In an oral history conducted in 1975, he revealed that Taft asked him to leave the studio because "he didn't like the way I went around embracing the girls in the place." He added, "they had all been women who were old enough to be my grandmother, and I certainly had no bad intentions."

Before Alférez left Chicago, he was hired as a sculptor to contribute to a number of preeminent art deco buildings in the city, including Holabird and Root's 1929

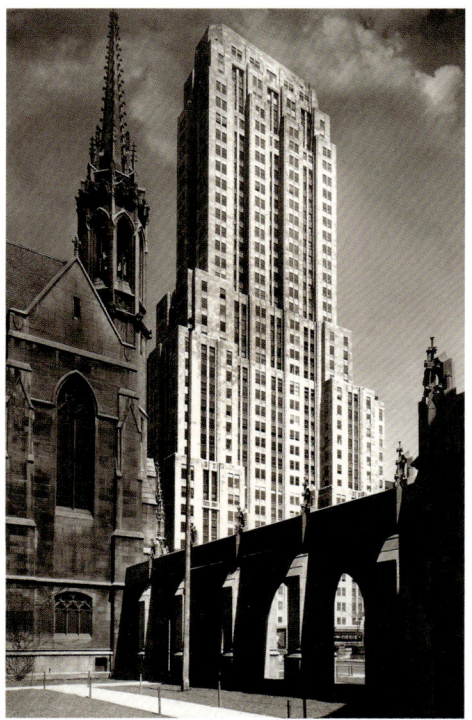

Palmolive Building
photo by Chicago Architectural Photographing Co.
COURTESY OF HISTORIC ARCHITECTURE AND LANDSCAPE
IMAGE COLLECTION, RYERSON AND BURNHAM ARCHIVES,
THE ART INSTITUTE OF CHICAGO

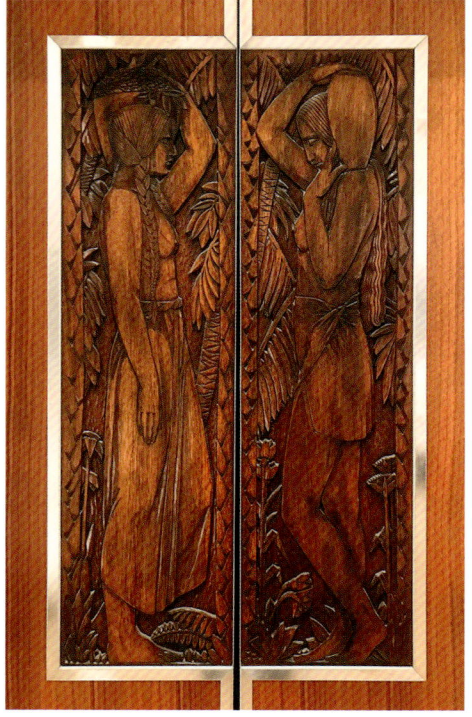

Palmolive Building elevator doors [1928]
photo by Lynn Stephens
COURTESY OF THE PALMOLIVE BUILDING

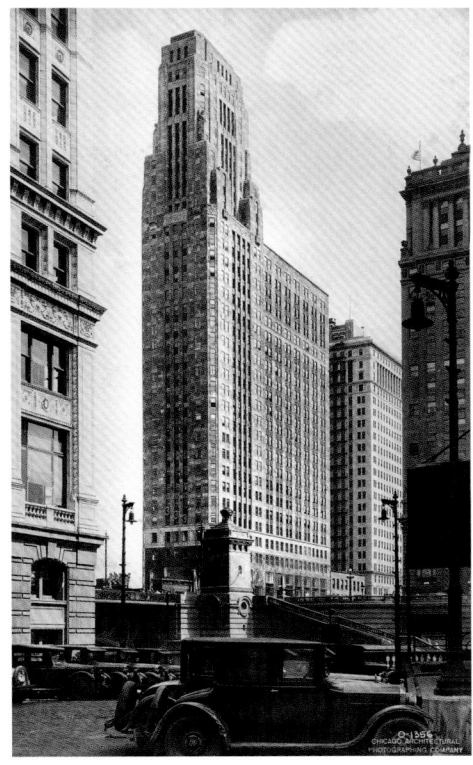

333 North Michigan Avenue
photo by Chicago Architectural Photographing Co.
COURTESY OF HISTORIC ARCHITECTURE AND LANDSCAPE
IMAGE COLLECTION, RYERSON AND BURNHAM ARCHIVES,
THE ART INSTITUTE OF CHICAGO

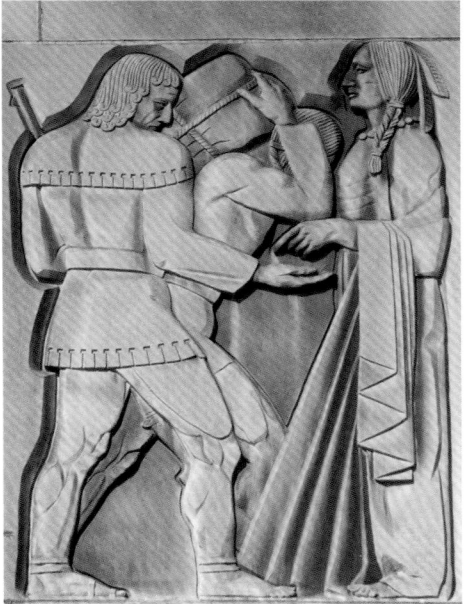

333 North Michigan Avenue exterior frieze
[1928]
photo by Gregory Jenkins, AIA

Palmolive Building (later the headquarters for *Playboy* magazine, now home to luxury condominiums) at 919 North Michigan Avenue. For this commission, Alférez carved eighty-four panels in walnut and oak for the elevator doors and cabs, many featuring women bathing and gathering water.[124]

Alférez also created architectural details for 333 North Michigan Avenue, which was completed in 1928. Fellow Midway Studios resident Fred Torrey was commissioned by Holabird and Roche, a precursor to Holabird and Root, to create a frieze on the exterior of the fifth floor of the building.[125] Alférez said he worked alongside Torrey on this project, and his résumé from 1930 indicates he created five of the reliefs.[126] Panels include historical and cultural figures relevant to the region, including "The Traders," "The Covered Wagon Era," "The Hunter," and "The Pioneer Woman." Alférez never received credit for his role in the frieze, which upset him so deeply that he recounted the slight in 1985, nearly sixty years after the fact, in a letter to his friend, the journalist and publisher Jack Davis. While Alférez leaned toward exaggeration and, in some cases, offered inaccurate details about personal aspects of his life, he neither joked nor intentionally misled about his art. There is no reason to disbelieve he completed panels for this project.

In his letter to Davis, Alférez also mentioned a second incident with Torrey. While on a visit to Veracruz in 1928, he received a letter from Lorado Taft's colleague, architect Otis F. Johnson, who invited him back to Chicago for a job. Johnson offered to pay his seventy-five-dollar fare. Alférez returned, believing he had been hired to design the reliefs for the facade of what he later referred to as a "memorial building" in New York: the art deco–style Norton Memorial Hall that Johnson and Taft had designed for the Chautauqua Institution, an arts education center and historic district in Chautauqua, New York.

Alférez was "excited to be a professional" and "worked like hell" for a few weeks, in Chicago, on the bas-reliefs for the hall. Torrey reviewed his designs and told him to make one figure "more ample"; Alférez refused. Torrey briefly left the studio and returned with a contract for the job, indicating that he, not Alférez, was in charge of the reliefs. Convinced that Torrey had been taking advantage of him, a furious Alférez went to speak to Johnson, who told him to charge Torrey and get paid, which he did.[127]

In his 1985 letter to Davis, Alférez indicated that he had created four reliefs for Norton Hall. This is inconsistent with his 1930 résumé, in which he claims to have created only one of the installed panels; the résumé also includes details about the dimensions of a panel. It seems likely that he misremembered the details decades after the fact. One of the extant panels stands out as possibly his.

Alférez believed that he lost the job to Torrey because Johnson thought Alférez didn't know anything about signing contracts. Whether he was implying that Johnson was questioning his language skills, experience, or genuine lack of business acumen isn't clear. Like his contributions at 333 North Michigan Avenue, though, he received no public credit.

Taft and his network opened up other opportunities for Alférez. On Sundays, when Taft would deliver lectures, the Midway Studios was abuzz. One such Sunday, the author and journalist Meyer Levin arrived at the studio and found Alférez and other students wearing Italianate costumes in the manner of Renaissance artists, an occasional practice during these weekend gatherings. Levin took a liking to Alférez and introduced him to other writers as well, including the poet Carl Sandburg and screenwriter and playwright Ben Hecht.[128] The friends set out to introduce Alférez to a world where art and literature prevailed.

Along with his writer friends, Alférez took weekend trips to visit Sandburg at his house in Harbert, Michigan. Once, traveling alone, Alférez requested a bus ticket "in his not too distinct English," and it was not until he arrived in Hartford, Michigan—nearly fifty miles from Harbert—that, with great distress, he realized the

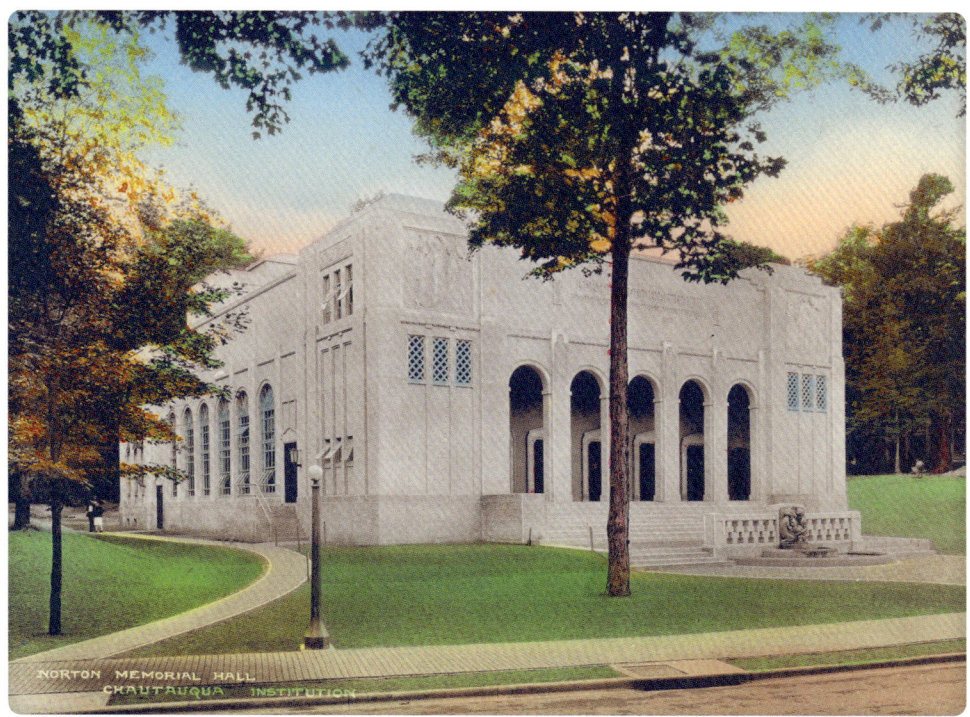

Postcard of Norton Memorial Hall at Chautauqua Institution [1930]
COURTESY OF CHAUTAUQUA INSTITUTION ARCHIVES, OLIVER ARCHIVES CENTER PHOTOGRAPHIC COLLECTION

error.[129] At a time when he was still struggling with his own language skills, teaching himself more English by reading and looking at the comics, it is befitting that he was also drawn to these experts of the written English language.[130] Additionally, Alférez and Sandburg shared a similar worldview that shaped their respective approaches to their art; both were drawn to public art and focused on the individual, the every-man. They stayed friends throughout their lives, and Sandburg visited Alférez in New Orleans at least once in the late 1950s.

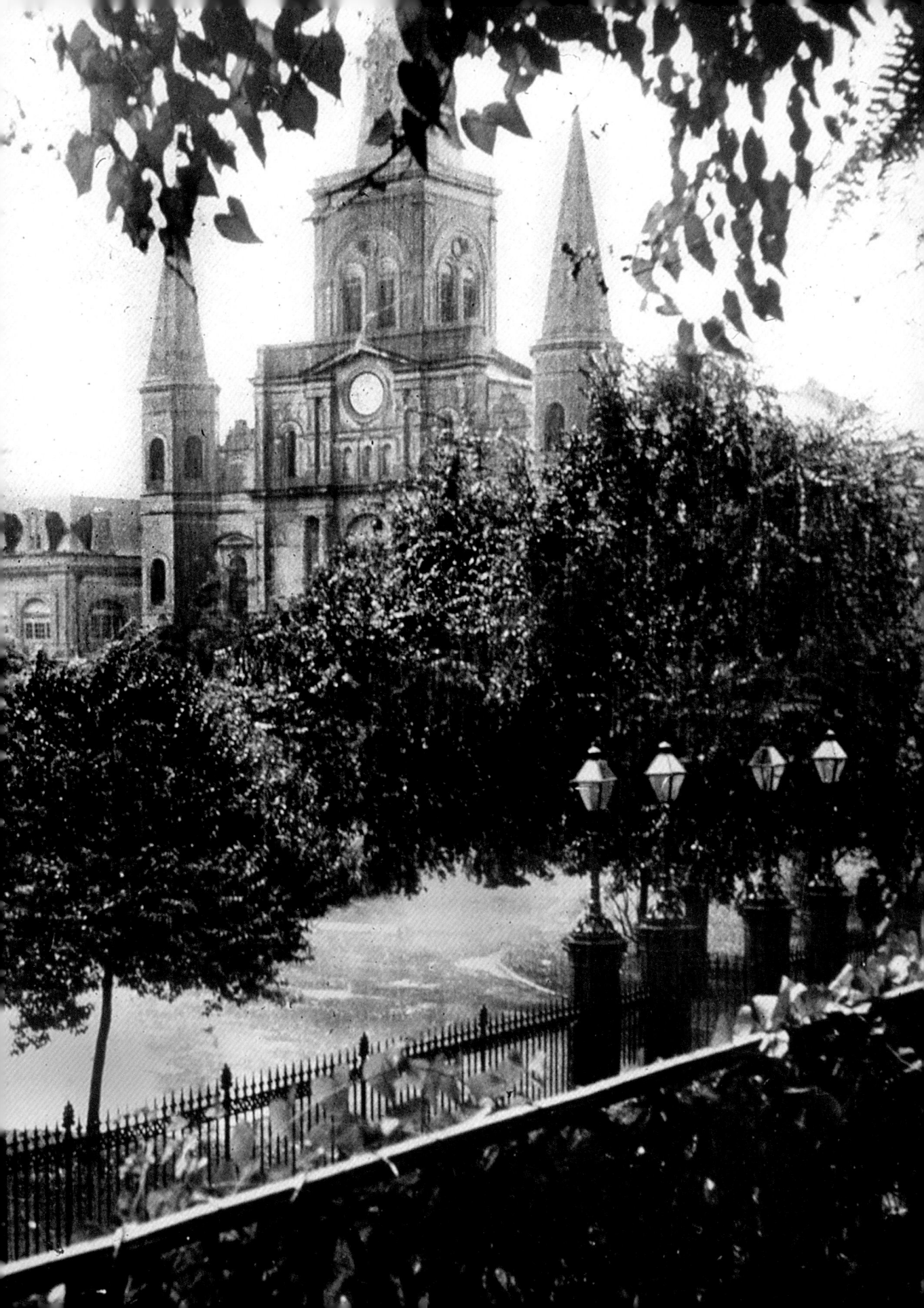

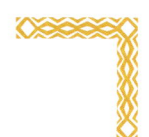

CHAPTER SIX

Arrival in New Orleans

ENRIQUE ALFÉREZ ARRIVED in New Orleans in May 1929. He consistently described his move to the city as a kind of happenstance: while still in Chicago, he had seen the port city of New Orleans as a midpoint in his travels from the Windy City to Yucatán, and he planned to stay only long enough to earn some money.[131]

When he arrived in the city, he found a welcoming, bohemian atmosphere in the French Quarter, which had come alive in the 1920s with a confluence of the arts: writers, visual artists, and musicians working and living in the historic district nested between the Mississippi River and North Rampart Street. Spanish, French, African, and Caribbean influences added layers and textures to the landscape: Creole cottages among Greek revival homes, stucco walls with exposed brick, and intricate cast-iron balconies. There was a cacophony of vibrant street life that persists today. One of the city's most famed chroniclers, writer and journalist Lyle Saxon, predicted that "soon we would boast of our Place d'Armes as New York does her Washington Square."[132] Among those writers whose articles and essays established the French Quarter as an intellectual center for the South and the world—a place where the unconventional was the convention—were Saxon, Sherwood Anderson, William Faulkner, and Natalie Scott. The *Double Dealer*, a literary journal published from 1921 to 1926, "bridged a gap between regional and national writing" and, despite its relatively brief lifespan, had long-lasting effects on southern literature.[133]

The artistic renaissance in New Orleans was inextricably tied to the Arts and Crafts Club, established informally in 1919 and formally chartered in 1922. The club, located in its heyday at 520 Royal Street, gave artists a place to meet, work, and learn. It hosted group exhibitions featuring local and regional artists and also brought

View of Jackson Square from Frans Blom's apartment in the Pontalba Building
FRANS BLOM PAPERS, BANCROFT LIBRARY, UNIVERSITY OF CALIFORNIA, BERKELEY

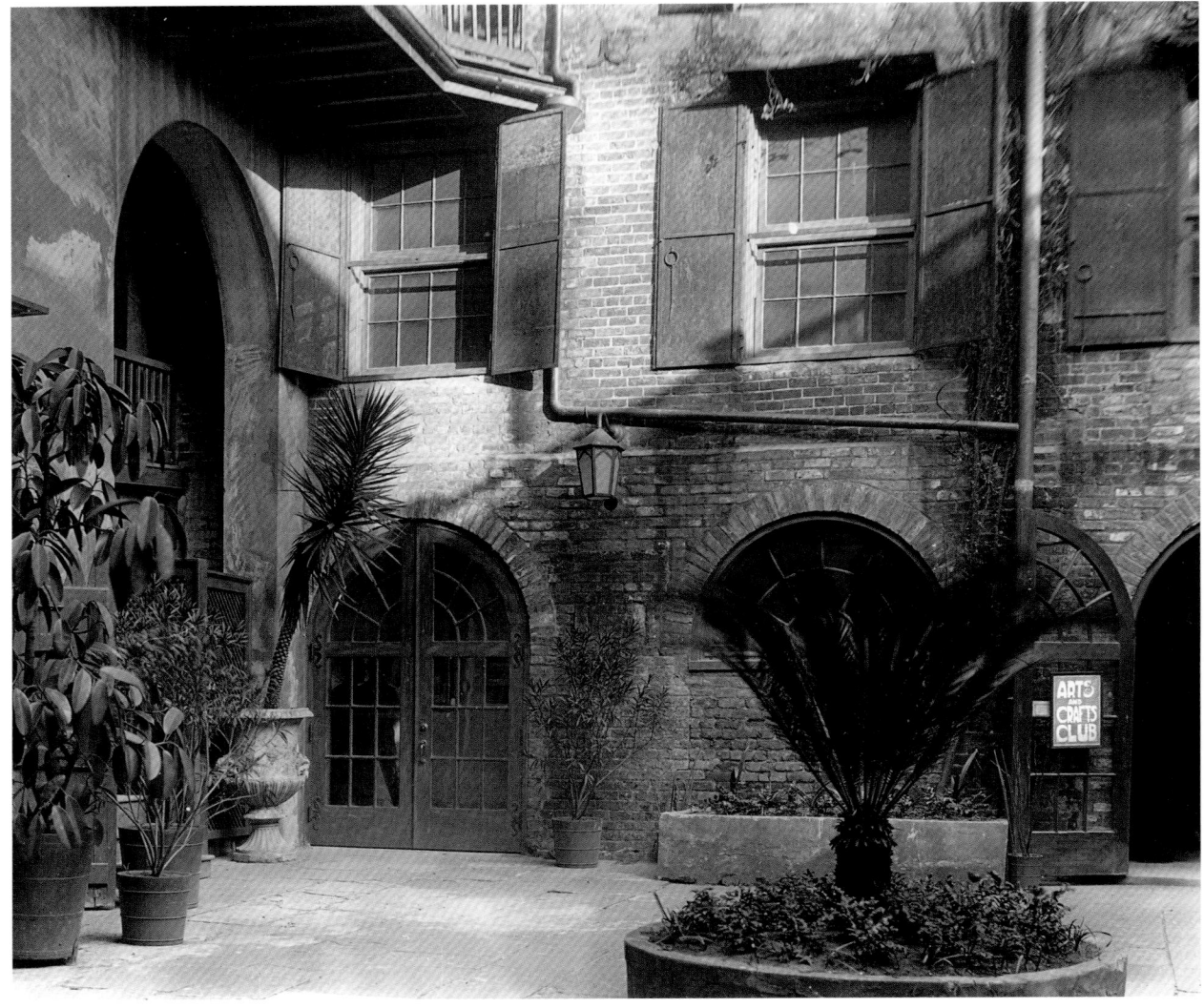

Courtyard of Arts and Crafts Club at 520 Royal Street [ca. 1929]

photo by Daniel Sweeney Leyrer
THNOC, GIFT OF ALLAN PHILLIP JAFFE, 1981.324.6.5

international exhibitions to the city. Alférez participated in group and solo shows at the club, where he also taught sculpture and figure drawing through its art school.[134] This space gave Alférez a wide net of artist friends, among them Paul Ninas and Xavier Gonzalez, as well as introductions to visiting artists. He remained active with the club throughout the 1930s and the early 1940s.

Alférez's first apartment in New Orleans was at Saint Peter Street and Cabildo Alley in the French Quarter, off Jackson Square. The apartment's prior tenant had been William Spratling.[135] Spratling had recently left New Orleans for Taxco, Mexico, a town southwest of Mexico City, known for active silver mines and silver craft traditions. An architecture instructor at Tulane University, Spratling had become intrigued by Mexico and pre-Columbian history, architecture, and culture through his Tulane colleague Frans Blom and anthropologist Oliver La Farge.[136] Blom took research trips to Maya sites throughout Latin America and frequently delivered related lectures and slideshows at the Arts and Crafts Club. Inspired, Spratling—who went on to become a successful silver designer—left for Mexico with support from Blom, who facilitated introductions to artists and cultural figures such as painters Diego Rivera and José Clemente Orozco; Frances Toor, founder of the journal *Mexican Folkways*; and Rafael Heliodoro Valle, editor for the *Excelsior* newspaper.[137]

New Orleans and Louisiana artists' interest in Mexico would continue to grow over the following decades. They were intrigued by connections between pre-

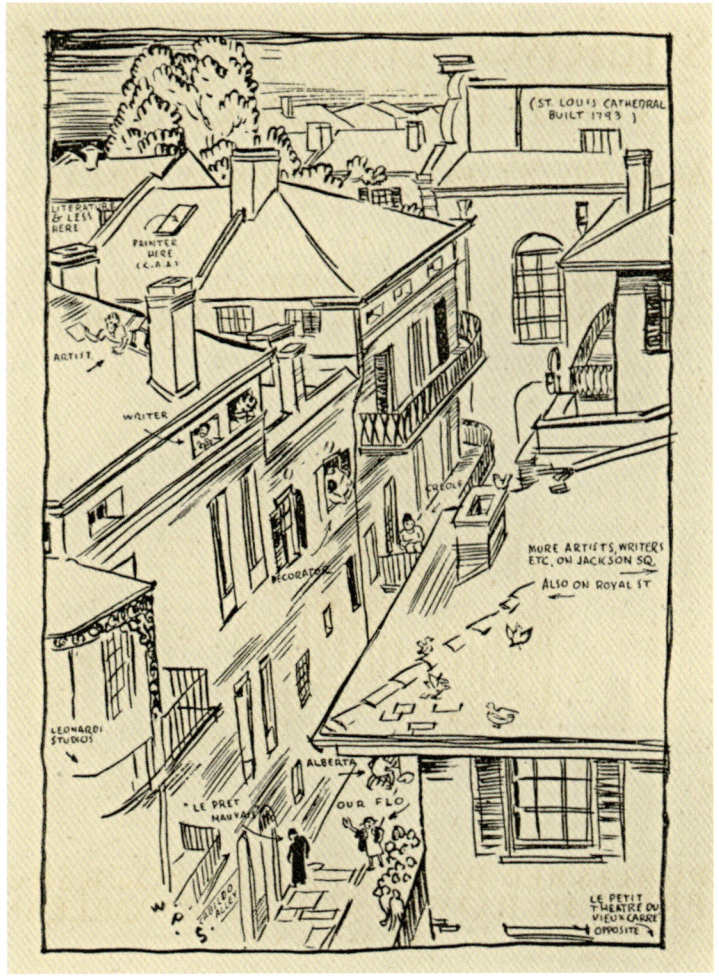

William Spratling's drawing of the block where he, and later Alférez, lived in the 1920s; from *Sherwood Anderson and Other Famous Creoles*

New Orleans: Pelican Bookshop Press, 1926
THNOC, 73-320-L

Columbian and Mesoamerican traditions and the post-revolution art scene.[138] Some went to Mexico to learn from artists including Rivera and Orozco. Others were driven by more practical concerns, drawn to Mexico out of a desire to live less expensively given the global economic downturn of the Great Depression.

The local vogue for Mexico helps explain Alférez's relative ease in being accepted by New Orleans's white artists. Nonetheless, the city was still very much separated by race, with white artists largely ignoring Black artists.[139] These disconnects put Alférez at a disadvantage—he *looked* quite unlike his French Quarter contemporaries, and he didn't fully fit in. His penchant for dramatic storytelling about his years as a Villista was no doubt charming and exotified him amongst his peers. Ultimately, Alférez's talent as a sculptor and the prevalence of the community's connections to Mexico led to a degree of acceptance among artists. Within just years of his arrival, he had a wide group of friends and was considered among the most important artists in the city—among contemporaries including Knute Heldner, Alberta Kinsey, Paul Ninas, Albert Rieker, and Ellsworth Woodward.[140]

In New Orleans, in May 1929, Alférez married Evelyn Kelly, a writer he had met in Chicago. Their marriage was short-lived, but the two remained in touch over the years. Kelly modeled for Alférez in Chicago when he was working on the Palmolive Building from 1928 to 1929, and throughout her life she was involved in the arts. She began her career as a journalist and was said to have been the second person on the scene at the infamous Prohibition-era gang-related St. Valentine's Day Massacre in Chicago.[141] She later wrote for the *Havana Post* in Cuba and became a fashion advisor and a philanthropist. Kelly went on to live in New York, Texas, California, Italy, and Mexico.[142] One of her signature styles, with her hair piled into a topknot, appears repeatedly in Alférez's female figures beginning in the late 1920s.

That first summer in New Orleans, Alférez, short on funds, found a job with architect Alexander Norman, who hired him to create four figures for the Gothic-style Holy Name of Mary Catholic Church being built across the Mississippi River from the French Quarter on Verret Street in Algiers, one of the oldest neighborhoods in New Orleans. Alférez worked for Norman from September until December of 1929, completing three figures for the church: a seven-foot Madonna in limestone, placed above the front door, as well as a Saint Joseph and Saint John. He also carved a sacred heart in oak for the interior. One figure, that of Saint Peter, remained unfinished when Alférez secured a life-changing opportunity: Frans Blom invited him to be lead sculptor on an expedition to study an important ancient Maya site, the

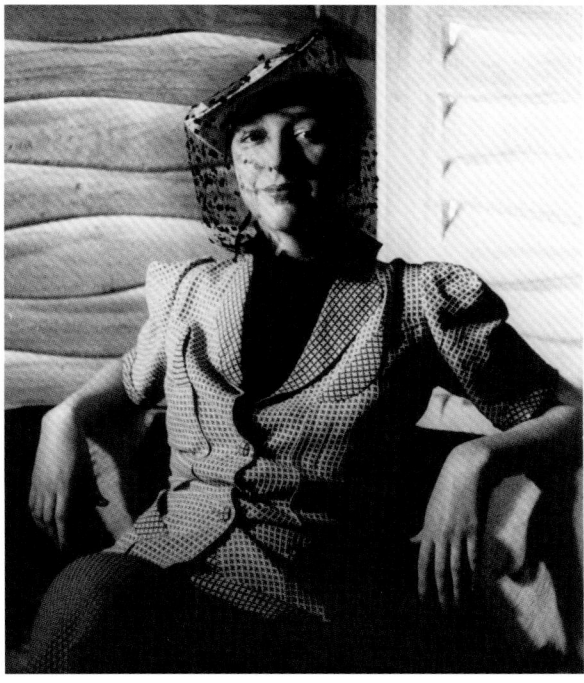

Evelyn Alicia Kelly Del Barrio in New York City [1938]
photo by Carl Van Vechten © Van Vechten Trust
COURTESY BEINECKE RARE BOOK AND MANUSCRIPT LIBRARY, YALE UNIVERSITY

Nunnery Quadrangle at Uxmal in Yucatán. Blom's group planned to depart in early 1930; Alférez would finish Saint Peter when he returned.[143]

Blom's professional ties in Chicago suggest that Alférez may have sought out Blom or had some kind of introduction to him through mutual acquaintances in Chicago. Additionally, Lorado Taft, Alférez's mentor in Chicago, had connections in Louisiana, most notably to Weiss, Dreyfous, and Seiferth, an architectural firm that Alférez would later work for. It seems unlikely that Alférez arrived in New Orleans without any information about potential professional connections, though he never made note of a facilitated introduction.

By the time he left in December 1929 for the Blom expedition, a number of crises—national and personal—were stirring. Earlier that year, Alférez had been arrested for disturbing the peace by assault, and Kelly, his wife of only one month, had to retrieve him from a police station around two in the morning. In July, New Orleans streetcar workers went on strike and by October the stock market crashed. With the onset of the Great Depression, prices fell for commodities including oil, cotton, sugar, and rice, all produced in the state and traded in the port city.[144] In short, like much of the country, New Orleans was experiencing economic and social turbulence.

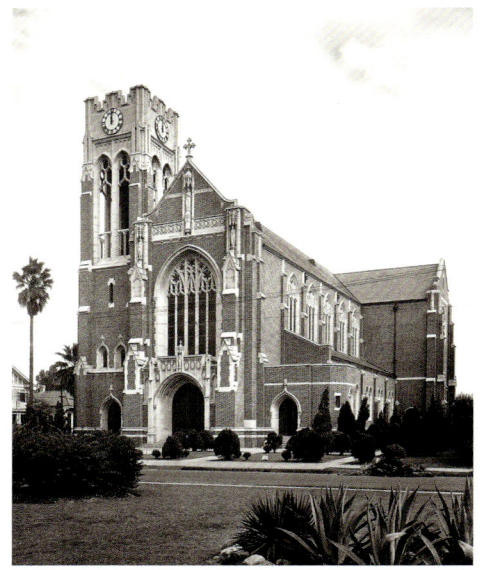

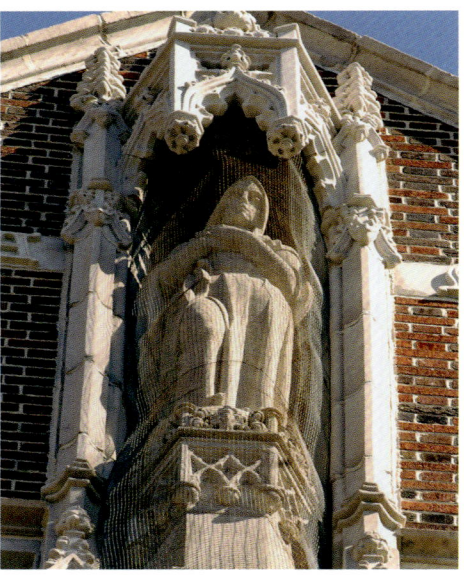

Holy Name of Mary Catholic Church,
in Algiers
photo by Charles L. Franck Photographers
CHARLES L. FRANCK STUDIO COLLECTION AT
THE HISTORIC NEW ORLEANS COLLECTION, 1979.325.2434

Statuary at Holy Name of Mary
Catholic Church [1929]
photo by Donn Young

By the fall of 1929, Alférez had become romantically involved with fellow Arts and Crafts Club artist Rose Marie Huth, who also modeled for him. When they met, she was nineteen and lived in Uptown New Orleans with her mother. Huth's mother didn't like Alférez; he said she "hated Mexicans," but his arrest record and the fact that he was married probably didn't help. She threatened to institutionalize her daughter to keep the two from courting. Although he had only finished three of the four works for Holy Name, the timing must have felt right to get out of town, and Alférez began planning an early, quiet departure for Yucatán in December, ahead of Blom's team.

Alférez called Norman, the architect of the Holy Name project, to ask for assistance leaving the city. Norman agreed to help and said he would pick up Alférez at the corner of Common and Canal Streets in the late morning. Alférez waited for hours in the cold. When Norman finally arrived, Alférez asked if he had had the car "oiled, filled up with gas, and washed."

"I told him he should have had it painted while he was at it!" Alférez said.

Norman and Alférez crossed the river by ferry and found somewhere to eat. The restaurant was crowded and the meal took a long time, although time might have also stretched the way it does when there's a desire to be on the road, or if one thinks one is being pursued: Alférez had learned that he was wanted for sending

Huth's mother a threatening letter, an accusation he denied. Norman then drove to Morgan City and from there, Alférez took a train to Beaumont, Texas, and placed a phone call to Blom. In Alférez's telling, Blom relayed good news—he had convinced authorities that Alférez had not written the threatening letter—and bad news: three federal agencies were still after him.[145]

Alférez, a natural storyteller, might have exaggerated just a bit in relating the story of his departure from New Orleans. While no evidence has been found to suggest he was quite so wanted—by three federal agencies, no less—his leave-taking nonetheless sparked concern. A US immigration office in New Orleans launched an investigation when it learned he had returned to Mexico.[146] Also, curiosity was piqued among his friends in the French Quarter, and the scandal of his disappearance grew. Adding to the drama: Alférez was still married to Kelly.

From Beaumont, Alférez traveled to Mexico City, arriving in Mexico in advance of Blom's team, which departed in February. Alférez corresponded with a friend in the French Quarter, and by March 9, 1930, another letter reached New Orleans, this one about Alférez rather than from him. Bertha Rolfe, proprietor of a French Quarter bookstore that Alférez and other young artists frequented, received a letter from traveling peddler Juan Vicente Alamos. The letter came from Veracruz, dated February 15. "Dear Sir," it read. "At the present writing I am sending you some fragments of paper. I encountered them very close to the place which lay the corpse of an individual and his saddle." The letter noted that the body could not be identified, but documents found nearby suggested that the corpse and saddle might have belonged to Enrique Alférez. It appeared that he had been robbed and murdered.[147]

The letter's arrival created a stir in the French Quarter. Although Alférez had lived there a relatively short period, he had already become a fixture. When the news began to spread, an article in the New Orleans *Item-Tribune* recalled his stories of "adventures as a Villista cavalryman and a Federal spy; of his escape from a firing squad, and his fear of returning to Mexico."[148]

His French Quarter friends contemplated what his death meant for Huth, whose whereabouts had come into question. Huth had recently been spirited away from a party in the French Quarter by two men who arrived suddenly. According to an *Item-Tribune* news story, Huth yelled, "Tell Rique, tell Rique," as she was carried away. French Quarter gossip suggested that Huth's mother had made good on her plan to separate Huth from Alférez, and indeed—though her friends may not have been certain at the time—Huth spent some part of 1930 at the House of the Good Shepherd, then a Roman Catholic reformatory for women who had been committed there either by the city or their parents. The 1930 US Census classified the residents as "inmates," and the women were given jobs such as housekeeping or laundry. Huth was assigned to sewing.[149]

Since friends didn't know where Huth and Alférez were, there was speculation about what one's disappearance had to do with the other's. Alférez's friend at the bookstore, Bertha Rolfe, wrote to Blom soon after she received the distressing letter. Inquiries were also made with Tulane University; the school's president, A. B. Dinwiddie, said that Blom remained in frequent contact and "undoubtedly would have informed us if any member of the party had failed to join." By March 11, a visitor who had recently returned from Blom's headquarters in Yucatán attested to Alférez's safety.

Though Alférez had recently recovered from a bout of dengue fever, the visitor noted that he was "in the best of health" by then. No one in New Orleans, living in the well of curiosity and concern, could have known at the time that Alférez had simply set out on horseback with an old friend to attend a wedding; he had ridden with a loaned saddle, and when he and his friend stopped to make a campfire, the horse was stolen—along with his loaned saddle and bag of clothes, leading to the case of mistaken identity.[150]

Replicating the Nunnery Quadrangle

The visit that Enrique Alférez made to Uxmal with Frans Blom in 1930 was an important early milestone in his career. It was the first large and complex project in which he was lead sculptor, and his close work with Blom strengthened Alférez's agency as a professional.

The Maya city Uxmal was founded around 500 CE and was likely the capital of the Puuc region as well as its trading center, and possibly a site of war. Its buildings bear architectural details and construction methods emblematic of the Late Classic Maya period and Puuc architecture common to the northern Yucatán: the use of limestone and carefully cut stones set into a concrete core, intricate friezes, and horizontal designs. Facades are replete with mosaic-like tiles and intricate ornamentation with carved patterns, motifs, and animal and human figures, as well as masks of the Maya rain god, Chaac. The overall design reveals a deliberate blending of Maya and other symbols prevalent in Mexico, including serpents and deities associated with Aztec traditions, such as Tlalocs and Ehecatls, to name a few.[151]

The central ruins are in an area that's approximately 150 acres, and a number of Uxmal's structures are noted for their size and design, among them the Governor's Palace, the Nunnery Quadrangle, the Pyramid of the Magician, and a ball court. At the quadrangle, buildings encircle a central open space that could have been used for public ceremonies. To the east of the Nunnery is the tallest building at Uxmal, the Pyramid of the Magician, which was built over a period of about four hundred years. Historically, parts of Maya buildings were painted, and though Blom's team found

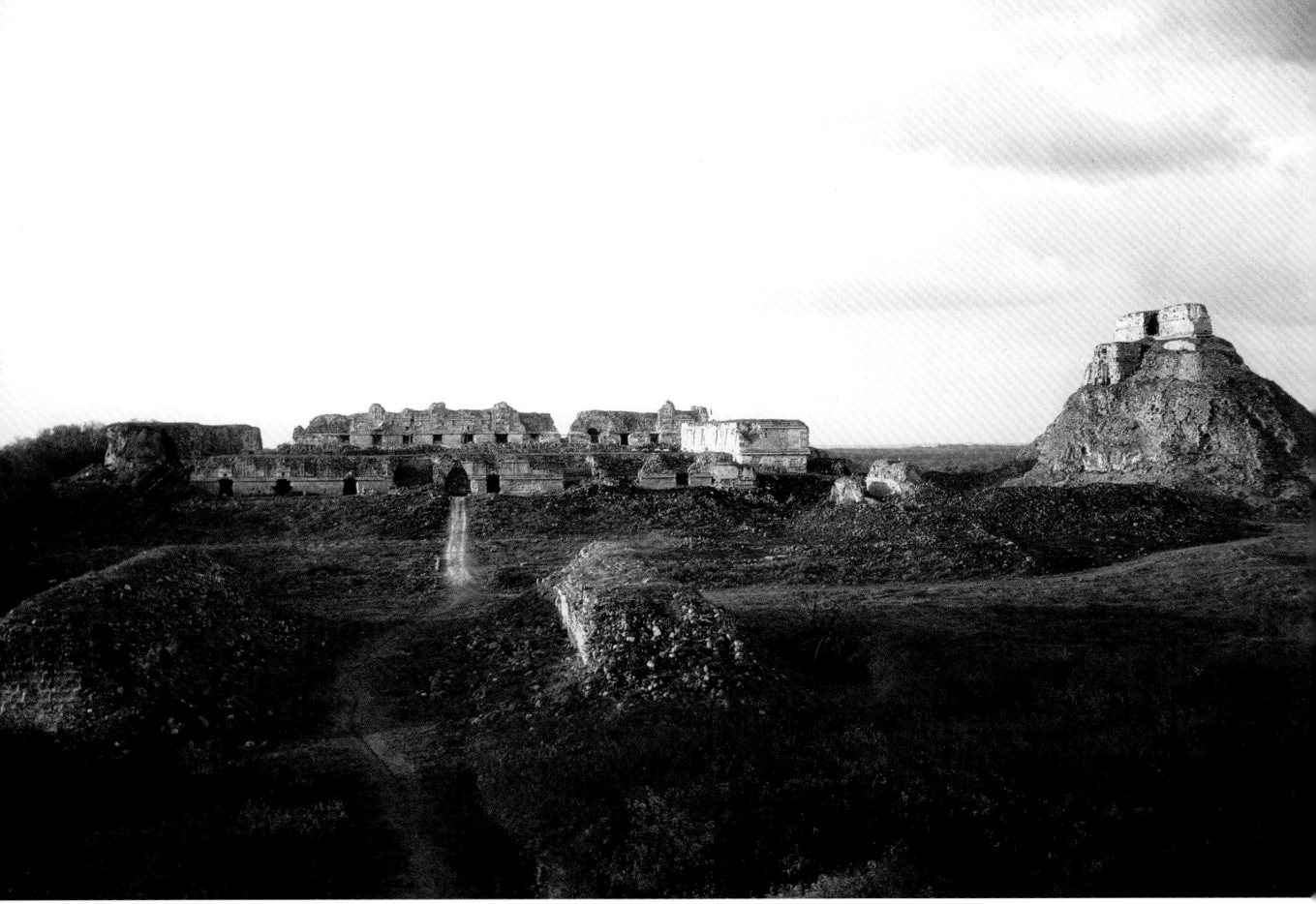

View of Uxmal from top of Governor's Palace: ball court (center, in foreground),
Nunnery Quadrangle (center, in distance), **Pyramid of the Magician** (right) [1930]
photo by Daniel Sweeney Leyrer
COURTESY OF THE MIDDLE AMERICAN RESEARCH INSTITUTE, TULANE UNIVERSITY

a few painted capstones, much of what they encountered was grayish- or yellow-white, as it is today, and overgrown following centuries of abandonment.

Blom's assignment was to replicate the Nunnery Quadrangle for the anthropological section of the 1933–34 Century of Progress Exposition in Chicago. Though the intent had been to reconstruct the entire Quadrangle, the project scope was reduced to focus on only one of the four buildings, replicated as the "Mayan Temple" exhibition near the 31st Street entrance to the fair in Chicago. Blom's group lived in the Quadrangle for about three months. In addition to Alférez, the team included an assistant sculptor, William Hayden; Robert H. Merrill, an engineer and surveyor who created contour maps of the area; Gonzalo Trujillo, a Mexican civil engineer; J. Herndon Thomson, head of Tulane's architecture school; photographer Daniel Sweeney Leyrer; and architecture students Herndon Fair and Gerhard Kramer. The group had two assistants, Mexican-born Ciriaco Aguilar, who had worked as an assistant on at least one previous expedition with Blom and who also worked at Baptist Hospital in New Orleans, and Pablo Pantoja, who spoke Maya, Spanish, and English.

Blom and Merrill left New Orleans on February 5, 1930, ahead of the other team members, arriving early to conduct an aerial survey. The rest of the team arrived on February 17, staying in fairly comfortable accommodations at a hacienda owned by the Péon family until their gear arrived.[152]

Their belongings and equipment arrived in 194 boxes and bundles on mule-drawn carts, which all members of the team helped unpack. They raised a Tulane flag and set about creating an extensive camp site inside the East Building of the Nunnery Quadrangle. They had spades and picks, buckets, two and a half tons of plaster of Paris, and other items including rubber bathtubs, cots, mattresses, linens, and sacks of food including potatoes and onions. "Noise and activity filled the long silent court of the Nunnery," Blom wrote in a field letter on March 10.

"At once we commenced to prepare the rooms of the east wing to receive our equipment," Blom wrote. "Bats and swallows had inhabited the silent temple rooms for many centuries, rocks had fallen from the ceiling, and large piles of branches and straw had been blown in by the wind."

Leyrer's photographs of the visit illustrate the men making camp in dusty conditions, achieving a relatively high degree of comfort among the ruins. Alférez, Hayden, and Leyrer roomed together in the first "apartment," as Blom referred to it, at the southern part of the East Building. Meals were taken in a room down one of two long halls, where they also had a kitchen and sitting room. Leyrer created a darkroom, one that Blom thought was as impressive as "any modern studio."

Inside, the group had shade and protection from the tropical heat and sun. They started their work outside at dawn to take advantage of the coolest part of the day and worked inside or rested during the warmest hours. By mid-afternoon, they returned outdoors for another two and a half hours. In addition to the heat, they faced thick brush and insects, and Alférez became very ill with dengue fever, running a fever early in the expedition. The fever lasted two days. When it broke, he improved but remained weak for days. Life in New Orleans must have seemed very far away from the Nunnery Quadrangle. In April, by the time Alférez recovered, Huth was at the House of the Good Shepherd.

On an average day, Alférez and Hayden either made drawings of the building facades or created plaster molds and casts of the facade and its figures. Leyrer took photographs and Alférez studied the carvings to identify patterns and the number of motifs to "simplify casting and avoid duplication of effort." Some of the plaster casts they made are extant and in the holdings of the Tulane University Middle American Research Institute.

In the evenings, the group sometimes gathered on a roof. They would look out over the growth "dotted with many great temples," with the Pyramid of the Magician rising "towards the clouds like a skyscraper," Blom wrote in a field letter.

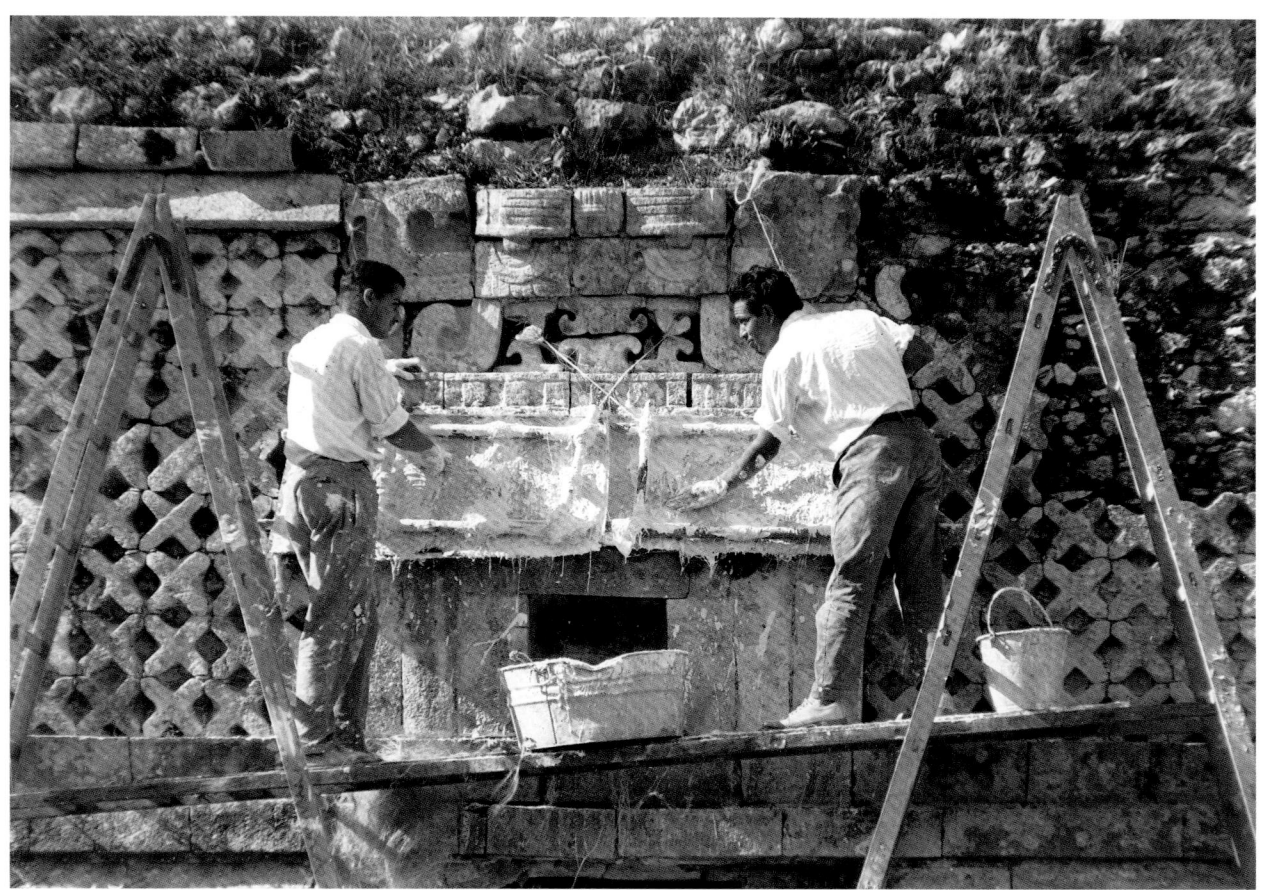

William Hayden and Alférez making a cast of the façade
of South Building at Nunnery Quadrangle [1930]
photo by Daniel Sweeney Leyrer
COURTESY OF THE MIDDLE AMERICAN RESEARCH INSTITUTE, TULANE UNIVERSITY

The sweeping view beyond the Quadrangle would have been filled with dense vegetation and outcroppings of temples and mounds still to be uncovered and examined, as well as the Governor's Palace in the distance. Throughout their months at the Nunnery, they made time to visit four other buildings. Blom hoped not only to re-create the Nunnery complex for the world's fair but also to report on "many buildings hitherto unknown to the archaeological world."[153]

Much of what is known of the expedition's time at Uxmal is gleaned from Blom's extensive notes, journals, and subsequent publications. There are significant holdings of his papers and materials related to the expedition at the Latin American Library at Tulane University and Tulane's Middle American Research Institute, as well as at the Bancroft Library at the University of California, Berkeley.

The research trip revealed to Blom that these sites, particularly the carvings and inscriptions, could be better seen and photographed at night using lights developed for the movie business, helping to eliminate shadows.[154] With centuries of dust and debris and thick vegetation all around, the view of the Nunnery must have been astonishing for all of them—and especially for Alférez, who saw himself as a shaper of light and shadow—in that moment after they first cranked a generator to light the facade with electricity.[155]

Alférez and other members of the team made observations during the expedition that intrigued Blom and influenced Alférez's art in the decades to come. First, the team discovered that though the Quadrangle appeared to be a perfect rectangle, this was an illusion; the north ends of the longer sides of the complex are slightly closer together than the south ends, and the floor is a few feet higher toward the narrower end as well. Additionally, Alférez identified another effect that Blom found compelling, the use of negative batter: while the buildings' walls are perpendicular to the ground, the embellishments slope slightly outward. Alférez described the effect: "The edges of the undercut places throw a heavy and solid shadow, thus making a contrast between the outer and deeper planes."[156]

Had the facades slanted backward rather than forward, or been vertical, "shadows would have been sparse," wrote Blom. He described the effect of this in a close examination of "scale-like eyelids" in a series of masks, noting that the shape of the eyelids "throws a sharp shadow into the eye-pit, and the spectator, standing below

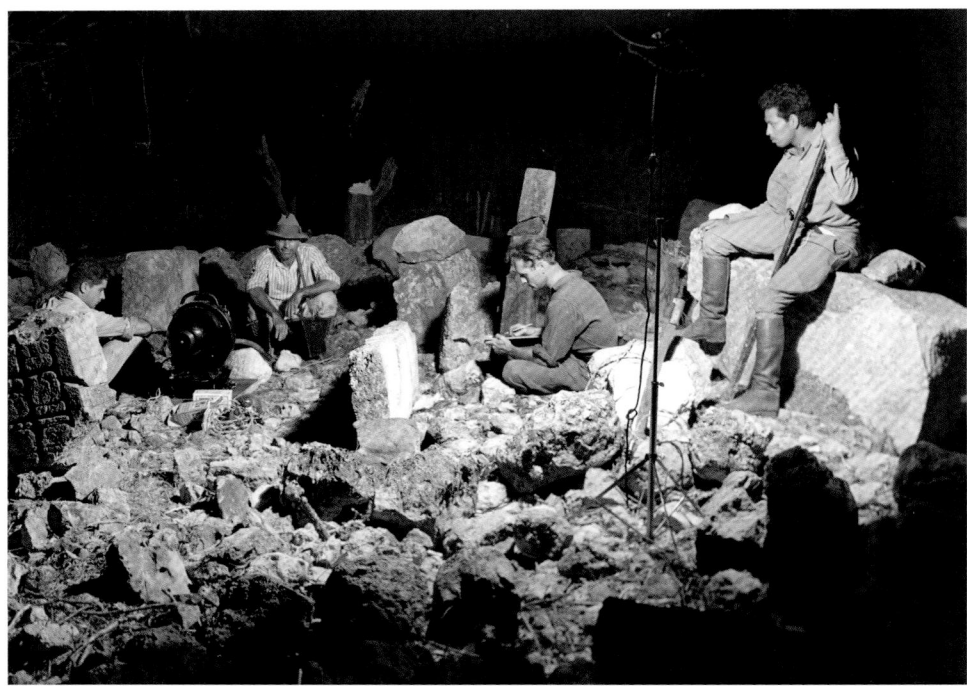

William Hayden, Gonzalo Trujillo, Frans Blom, and Alférez
working on stelae at night [1930]
photo by Daniel Sweeney Leyrer
COURTESY OF THE MIDDLE AMERICAN RESEARCH INSTITUTE, TULANE UNIVERSITY

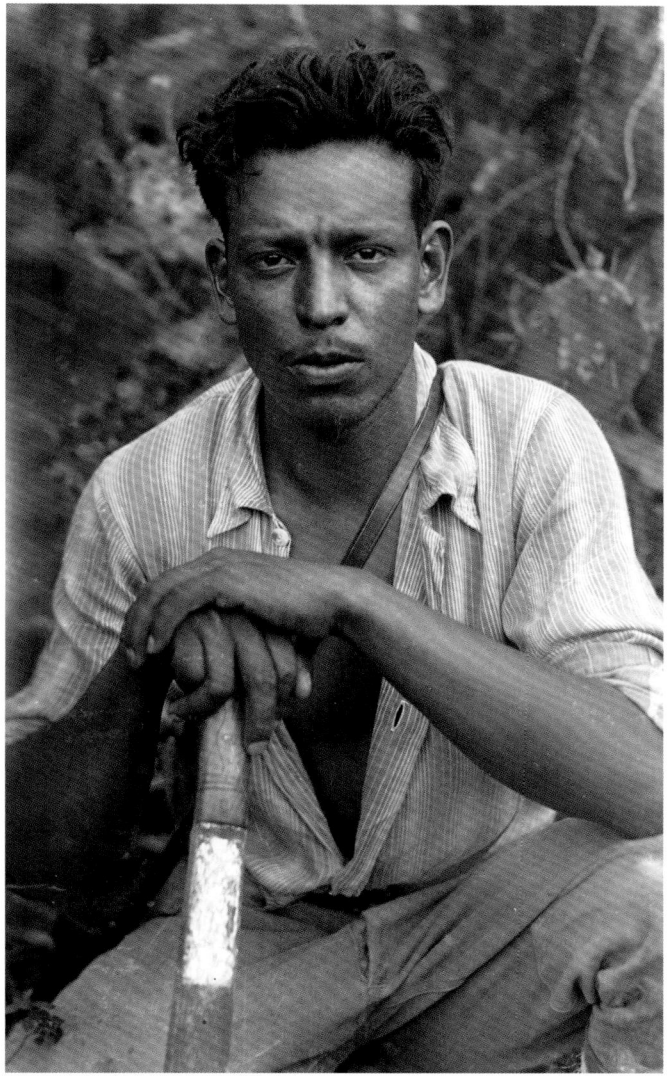

Portrait of Alférez at Uxmal [1930]
photo by Daniel Sweeney Leyrer
COURTESY OF THE MIDDLE AMERICAN RESEARCH INSTITUTE, TULANE UNIVERSITY

the panel and looking upward (as against the sunlight which comes from above) gets the impression that the monster is staring at him."[157]

This understanding—which Alférez would have come to through close inspection of the facade and by physically placing the plaster across surfaces to make its replica—reinforced lessons from Taft on light and shadow. The observation had a profound impact on Alférez's later work. He regularly used the cuts of a figure, with particular attention to eyelids, to control the effect of sunlight and shadow in creating expressions. Additionally, while many of his figures seem, at first glance, to

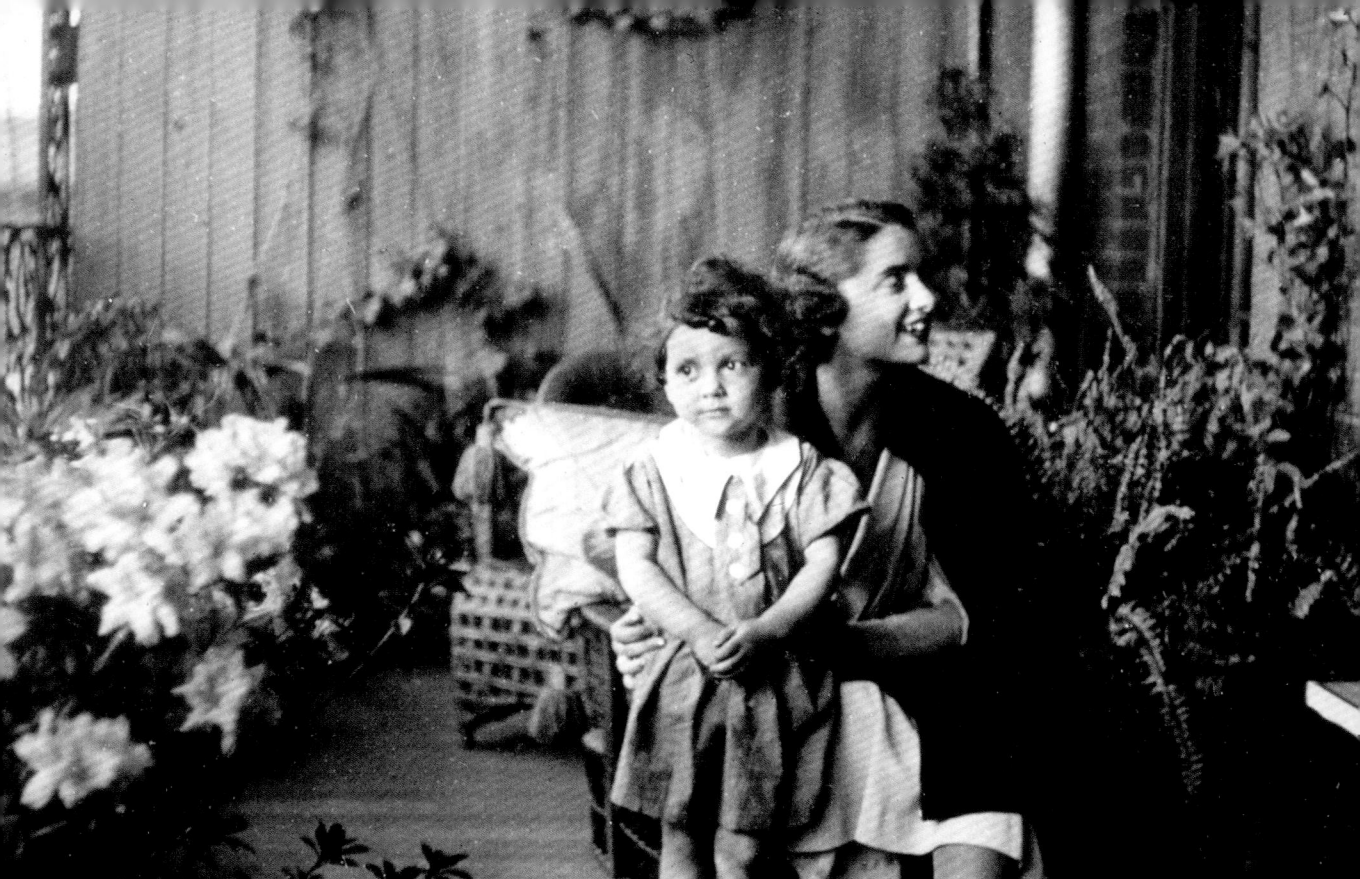

Alférez's daughter Cloe with Mary Sefton Thomas [mid-1930s]
FRANS BLOM PAPERS, BANCROFT LIBRARY, UNIVERSITY OF CALIFORNIA, BERKELEY

be proportional, he often made some elements such as a head, feet, or hands larger or smaller than proportion would call for in order to compensate for the viewer's perspective. Effects such as these were designed with consideration for the placement of the sculpture relative to the viewer.

The 1930 Yucatán exploration solidified the growing friendship between Alférez and Blom, and it was only the first of a few visits that the two made together to Latin America in the 1930s. During this period, Alférez also became friends with Blom's first wife, Mary Sefton Thomas. She and Blom lived in the Lower Pontalba Apartments in the French Quarter, just a stone's throw from Alférez; in the early 1930s, he moved downstairs from the Bloms and regularly visited with them, often drawing during gatherings in their apartment. Frans and Mary divorced in 1938. This coincided with a troubling period in Blom's life. He should have been at a high point of his career, given the respect he had earned for his research on Mesoamerican civilizations, but ten years after the Uxmal expedition, he was in crisis. After multiple awkward alcohol-induced run-ins with university administrators and colleagues, he was placed on "indefinite leave of absence" and demoted from director to associate in archaeology in November 1940. By November 1941, Tulane asked for his resignation.[158]

Blom's struggle with alcoholism also affected Alférez, who was not shy of a drink himself; it was during this period that Blom got rid of personal belongings that Alférez had temporarily stored with him, an incident that strained their relationship.[159] Among the items lost was a mask Alférez had made of his old friend Carl Sandburg. Alférez took out classified ads trying to track down the mask, but no evidence has been found to suggest he ever reconnected with it.[160] Alférez blamed Blom's carelessness on his alcoholism.

Despite the setbacks, Blom's life rebounded: He moved to Mexico, entering more meaningfully into a world he had previously studied, and had a second career studying Maya culture from his home, Na Bolom, an old monastery in San Cristóbal de las Casas in Chiapas. He had an enduring second marriage to Gertrude "Trudi" Duby Blom, a kindred spirit, documentary photographer, social anthropologist, and journalist.

Sefton Thomas and Alférez remained friends. Her family, owners of Harriet Hubbard Ayer perfumes and cosmetics in New York, were well connected in the city, and when Alférez moved there in the 1940s, she was instrumental in helping him find a place to live and work. Much later, in 1980, when Sefton Thomas was living in Charlottesville, Virginia, she donated fifty-eight drawings by Alférez to the New Orleans Museum of Art, including original drawings for Hermann B. Deutsch's 1923 novel *The Wedge*, loosely based on Alférez's life. E. John Bullard, director of the museum at the time, thought the gift would "nicely complement" an Alférez sculpture expected to be acquired later that year.[161]

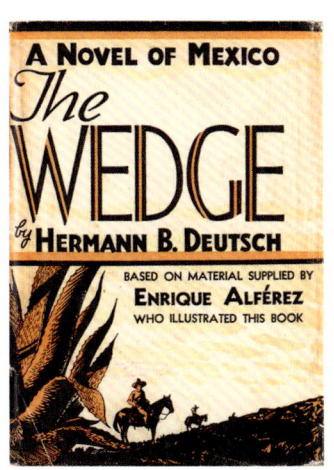
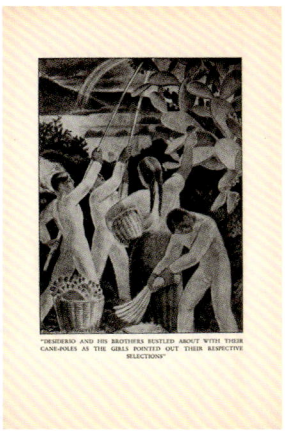
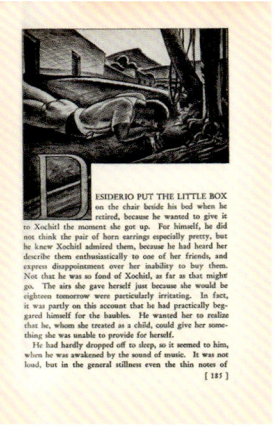

The Wedge: A Novel of Mexico
by Hermann B. Deutsch, with illustrations by Enrique Alférez
New York: Frederick A. Stokes, 1935
THNOC, 61-61-L.9

◇

Most of the members of the Uxmal expedition returned to New Orleans on May 19, 1930, arriving with 1,500 feet of film, "more than 500 photographs and scores of plaster casts," seven architectural drawings of the buildings, and a contour map detailing approximately 200,000 square feet of the site.[162] When they disembarked from the SS *Munplace*, they were greeted by Tulane president A. B. Dinwiddie. But Alférez was not with the returning party. When the rest of the group departed Yucatán for New Orleans, he set out from Uxmal for the city of Campeche on the western side of the peninsula.

The group had visited Campeche during their stay, and when Alférez returned, he took a room at the Cuauhtémoc Hotel. On June 3, 1930, he filed for divorce from Evelyn Kelly on the grounds that they were incompatible. Alférez then traveled about 135 miles to the port at Progreso, Yucatán, and sailed back to New Orleans on his own three-day journey aboard the SS *Munplace*.[163] Upon arrival in New Orleans, he was held for immigration questioning; ultimately the immigration officers allowed his return. On June 13, 1930, ten days after divorcing Kelly, Alférez married Rose Marie Huth in Gretna, Louisiana. His fellow Uxmal traveler William Hayden served as witness.[164]

Alférez returned briefly to Chicago in late May 1933 to attend the opening night of the Century of Progress Exposition and view the reproduction of part of the Nunnery Quadrangle. Though Frans Blom was cautious about publicly criticizing the exhibition, he was disappointed with its outcome, and it is possible that Alférez shared his friend's perspective. The reconstruction was smaller than originally intended, and seemed out of place, at odds with its surroundings. Made of stucco and plaster, the temple now had handrails for the steps and was painted to look like stone. The years of overgrown vegetation at Uxmal were not present in Chicago, another reminder of its artificiality. Blom expressed dissatisfaction with the exhibition but observed with a sense of irony that the public liked it.[165] Additionally, though the celebration of Mexico was likely well intentioned, the Mexican exhibitions were constructed largely without input from Chicago's sizable Mexican diaspora community. Historian Cheryl R. Ganz observed that the exhibitions were produced with an exotic flair by American businessmen who "established these venues to provide entertainment and produce revenue by drawing fairgoers to the charm of 'Old Mexico.'"[166]

Though Alférez had arrived in Chicago planning to attend the opening, he didn't do so; he skipped the celebration and spent the evening drinking with Carl Sandburg at Sandburg's cottage in Harbert.[167] About a week later, Rose Marie filed

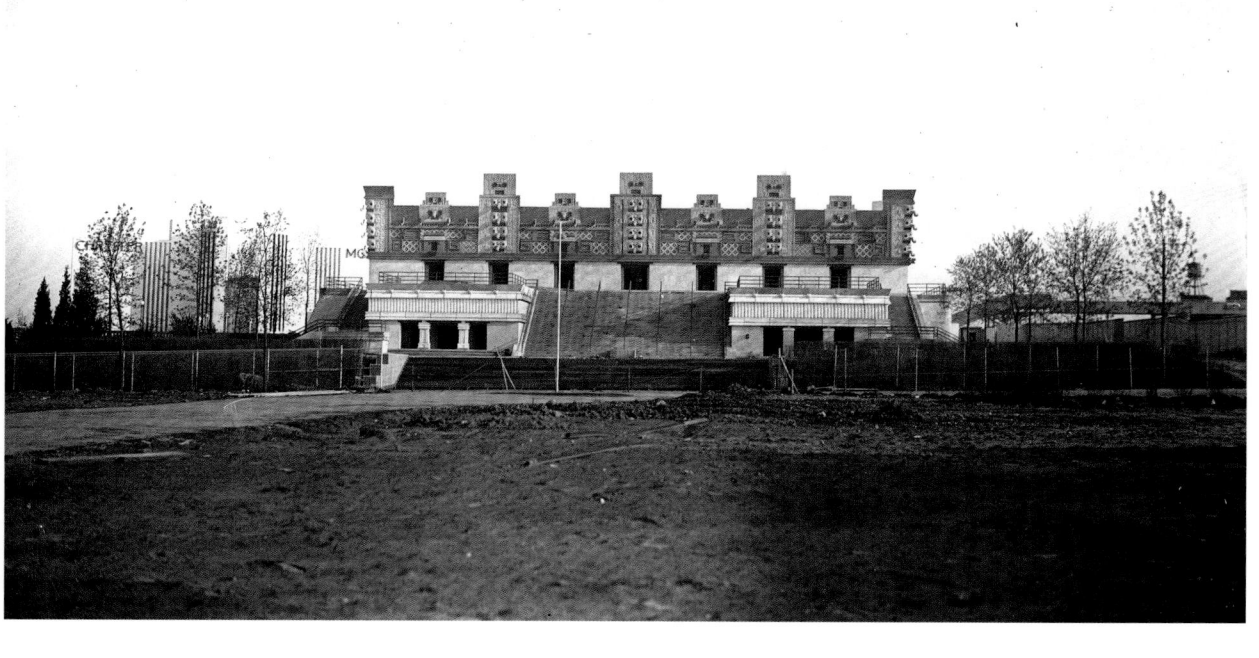

Maya temple contructed for 1933–34 Century of Progress Exposition, Chicago

photo by Frans Blom

COURTESY OF THE MIDDLE AMERICAN RESEARCH INSTITUTE, TULANE UNIVERSITY

for a separation from Alférez on the grounds that he had "absented himself" from their home on several occasions and that he "no longer loved her."[168] Huth requested custody of their child, Cloe, who had been born in April 1931—a request that was granted.[169]

After Alférez and Rose Marie divorced, Alférez's personal life stayed a bit stormy. He was arrested three more times between 1934 and 1937 for fighting and disturbing the peace.[170] The incident in 1937 resulted in high-profile publicity in the news, with Alférez accusing an officer of assault, beating, and wounding following an arrest in which he was beaten with a billy club, kicked into a cell, beaten with a broomstick through cell bars, and doused with buckets of water. A news account cites medical evidence that he suffered, and a photograph taken a day after the incident reveals physical injuries to his face.[171] The officer was cleared of wrongdoing, and the police superintendent said that "Alférez is a very lucky man that he has not been beaten oftener."[172]

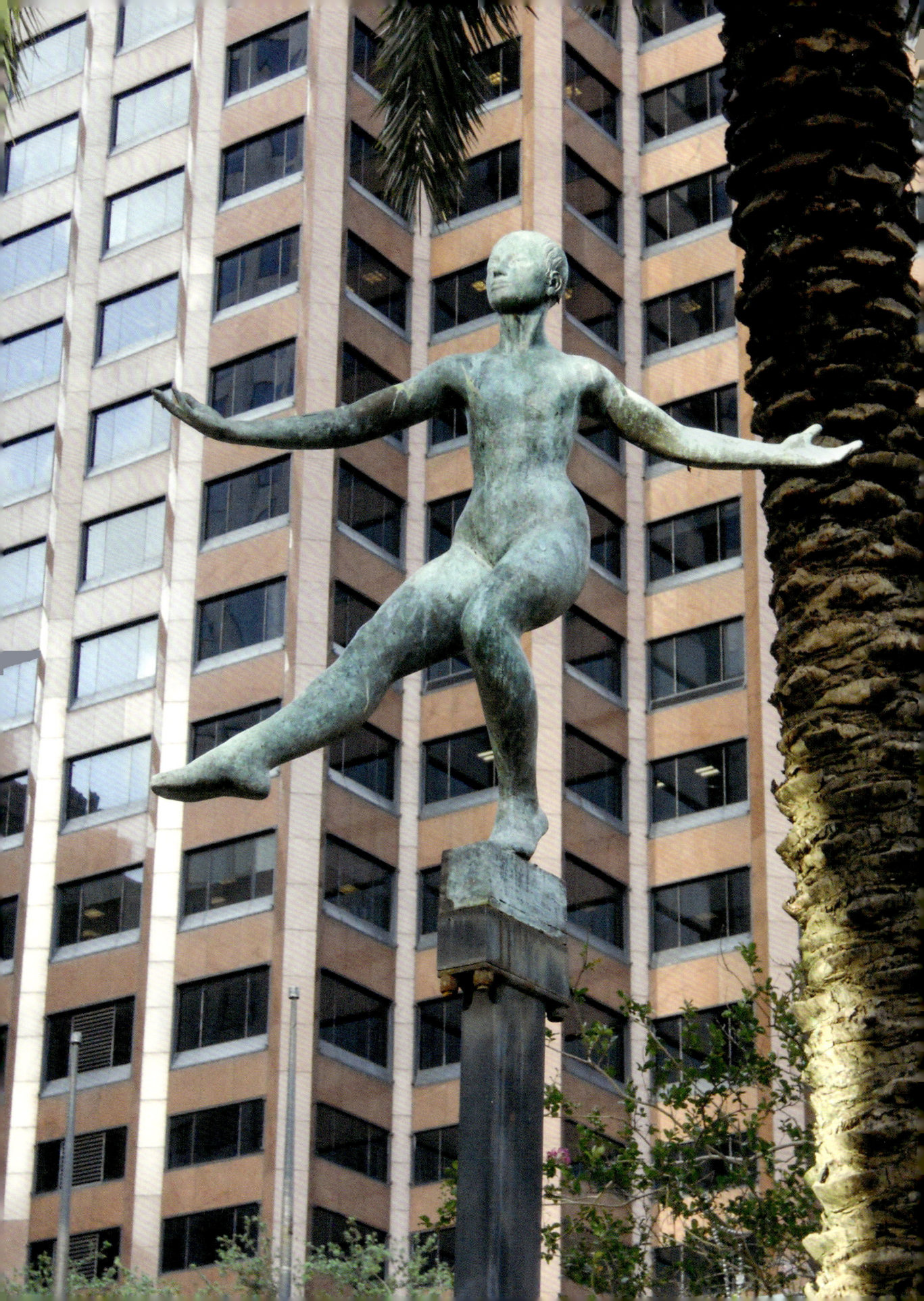

CHAPTER SEVEN

Shaping the New Orleans Landscape

OVER THE COURSE OF THE twentieth century, Enrique Alférez's hand shaped New Orleans and its environs. From City Park to the Central Business District, his work is infused into many aspects of daily life, featured in places where people socialize, conduct business, seek health care, study, and live. His sculpture can be seen outdoors, from Poydras Street to the Lakefront Airport, and it adorns exteriors and interiors of buildings across the area. In some instances, his sculpture is the main attraction, as in The Helis Foundation Enrique Alférez Garden at the Botanical Garden. In other venues, from Saint Martin's Episcopal Church to Touro Infirmary, his friezes, bas-reliefs, carvings, and small details fit into the character of a place, subtly setting a tone that makes these places more welcoming.

It is difficult to drive even a few miles around the city without encountering some trace of Alférez's influence. His work reflects the character of the city, reminding New Orleanians who they are. Multicultural carvings and bas-reliefs executed for the *Times-Picayune* headquarters and the Chapel at Christ Church Cathedral are indicative of the global nature of the city, one comprising people from many countries and cultures, together in a port city that remains a gateway to the world.

In the earliest stages of his career, Alférez was frequently subcontracted by architecture firms that were building, renovating, or improving sites. Often, these projects were funded through federal, state, and municipal funds. In some cases, he was one of a group of sculptors hired onto a project; at City Park, he worked as lead sculptor. Over the course of his career, he received assignments—from building details to standalone works—from leading architects in New Orleans, among them Alexander Norman, Moise H. Goldstein Sr., Edward B. Silverstein, and

Gymnast [1990–91]
photo by Alison Cody
THE HELIS FOUNDATION COLLECTION, POYDRAS CORRIDOR SCULPTURE EXHIBITION

Arthur Q. Davis, to name a few. He found his footing as a professional sculptor, though, through his earliest assignments with Weiss, Dreyfous, and Seiferth and with Richard Koch, from about 1930 until the early 1940s.[173]

Among the many Weiss, Dreyfous, and Seiferth projects Alférez pursued in the 1930s are the Lapeyre Miltenberger Home for Convalescents, 1932—where his bas-reliefs appeared alongside those of Albert Rieker, Juanita Gonzales, and John Lachin—and Shushan (now Lakefront) Airport, ca. 1932–34, which will be examined in depth.[174] He contributed to a number of other projects for the firm, including

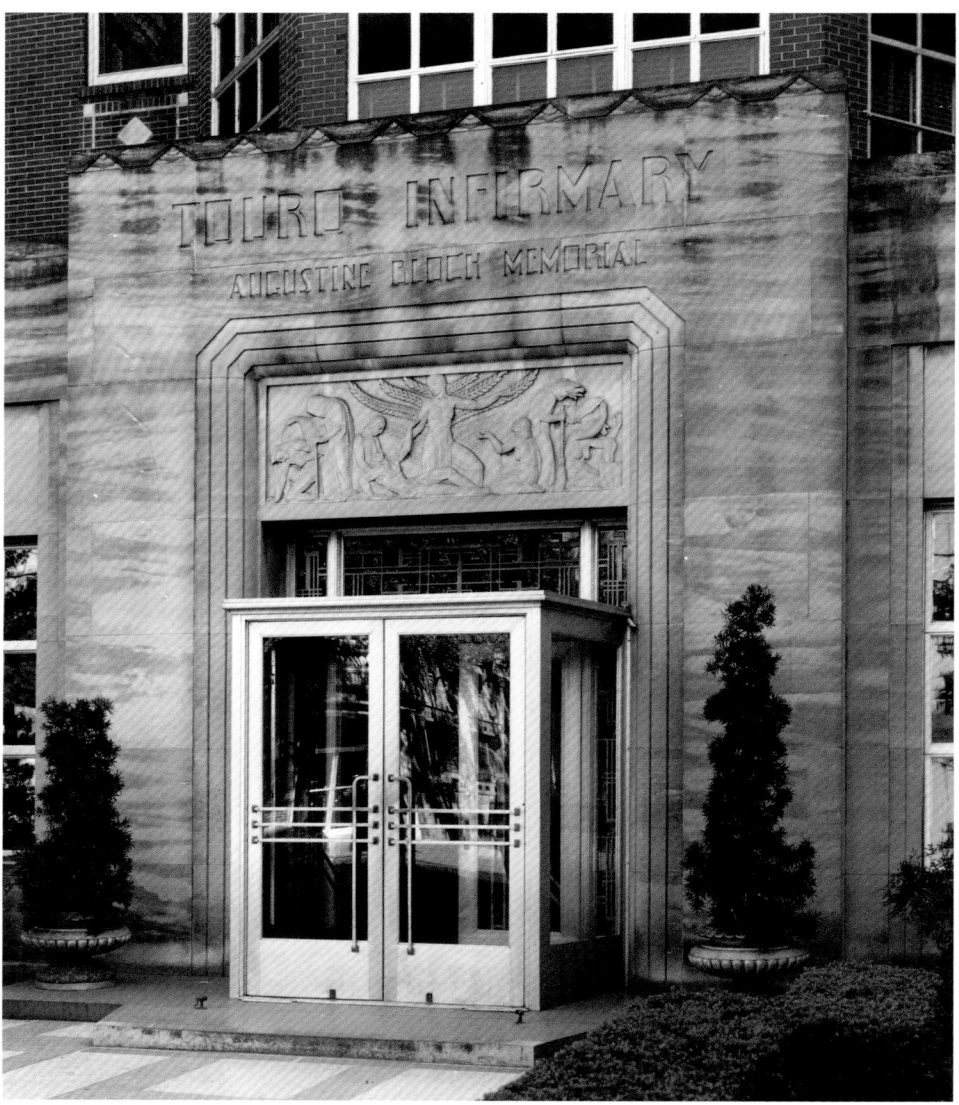

Entrance to Bloch building, Touro Infirmary [1935]

photo by Leon Trice, 1960

COURTESY OF TOURO INFIRMARY ARCHIVES

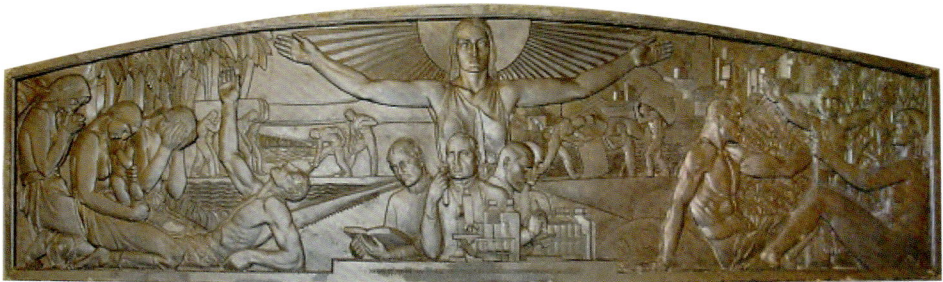

Conquest of Yellow Fever [1931]
photo by Jack Davis

Touro Infirmary, 1935; the Federal Land Bank on Saint Charles Avenue at Saint Joseph Street, 1937; the Saint Bernard Parish Courthouse, for which he carved a walnut panel featuring King Solomon, 1939; and buildings at Louisiana State University and McNeese State University.[175]

Most of these works are extant today. In some cases, his bas-reliefs and architectural details have emerged into more prominent view following building renovations. At Touro Infirmary, for example, his bas-relief panel over the main entrance on Prytania Street became a focal point of a renovation completed in 2011. The panel depicts "the struggle of humanity in ill health, reaching toward the help that medical science can give," with a tree of life and woman at center, offering rewards of life.[176] Alférez maintained an enduring connection to Touro for the care of his own family and other work by him appears in the hospital.

Sculptures such as these became markers of the history and character of New Orleans, both in their installation at important sites, and also in the narratives they tell of the city's history. In 1931, for example, Alférez created a tribute to the end of yellow fever outbreaks in the United States, the last of which occurred in New Orleans in 1905. His *Conquest of Yellow Fever* panel, a twelve-foot-wide, 600-pound plaster frieze coated in aluminum and banana oil, was initially installed in the lobby of LSU School of Medicine. Its central female figure is evocative of Hygeia. Before her, at center, stand four men, including Walter Reed and Aristides Agramonte, key figures in understanding the transmission of yellow fever by the *Aedes aegypti* mosquito, an advance that was important in ending yellow fever outbreaks in the United States. The doctors stand between two moments in history: at the left of the panel, a man is ill from yellow fever, and at the right, a city and a family flourish, free from the virus. The panel, restored in 1999, is now in the LSU Health Sciences Center Library Commons.[177] Though a gem more hidden than his outdoor reliefs, sculptures, and fountains, it is among the works that create an enduring link between Alférez and the history of New Orleans.

Shushan Airport

Alférez began working at Shushan Airport in late 1932 or early 1933.[178] The project was significant not only in his own career but also for the advent of art deco airports. The airport—now known as the New Orleans Lakefront Airport—was designed to surpass, in both style and facility resources, some of the most vibrant airports of the day, such as Croydon Airport in London and Tempelhof Airport in Berlin, and it was created as a symbol of promise in anticipation of the increase in passenger and commercial air travel between the United States and Latin America.[179] It was also the first airport to combine access by land and water, and was built as a destination unto itself, with restaurants, bars, dancing facilities, and more.[180]

The sculptural elements Alférez created illustrate a kinship with his mentor Lorado Taft, namely their shared interest in public sculpture that fit into its surroundings, both in the immediate physical sense, from an aesthetic standpoint, and also in its representation of a time and place. In considering how Alférez's work fit into this site, it's helpful to see the larger landscape in terms of geography and in terms of the goals for the airport. Huey P. Long, who was governor of Louisiana from 1928 to 1932 and subsequently a US senator, aspired to become president of the United States in 1936 (he was assassinated in 1935). Long undertook a number of measures toward that goal: creating jobs programs, building infrastructure, and making Louisiana and the vital port city of New Orleans gateways to the rest of the world. Long had a longtime confidant in Abe L. Shushan, a New Orleans businessman and president of the Orleans Levee Board. With Long's support, Shushan led the development of the new airport.[181]

Shushan oversaw the project from its origins through completion; before it could be built, though, a site needed to be identified, ideally with easy access to and from downtown New Orleans. In this case, Shushan and his colleagues reclaimed marsh that had previously been used for animal trapping and hosting fishing camps on pilings along the edge of Lake Pontchartrain, creating an artificial peninsula extending into the lake. A 1934 article in *Architectural Forum* suggested that the location was chosen in order to "avoid the legal tangles" of acquiring a site—instead using land "lying beneath the waters of Lake Pontchartrain" and thus "already owned by the city." The location allowed planners to meet the goal of creating an attractive and welcoming entry point to the city, with access to downtown.[182] Nearby, reclaimed land was also used for other community and neighborhood developments.

The architecture firm Weiss, Dreyfous, and Seiferth was chosen to oversee the project. They used a system that relied on crushed oyster shells and clay to create land, and they infused metaphors for flight throughout the site. Seen from above, the airport looks like a flying craft, with a central building flanked by hangars that look

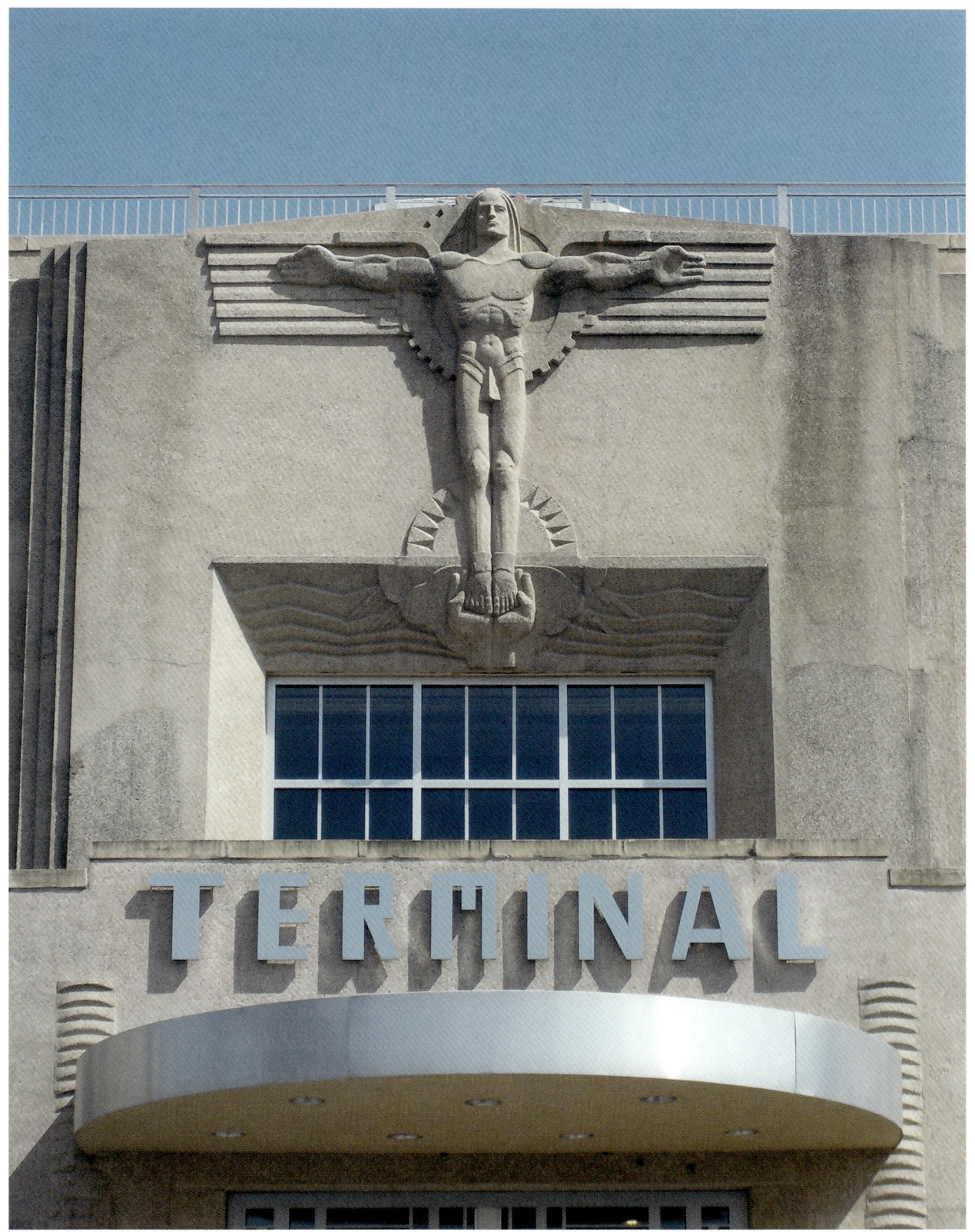

Sculpture above the entry to Lakefront Airport terminal [1932–33; restored 2013]

photo by Alison Cody

like wings. This metaphor was carried through to the bas-reliefs, frieze, and central figure that Alférez sculpted for the building's exterior surface decoration.[183] Inside are eight murals painted by Spanish-American artist Xavier Gonzalez, a friend of Alférez's, featuring famous flights and other travel inspirations.[184]

Alférez's work for the airport was guided and supervised by Weiss, Dreyfous, and Seiferth.[185] As was typical for such projects, Alférez would have received specs and concepts, or a synopsis, from the firm, and he would have submitted drawings to ensure that his designs met the approval of the architects. After receiving approval, he began modeling. The architects aspired to create a setting that would offer travelers a sense of worldliness and comfort; create a hospitable atmosphere that could also attract locals for social outings; and relay the safety and excitement of travel. The design needed to celebrate flight and signal toward its future.

The front of the building features a central figure placed between two sets of three matching bas-relief panels that create a narrative about learning to fly. Read from the outside edges of the building toward the central figure, the panels represent, first, man reaching for the heavens; second, the struggle to fly; and third, the achievement of flight, with a winged man standing above the sun.[186] In an interview conducted in 1975, Alférez said he created one of the three panels—the Indian shooting an arrow into the sun—and the large central figure above the portico. The other two panels were completed by William Proctor and John Lachin.[187] Alférez worked on the plaster reliefs at his studio on Saint Ann Street.[188] In the first panel,

New Orleans Lakefront Airport terminal
photo by Alison Cody

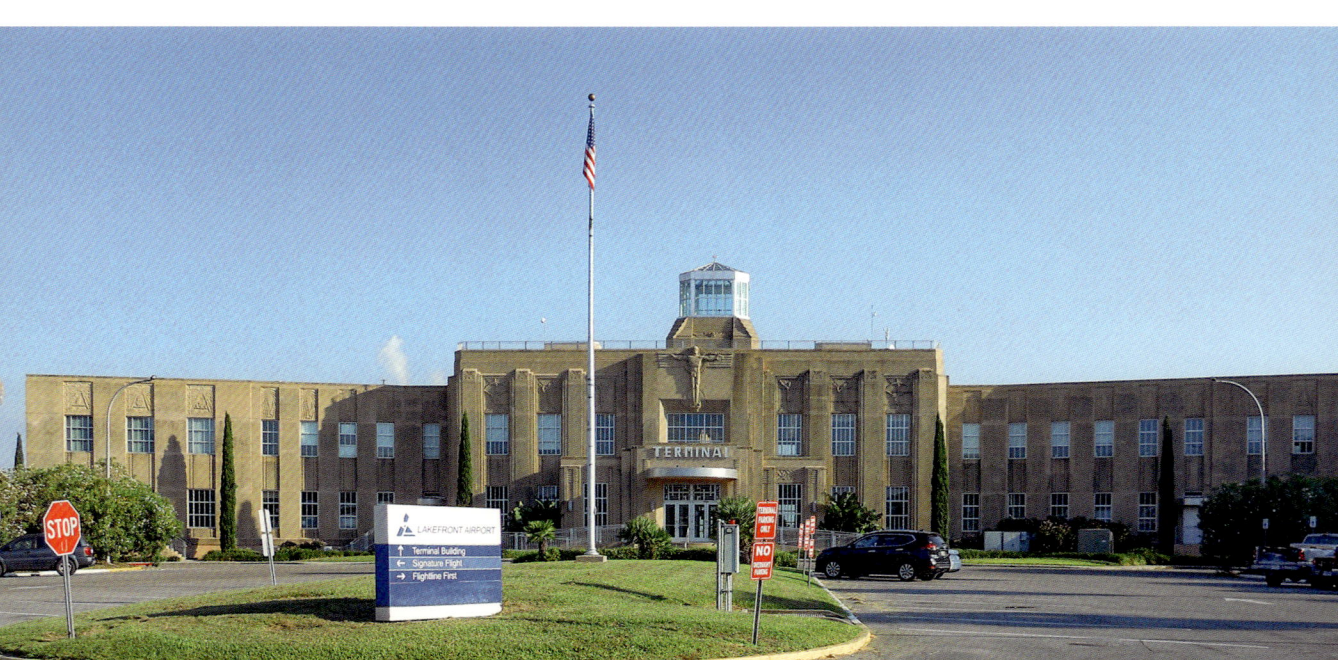

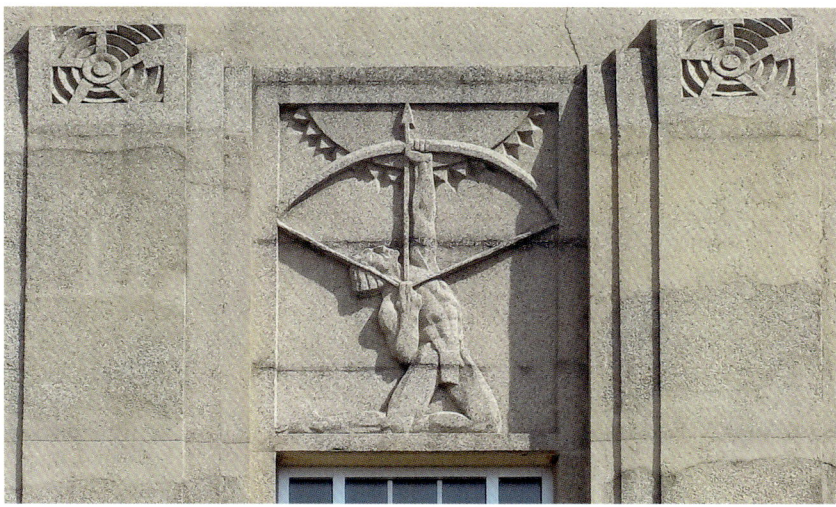

Bas-relief panel on Lakefront Airport terminal [1932–33]
photo by Alison Cody

Alférez's mythological figure aims his arrow toward the sun, symbolic of the dream to penetrate the skies. The definition of the muscles in the figure's torso, arms, and calves—reminiscent of the athletic boxer Alférez would later create for the wrought iron gate at City Park Stadium, now Tad Gormley Stadium—is an early example of the importance of the human figure in his work and how he portrayed the muscles and ligaments below the skin to inform shape. The arc of the bow, the waves of the figure's hair, and the simple and streamlined shape of the sun all have classic modernist signatures.

At the center of the panels, high above the entrance and second-floor windows, is the most dramatic piece Alférez made for the exterior, a cast-stone sculpture with mythological influence: *Man as a Flying Machine.*[189] It dominates the top of the building, and the figure seems to be soaring, his feet resting in a set of hands that are nestled in clouds. The figure features symbols of strength and power: lightning bolts extending from the clouds and disproportionately large hands and dramatically emphasized muscles. The figure's arms are outstretched at a ninety-degree angle from his body, like a perfect cross, leading an architecture critic to write that, although the sculptural details were "effective and appropriate," there was one exception: "the unfortunate crucifix effect over the main door."[190] The religious connection may have been intentional.[191] Whether or not the allusion was intentional, it persisted. When its restoration was unveiled in 2013, *Man as a Flying Machine* was referred to as the "Flying Angel," in addition to the "Spirit of Aviation."

Weiss, Dreyfous, and Seiferth wanted the interior of the building to match, or surpass, the grandeur of the exterior. There are decorative trim accents throughout the building, notably in the transoms and the balustrade. The main waiting area features art deco patterns and symbols of aviation on its terrazzo floor, as well as a central compass, the points of which make note of cities and their distances from New Orleans, inspiring visitors to imagine the far reaches of the world they could travel to and from by way of Shushan. The compass pointed not just to the distant cities but also toward Gonzalez's murals on the second floor. The murals showed feats including Charles Lindbergh's arrival in Paris in the *Spirit of Saint Louis*, accompanied by French fliers, and Richard E. Byrd and Floyd Bennett taking off from the ice for their flight over the South Pole.

In a 1975 interview with Jack Davis, Alférez was critical of Gonzalez's murals, suggesting that they were "travel brochure covers" rather than worthy examples of contemporary art. Alférez was referring to murals that infused elements of machination, a likely nod to Mexican muralism and its influence on US art. Though

Lakefront Airport terminal interior
photo by Donn Young

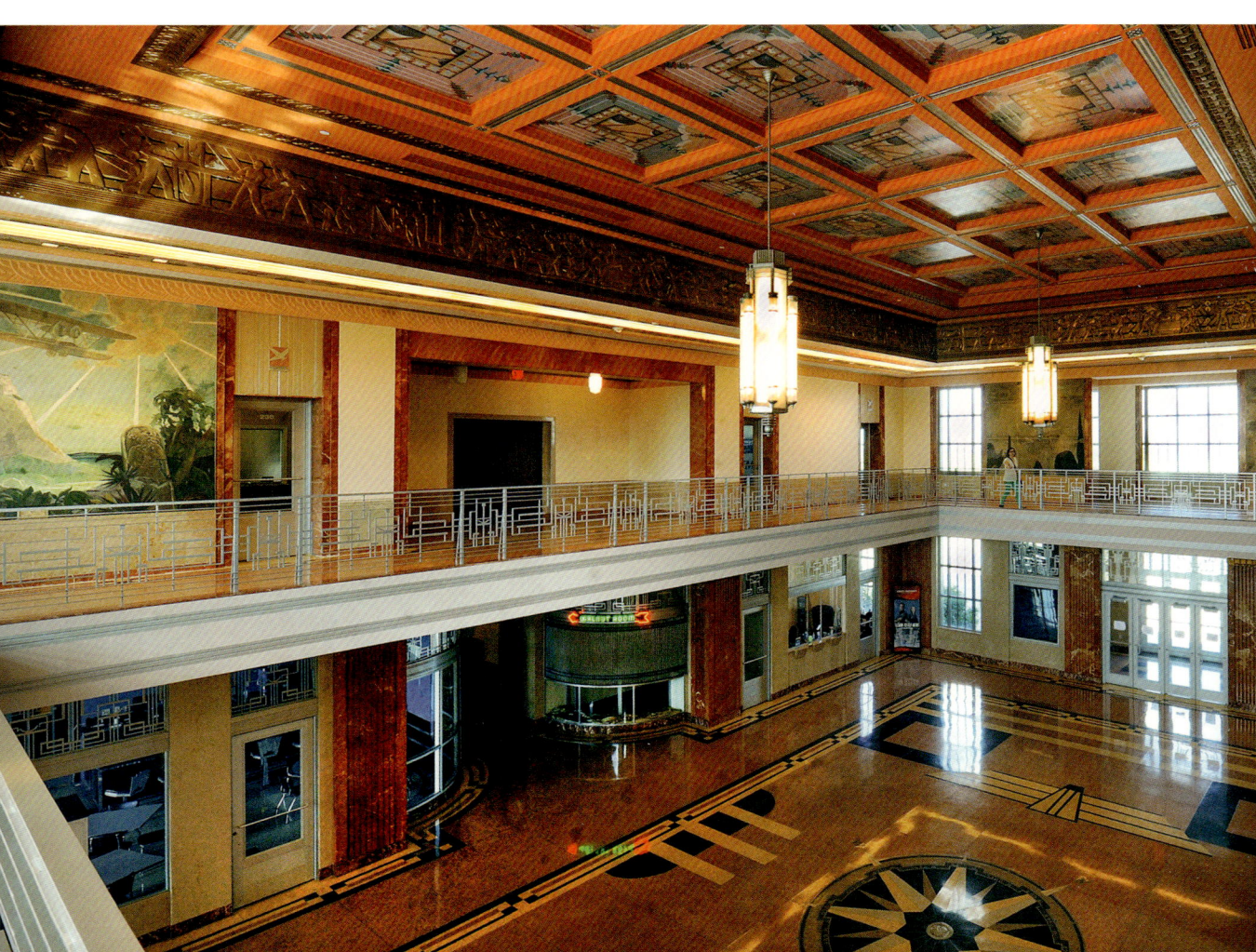

Alférez was critical of his friend's work, he also acknowledged that Gonzalez was producing what had been asked of him for this commercial project. Art conservator Elise Grenier, who oversaw restoration of the murals, notes that they would have needed to convey the relative safety of flying to an audience not yet fully comfortable with this innovation.[192] So, while Alférez's criticism—arriving long after the airport was completed and air travel had become more common—was true in a descriptive sense, it was also a bit unfair.[193]

In the waiting area, a frieze by Alférez encircles a recessed portion of the ceiling, above Gonzalez's murals. The frieze features figures at work with the tools and objects related to workers' contributions to the airport's construction. They are stylized but characteristically ambiguous art deco representations, with clean streamlined arcs and lines in their forms: an architect at a drafting table and workers amidst pulleys, belts, and wheels. Some have detailed muscles. Alférez's foregrounding of those who labored on the project is a theme that he would later repeat on bridges in New Orleans City Park.

Alférez's final work at the airport was completed in 1938. His *Fountain of the Four Winds*, installed about a hundred yards from the entrance to the airport, in what was then a small park, was designed in conjunction with a 1936–38 beautification program under the Works Progress Administration. Designed to further attract visitors and locals, the beautification project also included improvements to roadways, drainage, sidewalks, transmission lines, landscaping, a pump station, and the addition of a swimming pool and tennis courts.

Construction of the fountain began in 1937. Alférez was paid $350 to make the figures and molds, which no longer exist, and he had support from WPA workers for the casting.[194] He requested support from two laborers for about twelve hours each day.[195]

The main element of the fountain, four kneeling figures facing outward, is centered in an elliptical basin. The allegorical nude figures, three female and one male, represent the four mythological winds, each placed at its appropriate compass point. The figures are approximately nine feet tall and created from cast concrete, and they are expressed in graceful, smooth curves, with muscles defined in their arms, legs, and torso. Their hair is composed of well-defined raked lines, similar to the lines emanating from behind the central flying figure on the front of the airport and suggesting the movement of wind. The female figures' hair is tossed with slight waves, whereas the male figure's hair is defined by clean curves. The West Wind holds an owl with open wings in her cupped right hand, held beneath her outstretched left arm. The South Wind holds a cloud over her shoulder, as though lifting it as a vessel toward the sky. The only male figure, the North Wind, holds his hands together above his head. His hands are oversized, accentuating his strength

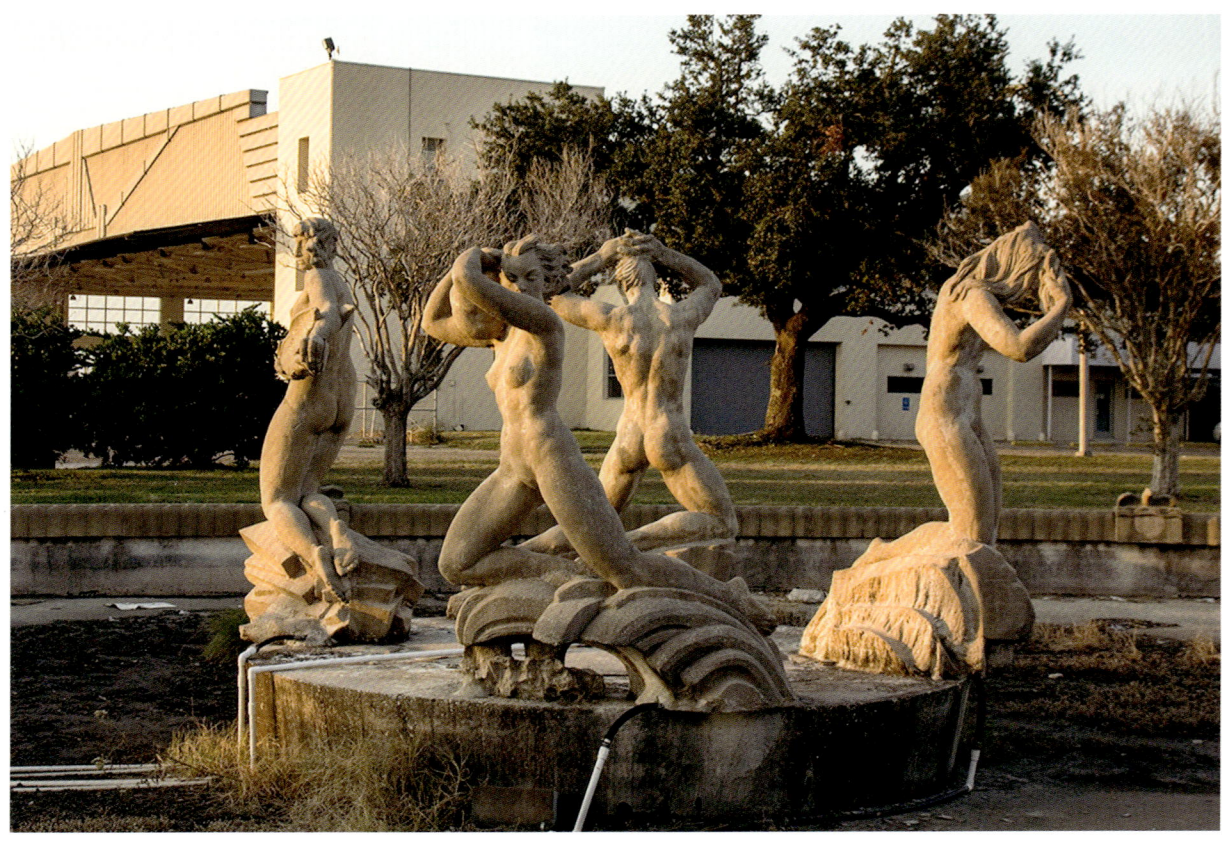

Fountain of the Four Winds, **Lakefront Airport** [1938]
photo by Ashley Merlin

and power and creating visual balance for the larger-than-life sculpture. The East Wind, the final piece Alférez modeled, represents the break of morning.[196] Her head is tilted toward the ground and a spray of water is blended with her hair in a downpour. When the fountain flowed, each figure released a stream of spray.

The figures look down toward the pool of water, which may seem at first curious for a sculpture dedicated to the symbolism of flight. But the figures' downward-cast eyes, could they see, would take in a reflected view of the sky overhead and planes in flight. From the air, their faces could be seen reflected in the water below. When the pool is empty, as it has been for decades, and the viewer stands at the feet of the figures, the sky appears to be on their shoulders and in their arms and hands. These distinctions are key to seeing how Alférez saw: both from a distance and close up, with an ability to control how his figures would appear from varied points of view. This consideration extended not just to the construction of the figures themselves but also to the added elements of light, spraying water, and the pool. In this case, Alférez also needed to envision how the fountain could be seen from above, by a visitor in flight. This perspective is one that Alférez might have begun exploring on that initial expedition to Yucatán with Blom, when they visited ancient sites that had been built to face the gods above.[197]

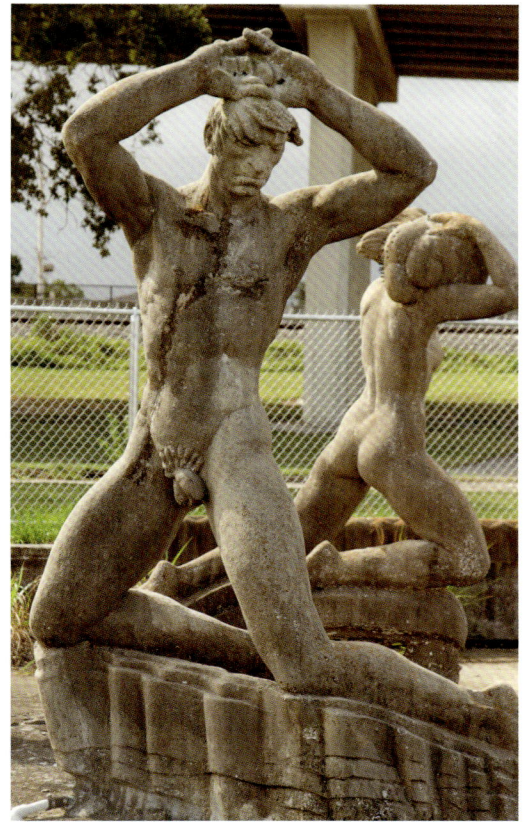

North Wind, *Fountain of the Four Winds* [1938]
photo by Ashley Merlin

The basin of the *Fountain of the Four Winds* has bas-relief symbols including stars, clouds, and birds in flight. Eight eagles, echoing the eight compass points in the floor of the airport's main building and Gonzalez's eight murals, are perched on the edge of the basin at equal distances from one another, facing the winds. At night, the pool was illuminated with colored underwater lighting for each figure.[198] The bases of the figures have hints of the shape of clouds or waves and were designed with functional and artistic purposes, as they also house water ducts.[199]

The figures were modestly distanced from one another, placed so that, when viewed from varied perspectives, there was an illusion of them overlapping.[200] Alférez considered this interplay essential, and he used artificial light and streaming water to further "mold" the work and allow for the moving lines of the water to complete the composition of the sculpture. But even with the connection provided by the streaming water and artificial lights at night, he wasn't satisfied with it as installed. The initial design for the fountain had featured a central globe with embellishments, partially submerged at the center of the circle of figures, but it was excluded from the contract. Dissatisfied by the fountain without this element, Alférez added the globe without additional payment. Even after the addition of the globe, though, Alférez felt the figures still needed "closer knitting."[201] Despite this self-criticism about the fountain, when he reflected more than fifty years after its installation, he still considered *Four Winds* the work he most enjoyed.[202] He also said it was his "favorite thing" done in his life.[203]

The figures were modeled in a studio at City Park Stadium, and by the middle of February 1938, Alférez was putting final touches on the *Winds* on-site at the airport. The fountain was first lit in July.

"The [*Four Winds* project] seemed to be going well until some puritanical SOB insisted that I was contaminating the morals of our WPA men because one of the figures was a nude male," Alférez told art critic and dealer Luba Glade.[204] According to Alférez, the offended official remarked that he wasn't going to let his workers "go over there and stand in front of that indecent thing," and he threatened to destroy the fountain with a sledgehammer. Alférez countered with a threat of his own: If anyone went to the fountain to damage it, he would go there too—armed with a rifle to protect his work. Alférez joked that he thought a man had a right to protect the way he makes a living, and, with similar amusement, acknowledged that he had also made up the law making that so.[205]

Alférez reached out to Lyle Saxon, editor of the WPA's *New Orleans City Guide*, hoping he would intervene. Saxon appealed to a higher authority: he wrote two letters, one to First Lady Eleanor Roosevelt, who was in California at the time, and the other to President Franklin D. Roosevelt in Washington, DC, and included photos of the North Wind. Mrs. Roosevelt, an ardent supporter of the arts, recommended that the fountain should be kept as it was.[206] Alférez took the letters to WPA administrators and to other leaders, and with the evidence of support, the controversy was settled.[207] The fountain is often considered Alférez's finest public work.

Its medium, cast concrete, has made upkeep a challenge over the years. Hailed as a stunning new medium during Alférez's early career, it has proved challenging to art conservators. There have been numerous discussions about the fountain's future, as well as valiant efforts to restore it. In 1991, the Orleans Levee Board approved restoration work in advance of the New Orleans Museum of Art's annual Odyssey Ball, which was to be held that fall at the Lakefront Airport.[208] Alférez, almost ninety

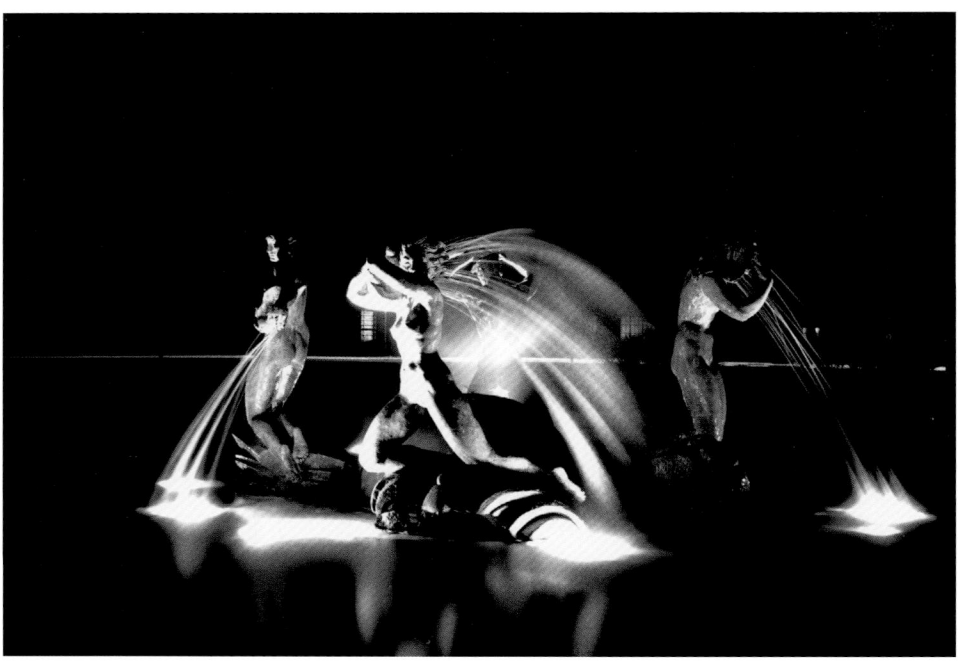

Original spray pattern, *Fountain of the Four Winds* [1938]
photo by Works Progress Administration
COURTESY OF WPA PHOTOGRAPH COLLECTION, LOUISIANA DIVISION/CITY ARCHIVES,
NEW ORLEANS PUBLIC LIBRARY

at the time, applied fixes in concrete, his work bucket carried for him because the weight had grown too heavy for him to bear on his own.[209] He also oversaw the demolition of the globe at the center of the fountain, likely done to gain access to pipes and plumbing.[210]

When Alférez saw the outcome of the 1991 restoration, he was pleased to see water flow again. But he and Peggy acknowledged that the original spray pattern had not been replicated. Thus, after the 1991 restoration, the Alférez family began pursuing the possibility of having the figures recast in bronze. Their interest had been sparked, in part, by discussions about a potential relocation of the fountain. Peggy was concerned that moving the fountain would put the *Winds* at further risk. "If it were to be moved," she wrote, "molds should be made of the figures to ensure that if they are damaged, they can be repaired or recast."[211]

Peggy also thought molds should be made even if the fountain was kept in its current location, and she began securing bids, from foundries in California, New Mexico, New York, New Jersey, and Pennsylvania. They provided assessments of the state of the fountain, as well as costs to produce rubber molds, cast the figures in bronze, and ship them to New Orleans. Jon Lash, a foundry supervisor at Johnson Atelier Technical Institute of Sculpture in New Jersey, observed that by 1995, the fountain had sustained "numerous alterations with natural elements and non-discretionary contact with some of the local citizens." In a letter providing recommendations on steps that could be taken to restore the fountain, Lash noted that the "natural leaching of lime precipitated by association of salts, water, and atmospheric conditions" had likely caused the breakdown of the concrete substrate. He also noted that some of the superficial improvements that had been made to keep up the figures' appearances did not address flaws below the surface, continuing to leave the structure at risk.[212]

The fountain was further damaged in Hurricane Katrina in 2005. By 2013, a board responsible for the fountain passed a resolution naming the *Four Winds* an "artistic masterpiece" and calling for its restoration, keeping open a dialogue with the Federal Emergency Management Agency (FEMA) about restoring the fountain to pre-storm conditions.[213] Once those steps were taken, the fountain could be ready for a more complete restoration. As of the publication of this book, early stages of restoration have begun.

Like the fountain that graces its grounds, the airport itself underwent considerable changes over the years. In 1964, during the Cold War, the architectural firm Cimini and Meric was hired for a renovation of the airport that would, in part, convert the building into a radiation fallout shelter. The art deco facade was covered with austere, thick, and windowless walls, absent of character. Alférez and Peggy, like many others, believed that the original facade was not just hidden, but destroyed.[214]

When Hurricane Katrina unleashed a storm surge that caused significant damage to the airport, the storm that brought such harrowing destruction also brought a more welcome surprise. When architect Alton Ochsner Davis began the project to renovate the airport after Katrina, he saw that Cimini and Meric had taken important steps to protect the building's detail by placing a steel skeleton between the 1933 and the 1964 facades. This allowed for the restoration of the exterior design, returning the building to its original elegance.[215]

Charity Hospital

The firm Weiss, Dreyfous, and Seiferth hired Alférez on another project, an important building in New Orleans's architectural and civic history: the sixth Charity Hospital building. From 1936 to 1938, Alférez created a number of works for the building, including bas-reliefs above the emergency entrance, carved in limestone, and an approximately seventeen-by-seventeen-foot aluminum grille, or window screen, called *Louisiana at Work and Play*, above the main entrance of the twenty-story hospital. When it was installed in November 1938, art critic W. M. Darling—struck by the grille's size relative to the massive building—described it as "a work in tiny detail."[216]

The sculpture was designed to reflect Louisiana culture as well as the people whom the hospital served. It includes a large figure at the center, his arms bent and hands held overhead, as well as a central tree of life. The figure is surrounded by scenes in low relief, illustrating common pastimes and professions: people playing baseball and golf and flying a kite; a woman cooking; two shipmen; and stevedores hauling sacks. There is an oil rig, and agricultural and fishery vignettes feature two men cutting sugarcane and two with nets. One element, a flying duck, got Alférez in trouble because of its symbolic connection to Louisiana politics.

By the time Alférez began his Charity projects, the institution was already one of the oldest hospitals in the United States, having opened the same year that Bellevue Hospital was founded in New York. From its outset in 1736, it was a hospital for the indigent. In 1928, within a month of Huey P. Long's tenure as governor, he proposed a bill to the Louisiana State Legislature giving himself the authority to reorganize the hospital board—just the latest manifestation of his autocratic approach to governance. Police and state employees were required to pay deductions, or "deducts," to Long's campaign fund, "donating" a portion of their income on payday. Hospital staff recalled providing 5 to 10 percent of their income—gathered in cash—for these required payments.[217]

Richard W. Leche, who became governor in 1936, continued taking the payments, which had become known colloquially as "de ducks." "De ducks are flying"

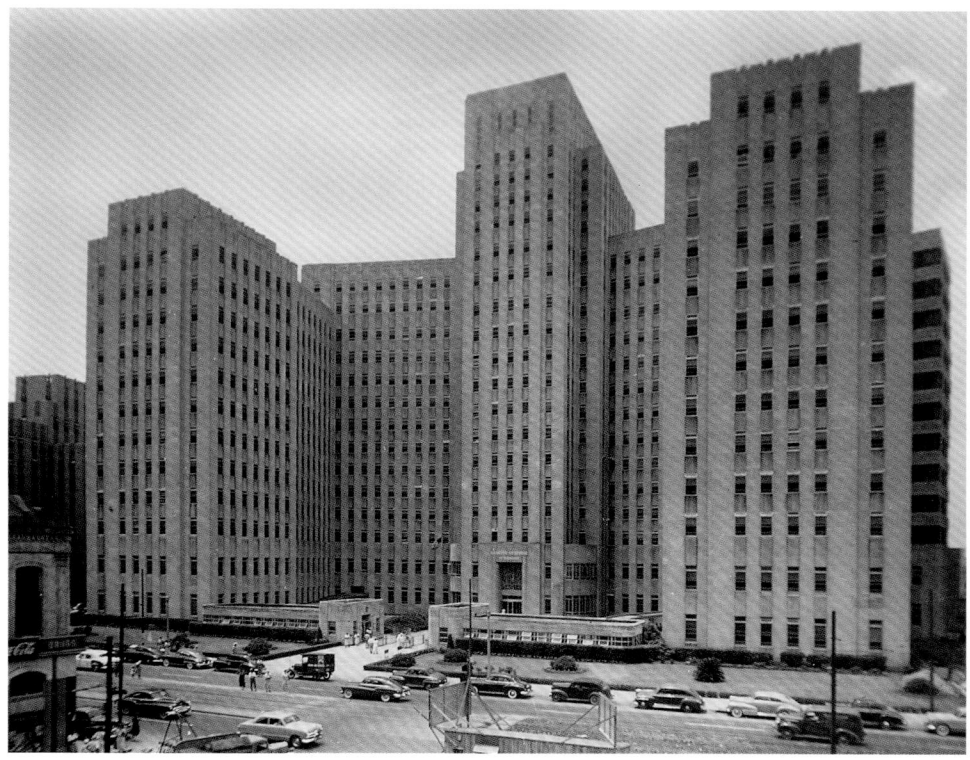

Charity Hospital
photo by Charles L. Franck Photographers, ca.1950
THNOC, GIFT OF ARTHUR PAINE, 2019.0118.26

was frequently said when the funds were collected. Leche was responsible for hiring Weiss, Dreyfous, and Seiferth, and when the hospital opened in 1939, it was mired in irregularities that had begun during construction. The bidding process alone prompted "at least four investigations" according to historian Robert D. Leighninger Jr.[218]

Alférez spoke of irregularities, from payoffs to the elimination of fire escapes to save money. In Leighninger's assessment, Alférez's allegations make for great stories, and may have occurred on other projects, but corner-cutting schemes would have been rectified as a result of investigations.[219] Nonetheless, Alférez couldn't resist referencing Long and Leche's unethical "deducts" practice with his inclusion of the duck in the grille design.

Alférez created the plaster model for the grille in his apartment in the Lower Pontalba Building, and he had it leaning against a wall when he received a visit from architect Felix Julius Dreyfous, who wanted to inspect the piece before it was cast. Alférez suggested that Dreyfous liked to offer criticism and always requested some kind of change, perhaps as a way of demonstrating his authority. Dreyfous saw the

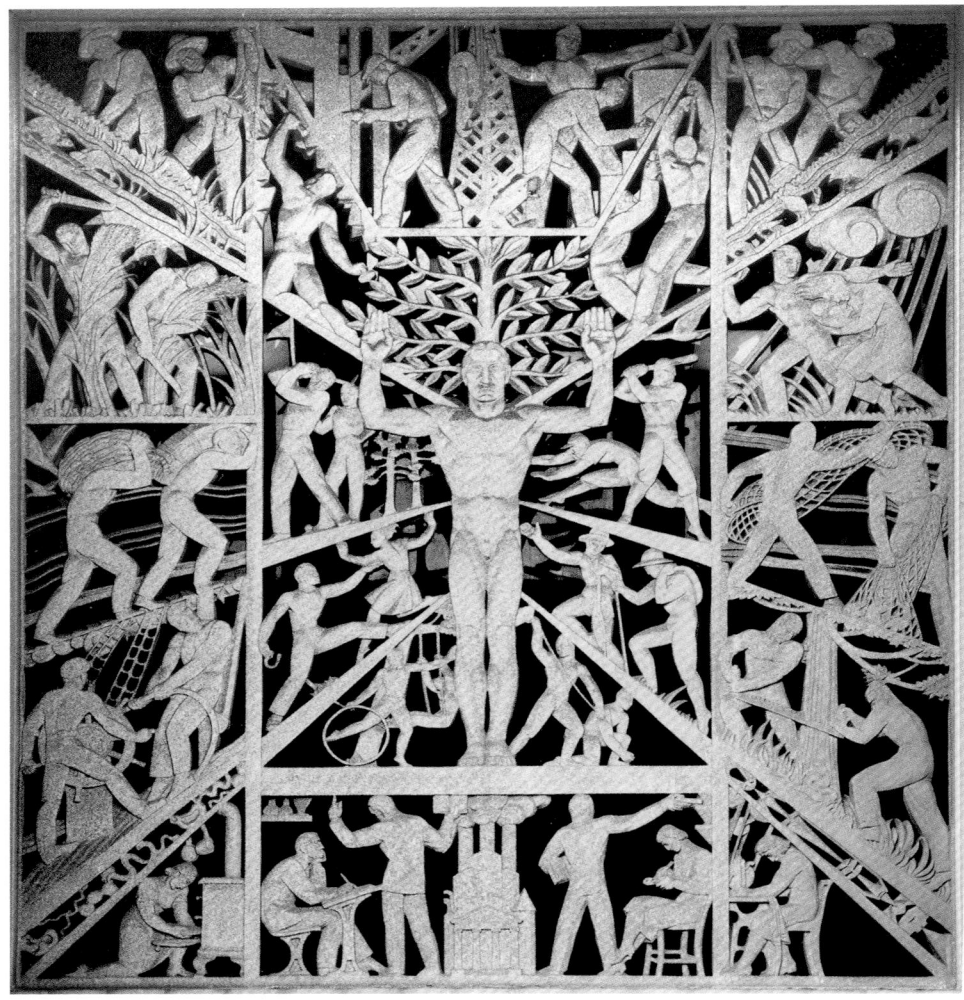

Louisiana at Work and Play [1938]
photo © Owen Murphy Jr., 1988

duck above the head of a baseball player and thought it was a leaf that had blown off the tree of life. He told Alférez to make the leaf smaller. Alférez didn't contradict Dreyfous or inform him that the leaf was in fact a visual pun. Instead, he picked up a chisel and a handful of plaster and gave Dreyfous the impression he was cutting to change the shape. Dreyfous then gave approval to cast the work.

When the finished aluminum screen was delivered, it was set on the first floor of Charity Hospital, which was still under construction, to await its placement above the entrance. Someone noticed Alférez's barely hidden message, and word began to spread.

Around New Year's Day, a police officer went to Alférez's home to pick him up and take him to the house of Leon C. Weiss, Dreyfous's partner. When Alférez arrived, Weiss was outside in his garden, with Dreyfous, among the winter blooms of his beloved camellias. Alférez noticed there was much bantering and back and forth between the men about which of them would tell him the news. He implored them to stop beating around the bush. Finally, they asked Alférez about the duck flying over the baseball player. He tried to tell them he had once gone to a baseball game and seen ducks flying, but no one was buying the explanation. Dreyfous reminded Alférez that he thought it was a leaf when he inspected the plaster model, and he suggested that Alférez might have changed it into a duck after the inspection. Alférez admitted that it had never been a leaf, and that Dreyfous simply didn't see it correctly to begin with.

Alférez was told to remove the duck, a nearly impossible task at that point. Years later, Alférez would recall that a man was sent to the hospital with a hacksaw to remove the duck from the grille, but a *Times-Picayune* journalist intervened by telling the man that it would be a federal crime to damage the piece since the hospital had been built with federal funds.[220] The duck remains on the facade of Charity Hospital today. A developer purchased the building in 2018, with a commitment to redeveloping the property and preserving art deco elements, including *Louisiana at Work and Play.*

The Family

Alférez's next major public commission was awarded after he moved back to New Orleans from New York around 1950. Architectural firm Curtis and Davis hired him to produce a sculpture that would be installed on an otherwise empty white marble exterior wall of a municipal court and jail at 501 North Rampart Street, between Toulouse and Saint Louis Streets on the edge of the French Quarter.

The firm requested a work that focused on the family, and Alférez chose as his subject a mother and father with an infant between them. *The Family* was cast in concrete and finished in zinc and lead. Alférez told New Orleans *States-Item* journalist Lanny Thomas that he thought the piece was "symbolic of family unity and strength."[221] It was suspended about a foot from the marble wall by iron rods that allowed the piece to cast shadows on the large and windowless white facade as sunlight changed throughout the day.

The Family was unveiled in a modest dedication ceremony with Mayor deLesseps Story "Chep" Morrison in attendance.[222] Within hours, Father Joseph P. Laux from the nearby Our Lady of Guadalupe Catholic Church and International Shrine of Saint Jude contacted Morrison's office to object to the nudity of the figures. New Orleans residents began sending letters to the editor, offering their perspective in the court of public opinion.[223] Only about 10 percent of these letters objected to the

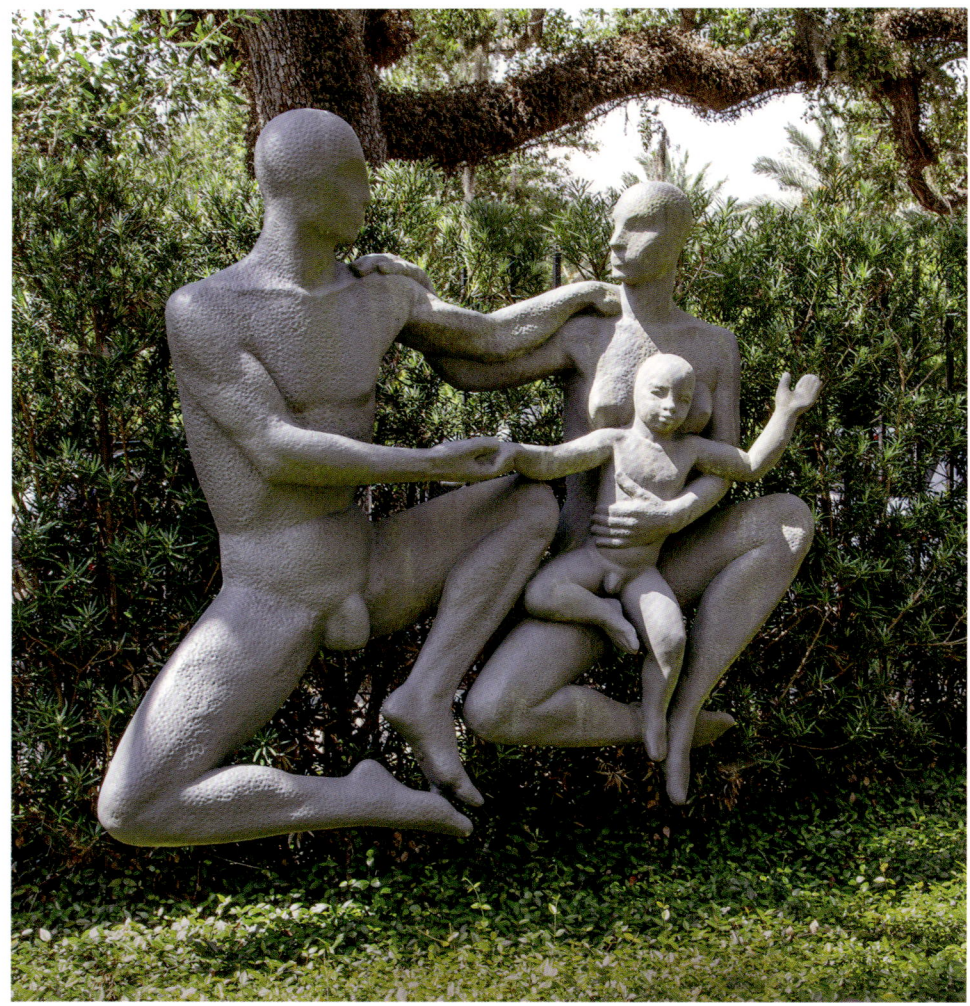

The Family in The Helis Foundation Enrique Alférez Sculpture Garden [1951]
photo by Keely Merritt, THNOC
DONATED BY MR. AND MRS. ALEXANDER CHARLES DENEUMOUSTIER

sculpture.[224] Nonetheless, controversy grew and publicity of the incident extended around the country and beyond, appearing in newspapers as far away as Delaware, Michigan, and Ottawa, Canada. The public debate would cause Alférez substantial stress, and he was already tense about *The Family* because of an incident that occurred while the figure was being staged.

As Alférez recalled it, his friend Xavier Gonzalez played a prank on him on the day of the unveiling. While a drape was still covering *The Family*, Gonzalez called Alférez over and told him to take a peek under the cover. When Alférez did, he saw that his friend had attached to the father a large and erect penis made of some kind of material like papier-mâché. Angered, Alférez knocked the attachment off the sculpture. Alférez's lingering anger over the incident may have deepened as a result of the drought in commissions that followed the controversy, and in time it led to a break between the two artists. When the Alférez family visited Gonzalez in New York in the 1980s, Gonzalez joked about the penis, something Alférez never found funny, and Alférez drew his family together and departed early from Gonzalez's home.[225]

It is impossible to know whether the phallic prank had any audience wider than Alférez and Gonzalez in 1951, and it is unlikely it had any role in heating the controversy around the sculpture. Alonzo Lansford, the director of the Isaac Delgado Art Museum (now the New Orleans Museum of Art), was among those who came to Alférez's defense. He observed that the sculpture had been approved by the city and architects before it was installed. "The people that are making the protests fool themselves into thinking they are righteous," Lansford said. "They're just ignorant."[226]

Others, though, thought the piece was immoral. Municipal Court Judge Harold Moore had chambers inside the building. He said, "Unless [*The Family*] is titled 'Bare Facts and the Naked Truth,' I can't imagine what that thing is doing on a courthouse." Mayor Morrison's executive assistant appeared to be in agreement. He thought it might be fine to place inside a museum, but "we can't have it out on the street!" Judge Paul Garofalo also sided with those opposed to the display of *The Family*: "If the architect says it symbolizes the family, I guess that's understandable," he said, "but is it necessary to portray the *origin* of the family quite so graphically?"[227]

Mayor Morrison contacted the architects to see if they could get Alférez to add a fig leaf to cover the father figure's genitals. The architects didn't think this was necessary, but they tried to persuade Alférez nonetheless.[228] Alférez refused. He offered to buy the figure back, but the offer was not accepted. Instead, it was covered in burlap and then removed from public view within three days of its installation. *The Family,* about five by six feet and weighing more than a thousand pounds, was moved to a city warehouse.

Soon it was announced that the work would be auctioned at Lafayette Square, with the tempting caveat that the nude figures would not be shown any longer than was necessary to make the sale. An announcement said, "The statue will absolutely not be on view until 11 a.m. sharp, the time of the auction." *The Family* was placed on a platform in the square and covered with sheets from the city jail. About a thousand people gathered outside in the 96-degree heat for the auction, Alférez among them. He brought treats—a baked ham, cheeses, bread, red wine, and a watermelon—to help endure the weather and auction, and spread his repast on a picnic blanket.[229]

Judge Moore, who had been among the sculpture's opponents, was also among the bidders. He offered a hundred dollars, saying that if he won the sculpture, he would "throw it in the river."[230]

The piece was sold at a price $600 greater than the city had paid for it. A bidder paid $2,400 for *The Family*, and later installed it in the cocktail lounge at a hotel he owned, the Saint Francis Hotel on Common Street.[231] It would change hands again, passing to Alexander Charles "Denny" Deneumoustier. It ended up in storage in the back room of Denny's son-in-law's dinner club and cocktail lounge, O'Dwyers, in Jefferson Parish, Louisiana, and was later moved to the family's backyard, where it leaned against a garage wall for decades. Over time, its weight, in combination with the soft, sinking ground, caused it to become partially buried. Alférez visited *The Family* in this condition at least once.[232]

Alférez's ham, wine, and watermelon might have appeared witty enough to belie his feelings about the incident; in truth, he was very distressed about the controversy. At least once, he suggested that he considered *The Family* among his most accomplished works. His impression might have been more of an indicator of a feeling he brought to creating the work and an emotional response to the stress caused by the fallout than an assessment of the sculpture in comparison to other figures he created—because it isn't among Alférez's best works, nor would it have become an iconic figure had it not been mired in controversy. A similar family, carved in mahogany for an Alabama hospital about a decade later, was a more refined and emotive version of a mother, father, and child.

Alférez thought the removal of *The Family* and the attendant controversy meant that his career in New Orleans was over—and given how far the news had reached, he thought he would never again be hired as a sculptor. Indeed, commissions for work in public spaces didn't pick up for Alférez until the 1980s. The art world had changed considerably since the end of World War II, with a decline in funding for public works, but incidents surrounding *The Family* may have also contributed to his diminishing commissions.

Symbols of Communication

Alférez's work was featured prominently in another building important in the public life of New Orleanians, the *Times-Picayune* building on Howard Avenue. Though he was embraced by the community and celebrated publicly toward the end of his life, Alférez often felt like an outsider. Some of the contributing factors were addressed in chapter 2, "Culture and Belonging," and the work Alférez created for the *Times-Picayune* building was an important illustration of his views on connections between cultures. His *Symbols of Communication*, a series of bas-relief panels he executed for the *Times-Picayune* building in late 1967 through early 1968, features a blending of culture, through the representation of languages. Architect Edward B. Silverstein designed the newspaper's headquarters with an entrance atrium that was open to the

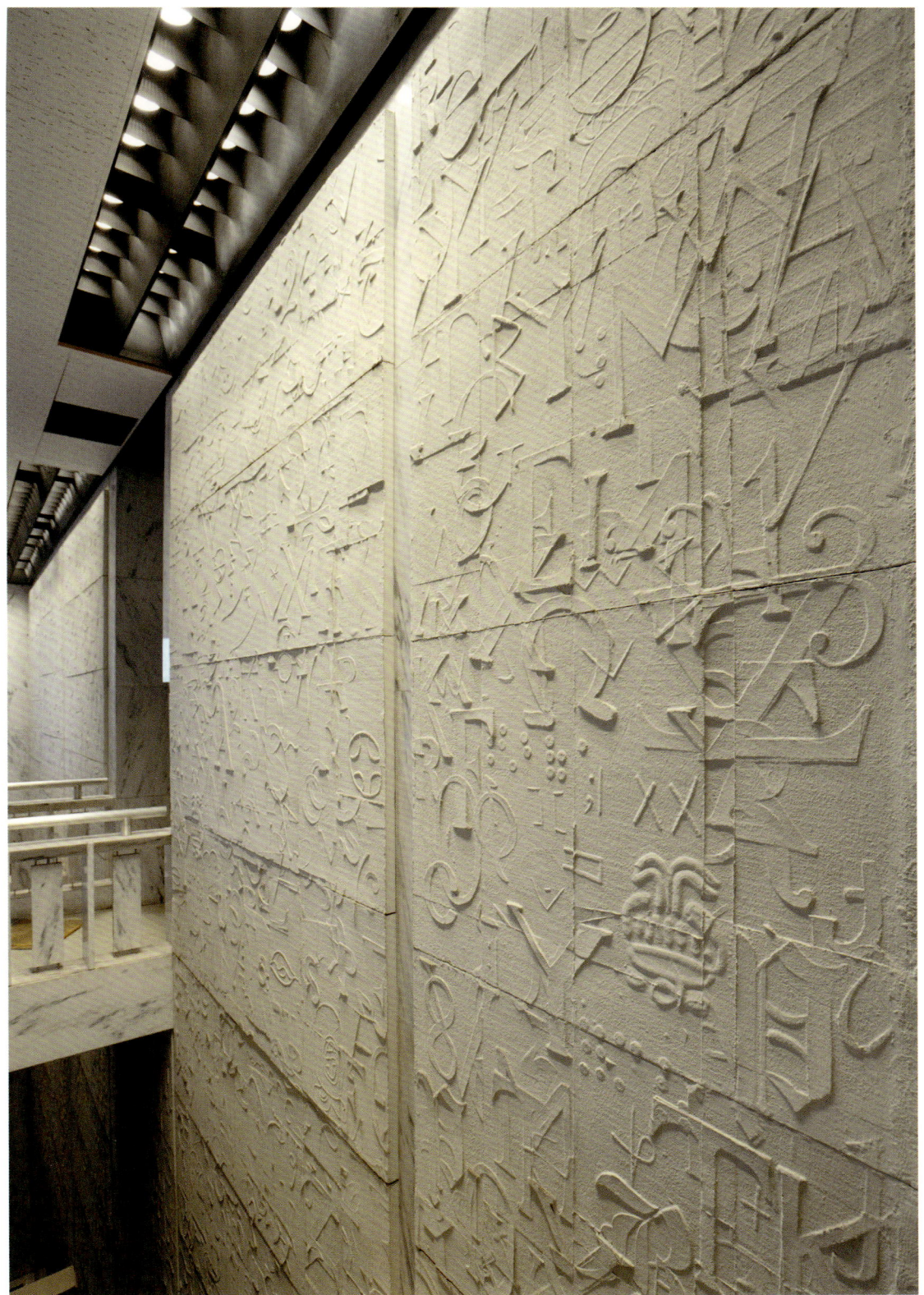

Symbols of Communication (detail) [1968]

photo by Max Becherer

NEW ORLEANS ADVOCATE, JANUARY 22, 2018, CAPITAL CITY PRESS/GEORGES MEDIA GROUP, BATON ROUGE, LA

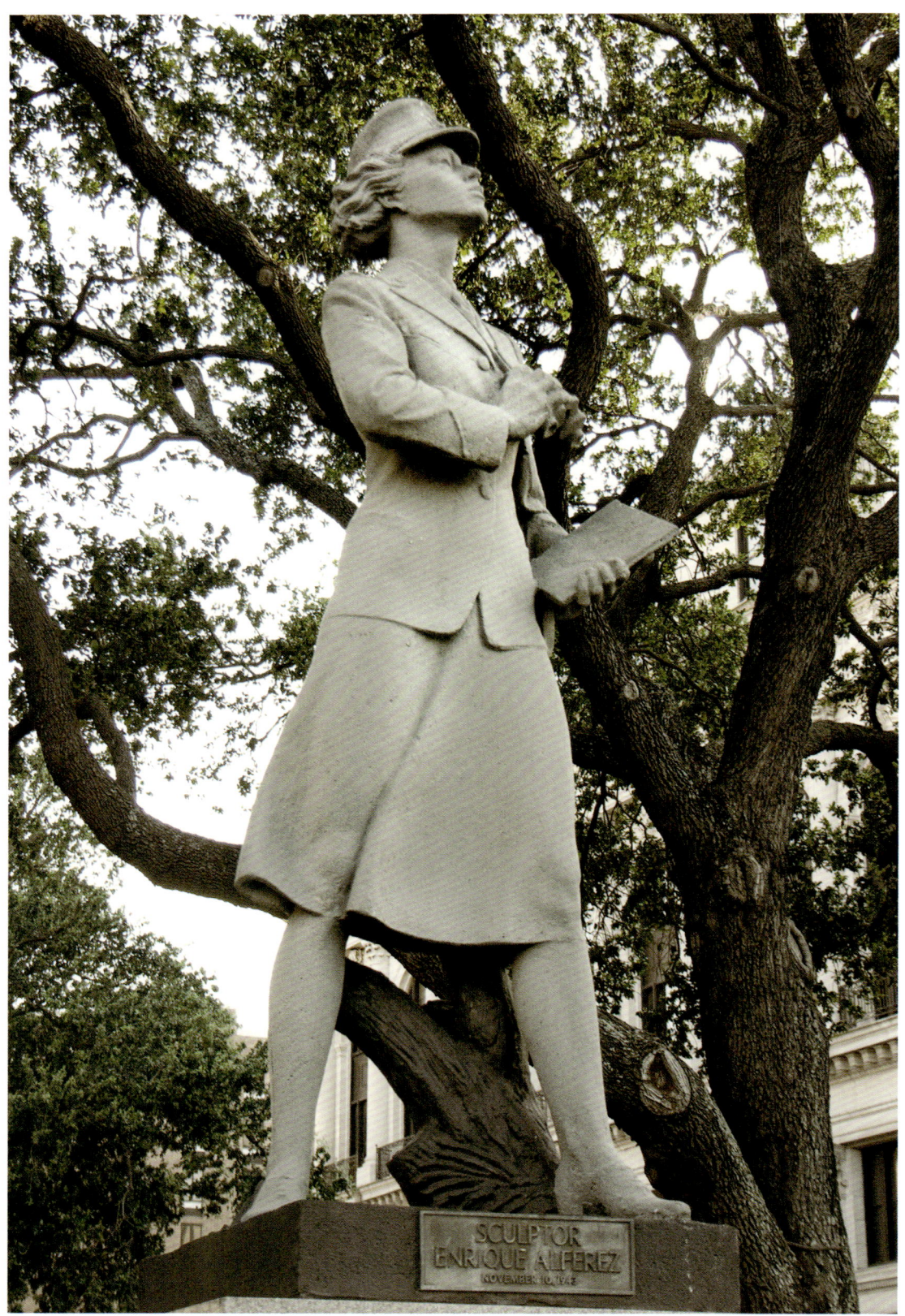

Molly Marine [1943]

photo by Ashley Merlin

ceiling of the third floor, with a line of vision from the first floor to the top floor, framed by the escalators. Riding up or down, a traveler was just a few feet from Alférez's panels, which Silverstein commissioned in order to provide texture without overwhelming the space.[233]

Alférez created patterns on fourteen massive plaster panels, some thirty-seven by eight feet and others twenty-two by six feet, designed so that they could be disassembled in smaller sections. The installation includes letters from Roman and Greek alphabets as well as hieroglyphics from ancient Egypt; Chinese, Japanese, and Arabic characters; and the dots and dashes of Morse code and Braille, to name just a few. The letters and characters are nested together aesthetically, not to create a decipherable message, but to bring languages and cultures together. It's also possible to find at least one embedded message, a signature reminding the viewer who created the panels. Heading from the first floor by escalator, a viewer could see the name "Enrique" when approaching the second floor.

The plaster panels were cast in a rented warehouse where Alférez had a large enough space for the thirty-eight-foot table required to hold a single panel. After casting, the fourteen panels were then transported to the Howard Avenue building, where Alférez oversaw the assembly on-site.[234] In 2018, *Symbols of Communication* was disassembled and placed in storage in advance of the demolition of the building, which occurred in 2019. In 2020, the panels were acquired by the New Orleans Museum of Art.

While many works by Alférez are in public spaces, he rarely created monuments to public figures. Further, most of the portraits he created are small pieces in private collections, created for family, friends, or on commission. He did, however, sculpt a few public monuments and statues that honor individuals. In these cases, the subjects are civic and political leaders who embodied values Alférez held dear. One monument, *Molly Marine*, was created to honor a group of women rather than an individual. The modest representation of these kinds of figures in Alférez's work was intentional, as he preferred to focus on the everyman or everywoman rather than statesmen, generals, or public figures. Nonetheless, there are a few such works to examine in New Orleans and Morelia.

Molly Marine

Molly Marine, the first monument to women in the military in the United States, was dedicated on the US Marine Corps's birthday—November 10—in 1943, following the 1942 establishment of the Marine Corps Women's Reserve.[235] Today the statue stands in a small garden in the median on Elk Place near the intersection with Canal Street; the figure's head is held high, a book in one hand and binoculars in the other.

Charles Gresham, a technical sergeant and recruiter for the Marines in New Orleans, was interested in having a monument made to recognize women in service. He encouraged Alférez to make the figure. Alférez wanted to join the military during World War II, and according to his family, he believed that donating his time, effort, and clay to sculpt the homage might increase his chances of becoming a Marine.[236] Although this dream wouldn't come to fruition, Alférez did serve in the US Army Transport Service and was named an honorary Marine for his gift, and his lifelong connection to the Marines was a source of pride for him.

Alférez created the twelve-and-a-half-foot *Molly* by working with five models, including his neighbor Judy Mosgrove, and four female Marines.[237] *Molly* was cast with donated marble chips and granite blended into concrete, eliminating the need for wartime-restricted metals.[238] By the early 1960s, the statue was in need of cleaning and repair.[239] In 1966, the monument received a new marble pedestal and a bronze wash over the cast concrete; by 1988, the bronze wash had begun to chip, so the statue was sandblasted, cleaned, and given a new spray coating of bronze. In 1999, plans were made to reproduce and restore *Molly* again. Alférez made a mold of the statue on-site at Elk Place so that copies could be cast in bronze. Two replicas were installed, at the Marine Corps Recruit Depot at Parris Island, South Carolina, in 1999; and at the Marine Corps Base at Quantico, Virginia, in 2000. Though he was unable to see these figures on-site, he was presented with a Meritorious Public Service Award from the Marine Forces Reserve in his hospital room in 1999. When the Quantico copy was installed, in conjunction with the Women Marines Association Biennial Convention, Peggy and Tlaloc traveled to attend the dedication. *Molly Marine* continues to serve an important role in the US Marine Corps—the Molly Marine Award is annually presented to an exemplary female recruit at Parris Island.

Sophie B. Wright

A monument to Sophie B. Wright, seen in the eponymous park at the intersection of Magazine and Saint Andrew Streets, is among Alférez's few statues of public figures. Wright (1866–1912) was an educator, philanthropist, community advocate, and prison reformer. She began teaching students in her family's house when she was fourteen years old and later opened a school for girls and a free night school for boys and men. Wright lived a life based on values that resonated with Alférez, who thought education was "the most important human activity"—and the monument carried great meaning for him.[240]

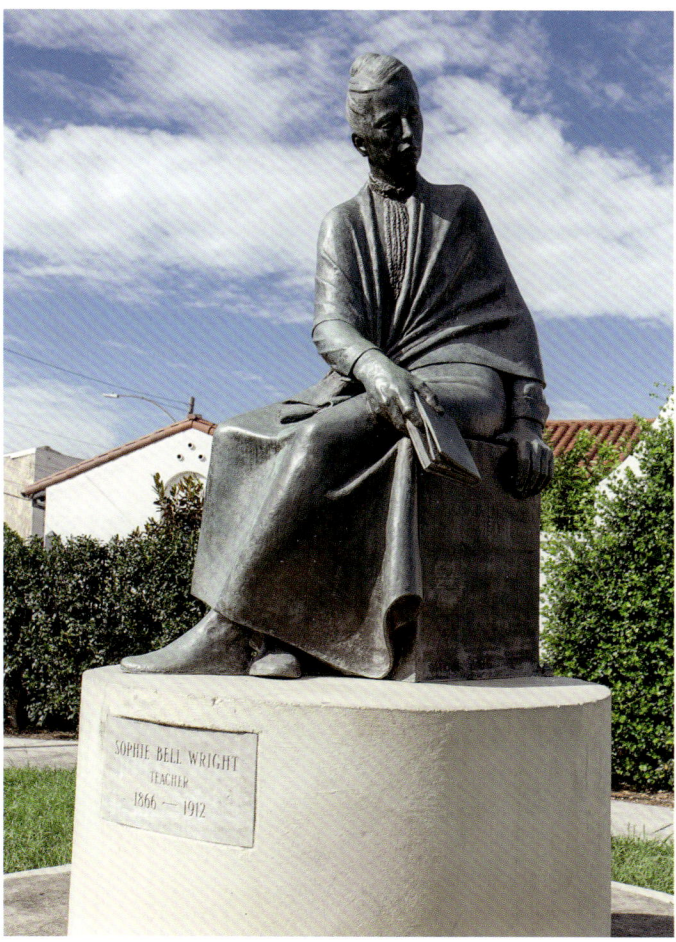

Sophie B. Wright [1986–87]
photo by Ashley Merlin

The work was commissioned by the Sophie Wright Monument Committee, which formed in 1986 and raised private donations to fund the project. Alférez modeled the seven-foot statue in plaster in late 1986 to early 1987, and it was cast in bronze. The figure holds a book, symbolizing Wright's career as an educator, and she is shown in a seated position, a subtle illustration of a disability caused by a childhood accident. The monument was dedicated in a public ceremony on April 17, 1988.

Benito Juárez and *David*

Alférez rarely created works that celebrated machismo or military prowess. In the 1980s, however, he created two strikingly similar tributes to masculine strength, both in cast bronze. *Benito Juárez*, a portrait of the president of Mexico between 1861

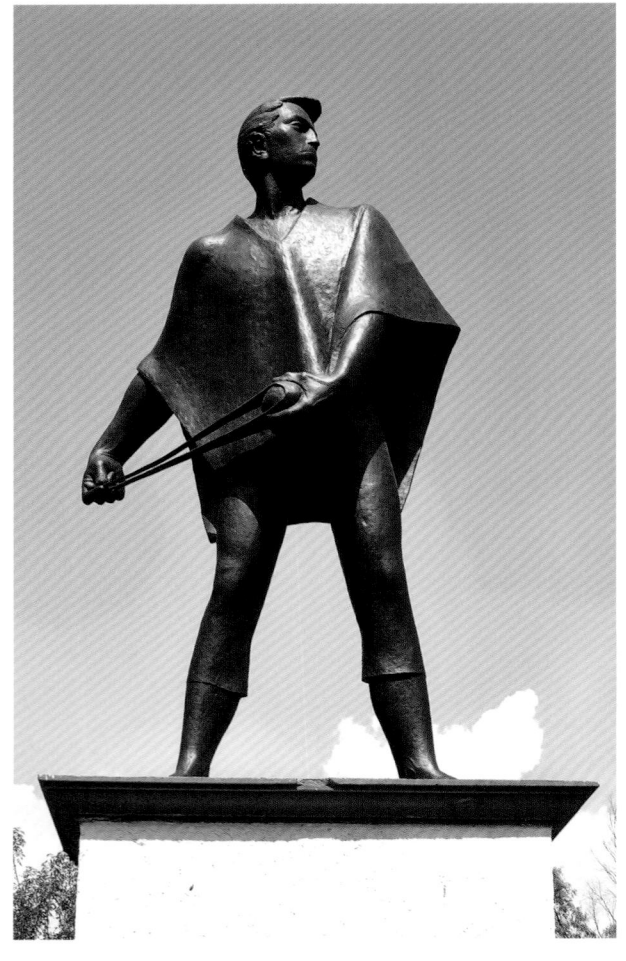

Benito Juárez [1984]
photo by Donn Young

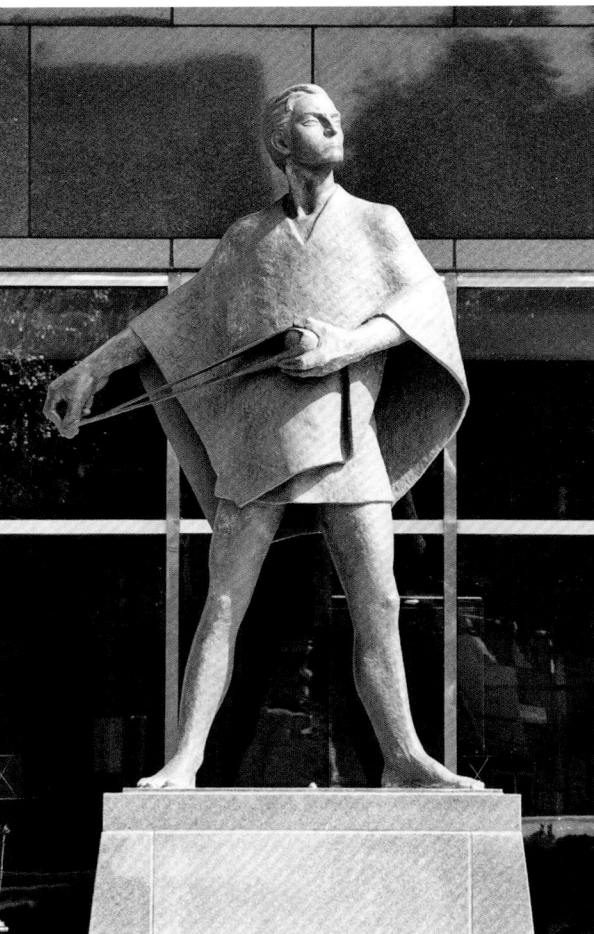

David [1988]
photo © Owen Murphy Jr., 1988

and 1872, was unveiled in Morelia in 1984, and *David,* a portrait of the young bibli-cal shepherd, was unveiled in New Orleans in 1988.

Although Alférez was not religious, he was familiar with the Bible and biblical stories, and he was drawn to images of the shepherd as protector. In this light, he associated Benito Juárez with David, a connection he began to draw at least as early as 1980.[241] Juárez was one of Mexico's most respected national figures, and Alférez had great admiration for him, once observing that Juárez was the only "hero" he sculpt-ed.[242] Juárez occupies a place in history and memory in Mexico that sets him apart as a leader of the people and for the people. Seen as a reformer who modernized the country, he overcame the poverty of his youth as son of a herdsman in rural Oaxaca and went on to become president.[243] Perhaps Alférez saw a connection to the leader, given that both men had close ties to New Orleans: on two occasions, when exiled from Mexico, Juárez sought shelter in the city. In 1965, a monument to him—not by Alférez—was given to New Orleans and placed at Basin and Conti Streets.[244]

When Alférez created his Juárez statue, his interpretation of this historical figure led one writer to consider the final portrait to be "unlike any other interpretation of our national hero anywhere in Mexico." Instead of appearing as a dignified older statesman, Juárez was shown as a young herdsman with a slingshot, recalling the shepherd David.[245]

The parable of David and Goliath is among the most well-known biblical stories: the young David battles the Philistine giant Goliath after Goliath belittles the Israelites. David, of course, slew Goliath with a rock from his slingshot, and the story has lent itself to allegories of courage, faith, and determination against oversized challenges.

Alférez created the two figures in similar fashion, but gave nuanced attention to the planes, styles of their clothing, and physical gestures. Both figures stand firmly, with their legs slightly apart, although there is a subtle difference in their torsos and shoulders. The plane of *David*'s shoulders is at a more accentuated angle, invoking a sense of defiance and courage, with the figure's chin thrust upward to see his giant foe; the statue of Juárez is more squared off to face a peer at eye level. There are differences in their attire as well, designed to match their time and place, with *Benito Juárez* in a serape and *David* in a cloak, or cape. Both ten-foot figures were unveiled with ceremony in their respective locations.[246] In 1984, Mexican President Miguel de la Madrid presided over the unveiling of *Benito Juárez* in a prominent area near the Zoológico Benito Juárez on Calzada Juárez in Morelia. In New Orleans, influential leaders joined businessman Joseph C. Canizaro for the unveiling of *David* and the *Lute Player*, which flank the entrance of the building at 909 Poydras Street.

City Park

City Park is where Enrique Alférez's imprint on New Orleans can be seen most extensively. In the 1930s and again in the 1980s and 1990s, Alférez created works throughout the park, from fountains, figures, and bas-reliefs on bridges to smaller details: benches, a sundial, and light standards.

Alférez's role at City Park in the 1930s came at an important turning point in its long history. Though improvements had been made since the original plot of land was bequeathed to the city in the 1850s, significant expansion in the 1920s made it one of the largest urban parks in the United States.[247] Other circumstances also influenced the rebirth that was to come: in addition to the new land, the park received private gifts, including a 1928 bequest from sisters Rebecca Grant Popp and Isabel Grant. This gift allowed for the creation of Popp Fountain, shelters, outdoor lighting, and a new master plan, which would ultimately change the park's landscape.[248]

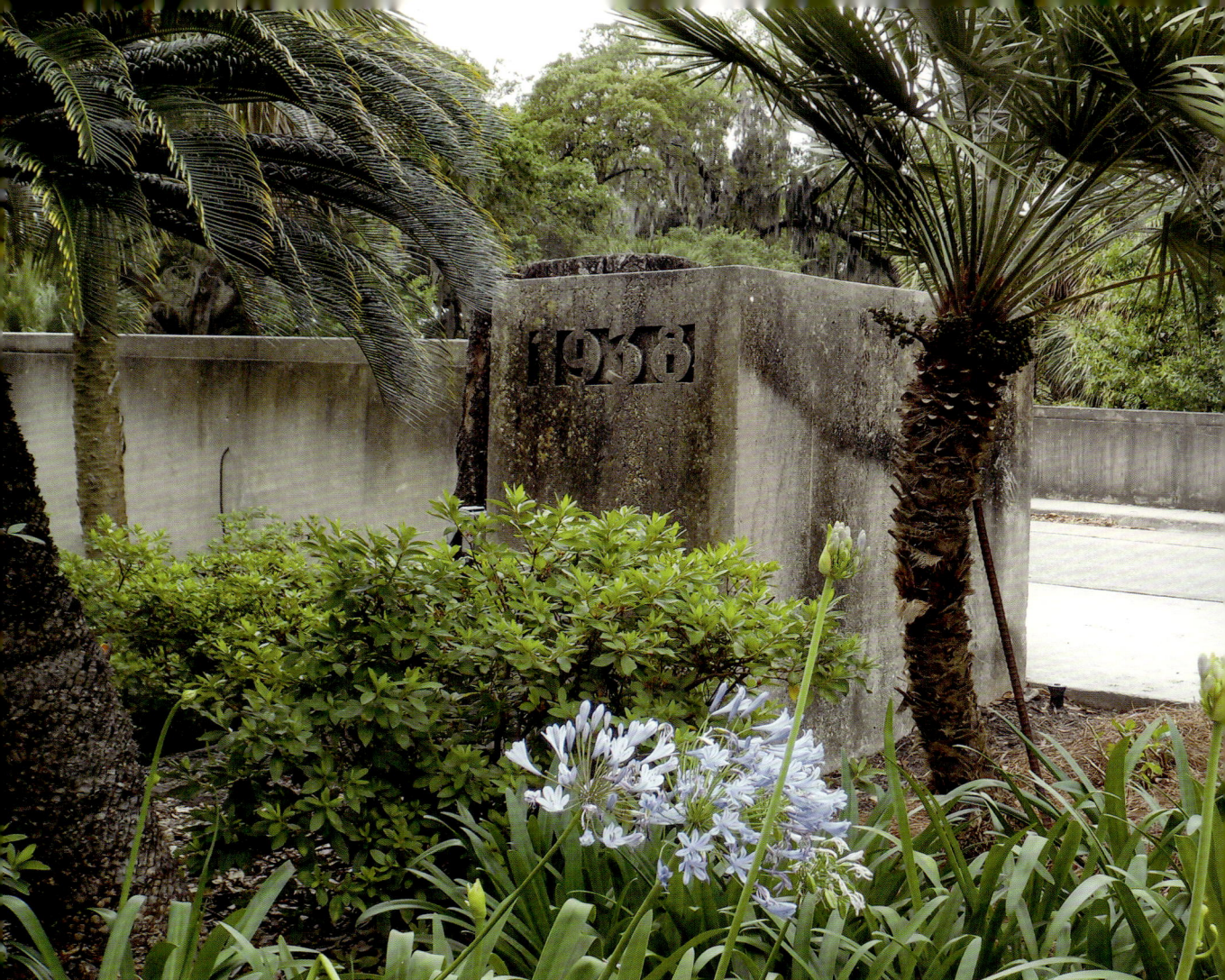

Anseman Bridge, City Park [1938]

photo by Alison Cody

In 1927 the City Park board convened an aesthetics committee comprising three board members: architects Richard Koch and Felix Julius Dreyfous and engineer Marcel Garsaud. Together, they laid the foundation for the park as it exists today. They selected the Chicago-based firm Bennett, Parsons, and Frost to produce a master plan for the park and implemented it.[249] There was some irony as the board conducted its multimillion-dollar planning: by 1931, when they had the master plan in hand, the park was no longer reaping benefits from a financial surplus and the country was falling deeper into economic distress. Though they lacked the funding to fulfill their goals in the short term, the effort they put into creating the plan would prove fortuitous; it served as a roadmap for the park's future by the time federal relief funding began becoming available, later in the 1930s.[250]

When President Franklin D. Roosevelt and Congress ushered in federal New Deal programs in response to widespread unemployment and economic despair during the Depression, the park was well positioned. Federally funded projects included the development of national and state parks by the Civilian Conservation Corps and parks, playgrounds, and airports by the Civil Works Administration and the Works Progress Administration (renamed the Work Projects Administration in 1939). New Orleans was the beneficiary of federal funding made available through New Deal programs, including a renovation of the Lower Pontalba Building and Presbytère, a restoration of the French Market, and the construction of the Huey P. Long Bridge.

Seen in this context, City Park's $13 million revitalization was part of a much larger endeavor to put people back to work. Improvements from infrastructure support to new buildings and bridges were funded through the Public Works Administration, Civil Works Administration, Federal Emergency Relief Administration, Works Progress Administration, and other agencies.[251] Approximately 20,000 people were employed through programs at City Park.[252]

Though having a master plan in hand in 1931 allowed the board to compete for its initial federal funding, part of what made park administrators and the board so successful in obtaining additional funding was their continuous work to develop new project plans. As Congress enacted legislation to provide relief monies, the board proactively identified projects that could qualify. Richard Koch drew building

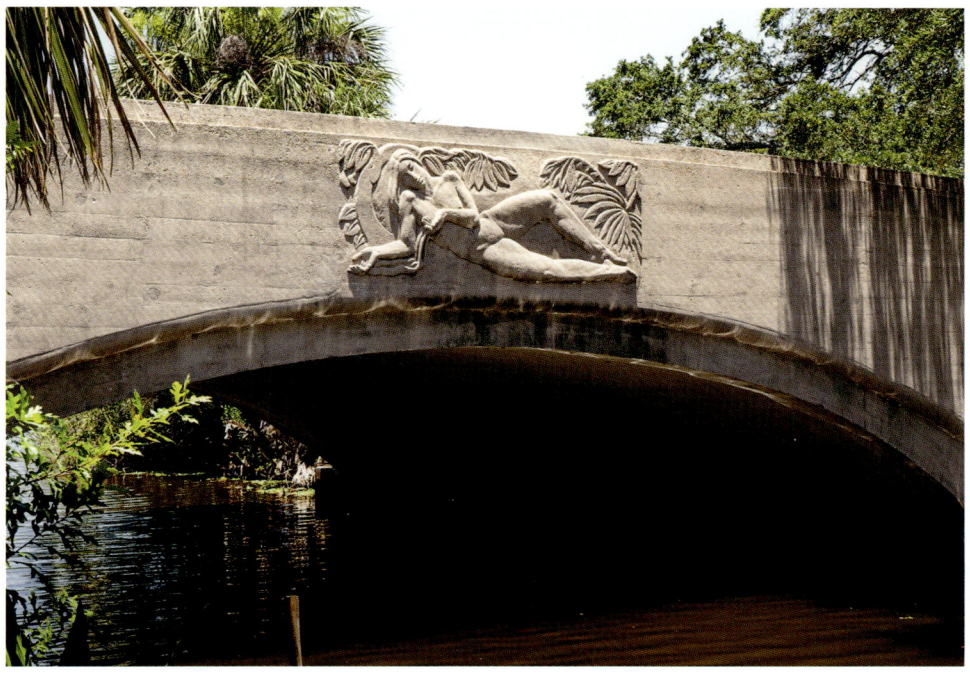

Bas-relief decoration on Bridge #7, City Park [1930s]
photo by Keely Merritt, THNOC

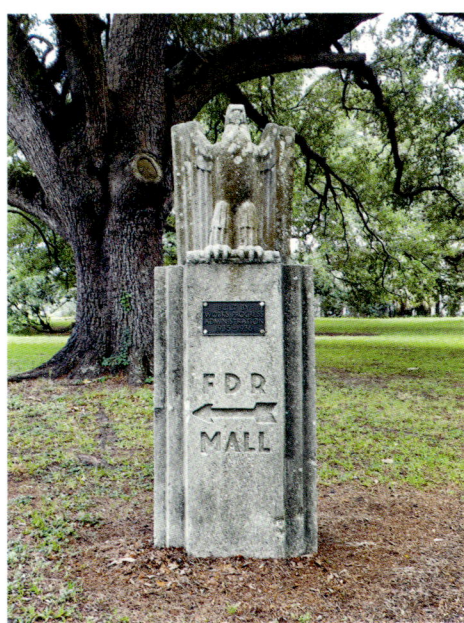

Directional eagle, City Park [1930s]
photo by Alison Cody

plans in collaboration with Samuel Wilson Jr.; architect David Geier worked on-site in the park to lead a team of draftsmen. The landscape was designed by William S. Wiedorn. Park historians Sally K. Evans Reeves and William D. Reeves considered Koch and Wiedorn the "major craftsmen" of the park's development in the 1930s, their vision leaving a lasting imprint on its character.[253]

Koch hired Alférez to lead the sculpture program at the park. Alférez made fifteen dollars a week, and he walked from Jackson Square to City Park each day, almost seven miles on foot roundtrip.[254] Some of his students from the school of the Arts and Crafts Club also worked with him at the park. Alférez created elements for important sites, from Popp Fountain to City Park Stadium (now named Tad Gormley Stadium). His work can be seen in more secluded areas as well. It is visible through foliage while visitors stroll park paths or paddle boats below lagoon bridges crowned with his bas-reliefs, and beside the road on Roosevelt Mall, where cast-concrete eagles look as though they're protecting their stretch of road.

The densest representation of Alférez's work is in the Botanical Garden, known as the Rose Garden when he first began his work at the park. There, he created fountains and figures as well as details that set the tone for the garden: cast-stone benches that feature frogs, crickets, foxes, and other creatures; cubist-influenced drinking fountains; art deco light standards; and poles embellished with figures of a satyr and a nymph.

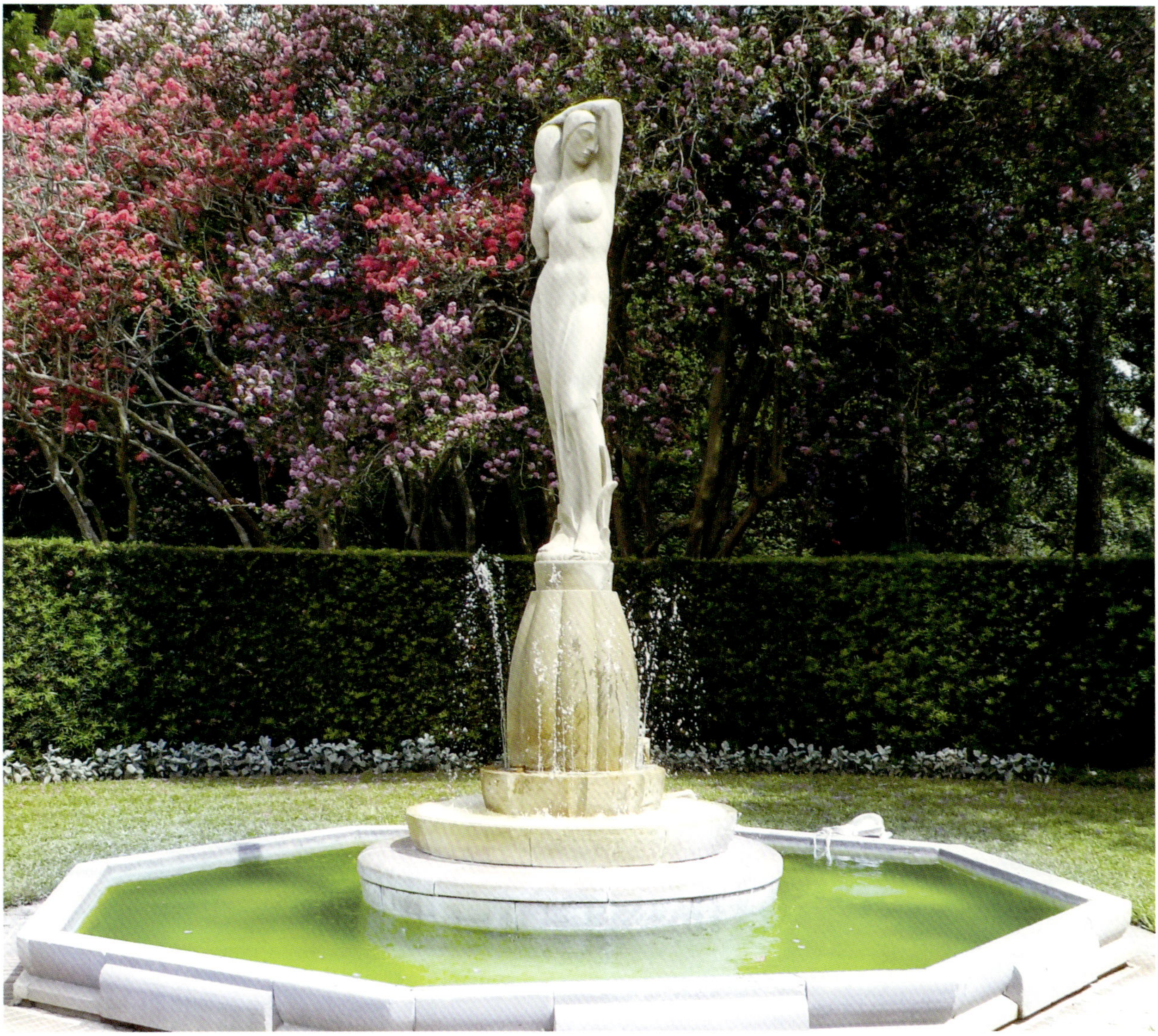

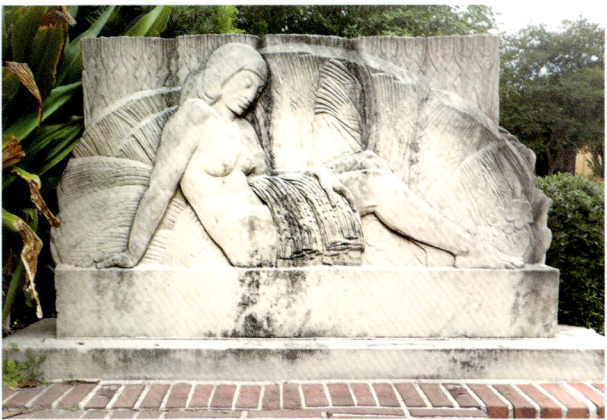

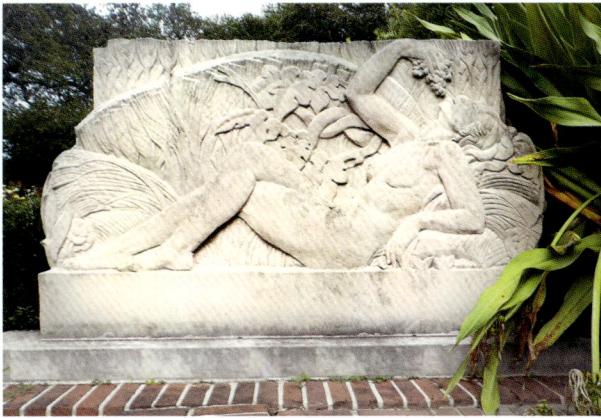

Shriever Fountain with water maiden (top); bas–relief panels of reclining nude (bottom left)
and reclining nude eating grapes (bottom right); New Orleans Botanical Garden [1932]

photos by Alison Cody

One of Alférez's earliest and most iconic pieces in the Botanical Garden is Shriever Fountain, named for Mrs. Gerhard Shriever. The fountain's central female figure holds a vessel on her right shoulder, and she is surrounded by an octagonal pool. The female figure is reminiscent of others that appear in profile in the carvings Alférez executed for the Palmolive Building in Chicago, where a similar figure holds a vessel on her shoulder, one hand beneath it and the other arm extended overhead to balance the vessel from above. The Shriever Fountain figure was created from a seven-foot block of limestone.[255] It stands in a parterre surrounded by foliage and flanked by two cast-stone bas-relief panels, also by Alférez, featuring reclining nudes. In addition to the fifteen dollars he was paid each week, Alférez was allotted $1,500 to produce the central figure.[256] With that budget, he bought the stone, carved it, paid the plumbers, and installed the work.

Another iconic sculpture in the Botanical Garden is often attributed incorrectly to Alférez. He is often assumed to be the creator of the cast cement *Undine*, a signature figure in the lily pond in front of the garden's conservatory. *Undine* was in fact created in 1942 by Alférez's second wife, sculptor Rose Marie Huth, years after they divorced.

By early 1936, Alférez had begun working on bridges for City Park in conjunction with development near the stadium. Considered "unusual and striking" at the time, the detail on the bridges marked a shift from more common stone statuary to figures and relief work in cast concrete, the same material used for the bridges.[257] Alférez's work on the lagoon bridges appears in three areas: on the facades, most easily viewed from a boat; on the wing walls; and on the entry points to bridges.

Some bridges have romantic reliefs on their facades, featuring floating women for example, and others have embellishments at entry points, with icons for tools, a symbol of the handwork accomplished at the park. Other designs were controversial. On one bridge in the northern part of the park, Alférez included a series of male figures as tributes to the labor and expertise of those who worked on the park's development. Each figure uses a tool—shovel, wheelbarrow, or surveying equipment, to name a few—and Alférez included African American figures. At the time, white society banned African Americans from the park, a restriction that remained in effect until 1958. Alférez said that he "got in trouble" for including the figures and that he received letters from irate residents who thought that African Americans should not be portrayed.[258] But Alférez observed that there *were* African Americans working at the park; he referred to them as Negros, in the language of the day, and said they were talented craftsmen. "They had pride in the work," said Alférez. "I know because I was with them."[259] With these words, he wasn't just referring to his work alongside African Americans; he was also commenting on how he was subject to similar social penalties. In projects like this, with the access that his expertise as

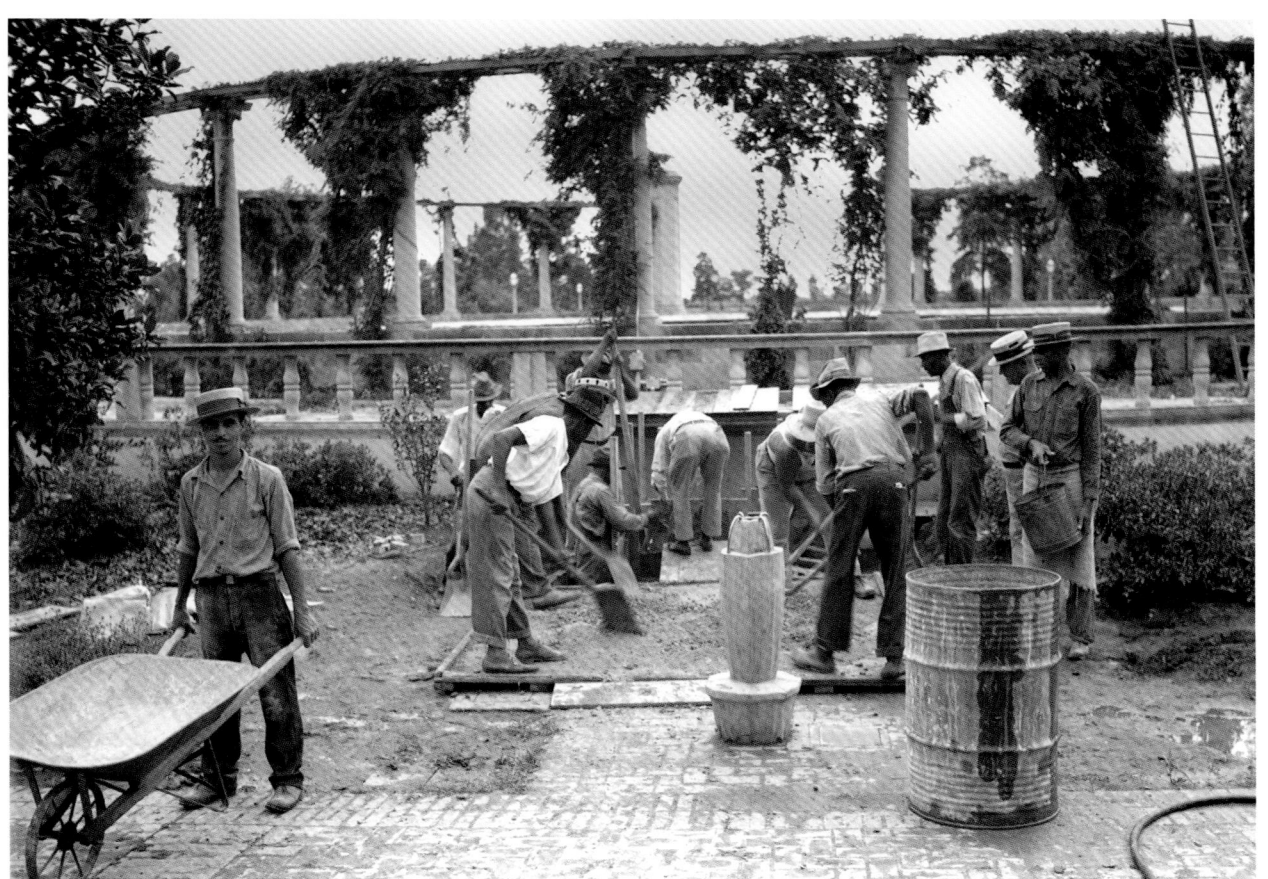

Workers installing auxiliary pumps for Popp Fountain [1938]

photo by Works Progress Administration

COURTESY OF WPA PHOTOGRAPH COLLECTION, LOUISIANA DIVISION/CITY ARCHIVES, NEW ORLEANS PUBLIC LIBRARY

a sculptor gave him, he rebelled against racist social constructs and created artwork that reflected the public more broadly. Alférez's making monuments to the people who built City Park was a radical act at the time.

One intriguing plan for the park went undeveloped. When Koch was planning his design for City Park Stadium, he anticipated including a "large group of massive statuary" outside the entrance to the stadium, providing a "striking and impressive picture" as visitors approached. Alférez was tasked with sculpting eight to ten figures, each about twelve feet tall and placed on pedestals that rose approximately twenty feet above ground level. The figures would hearken to Louisiana labor, with representations of a stevedore, cotton picker, and fisherman, among others. The project was never executed, but a couple of relics remain: The Historic New Orleans Collection

FOLLOWING PAGES:

Bas-relief images of WPA workers on Bridge #5 wing walls, City Park [1930s]

photo by Alison Cody

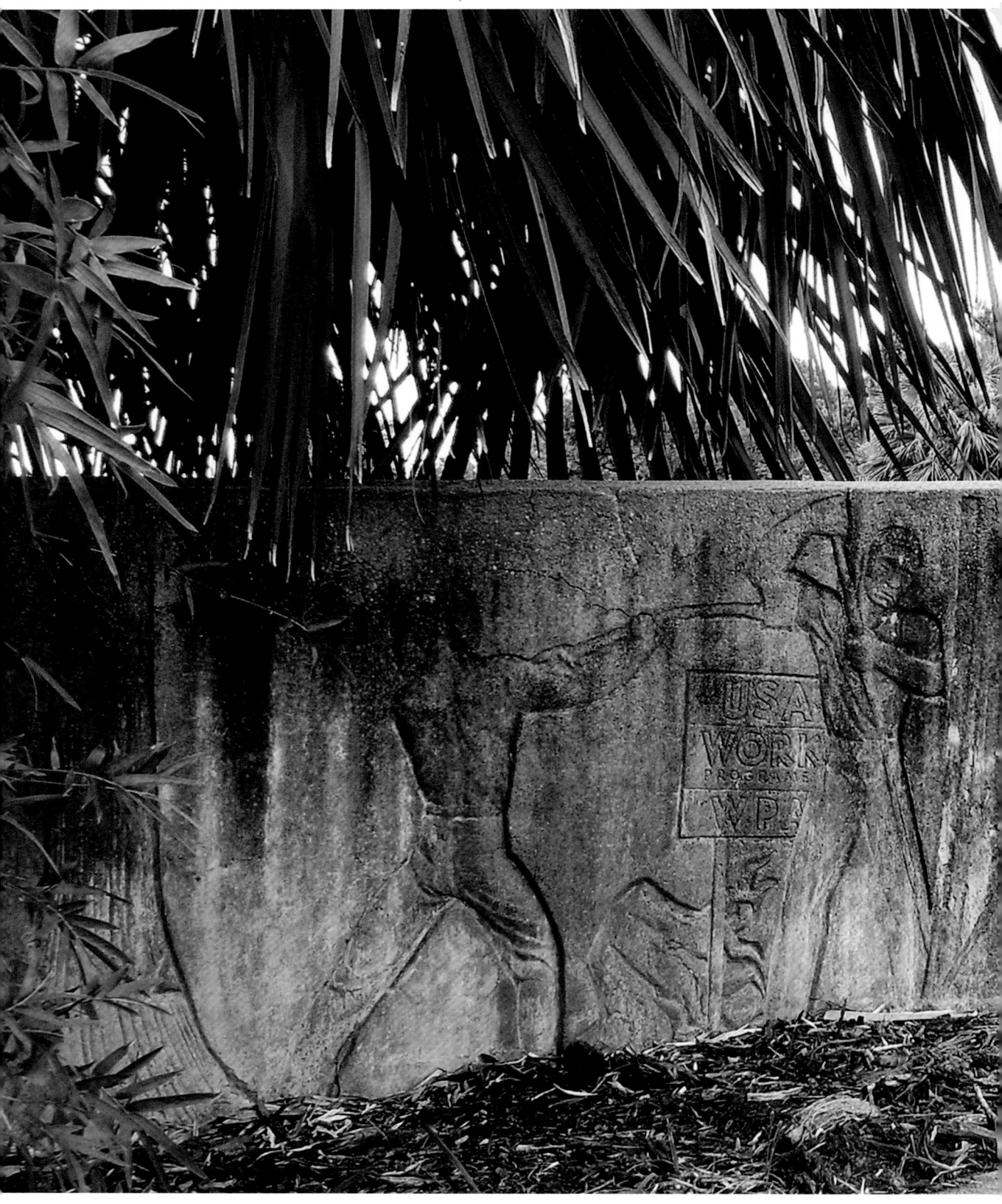

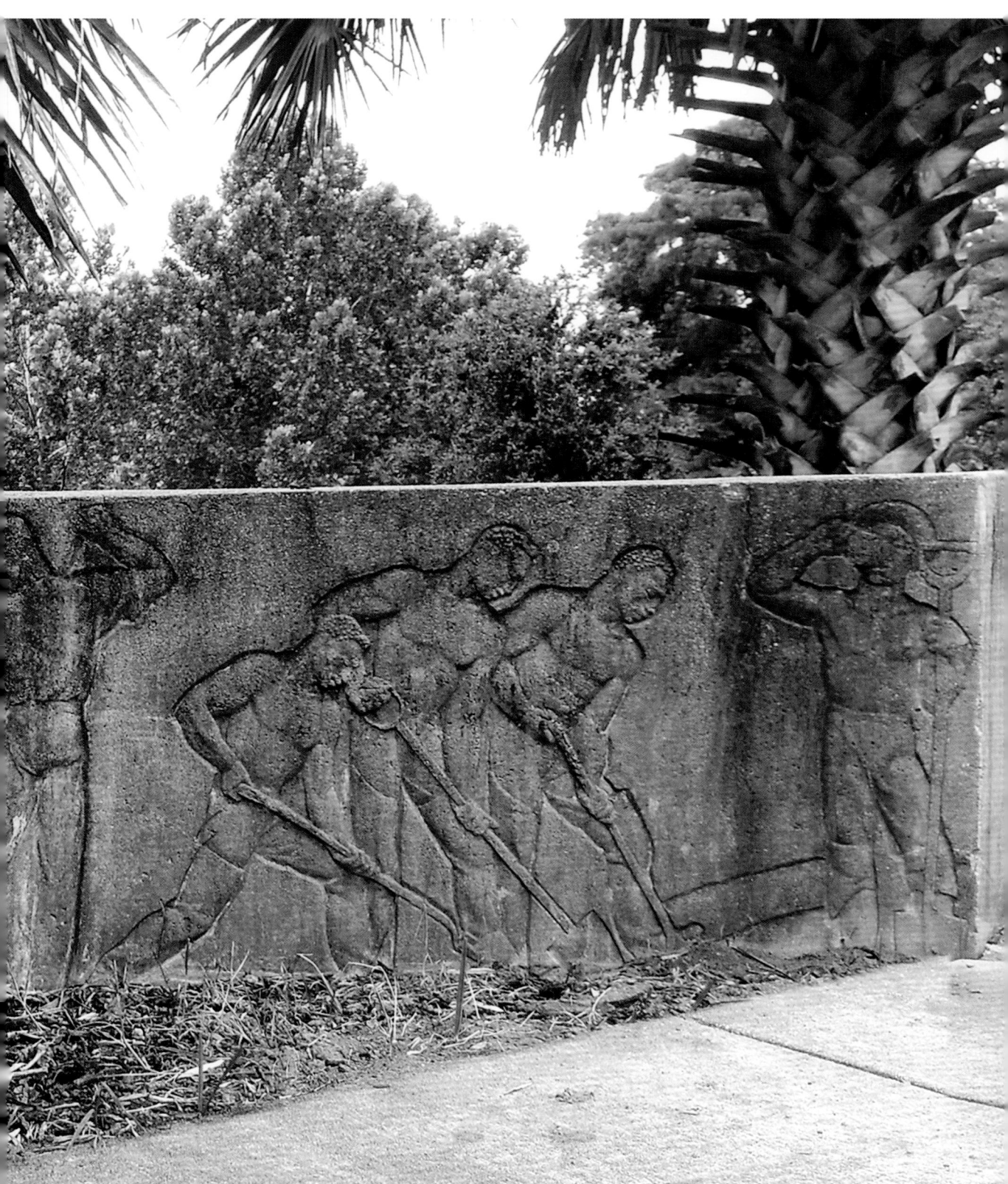

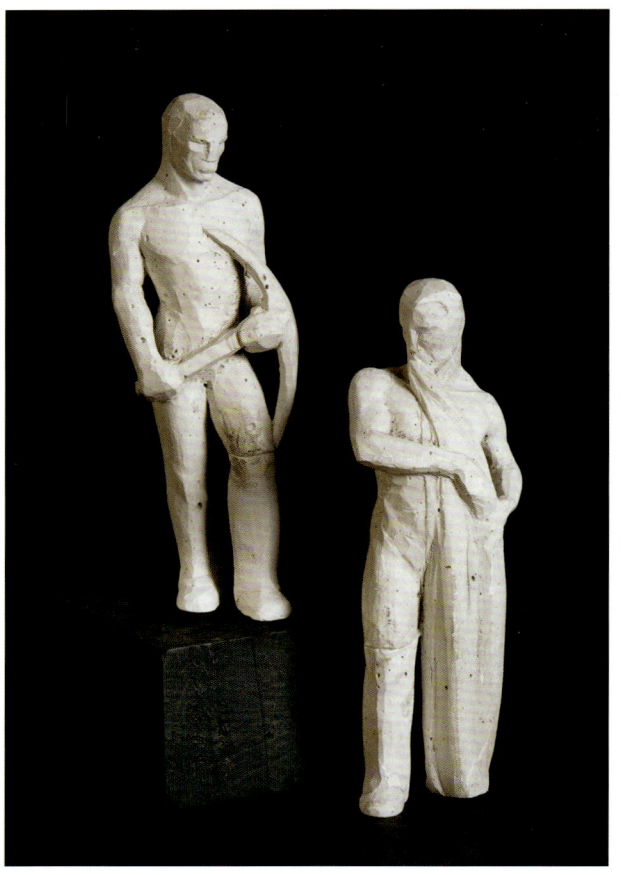

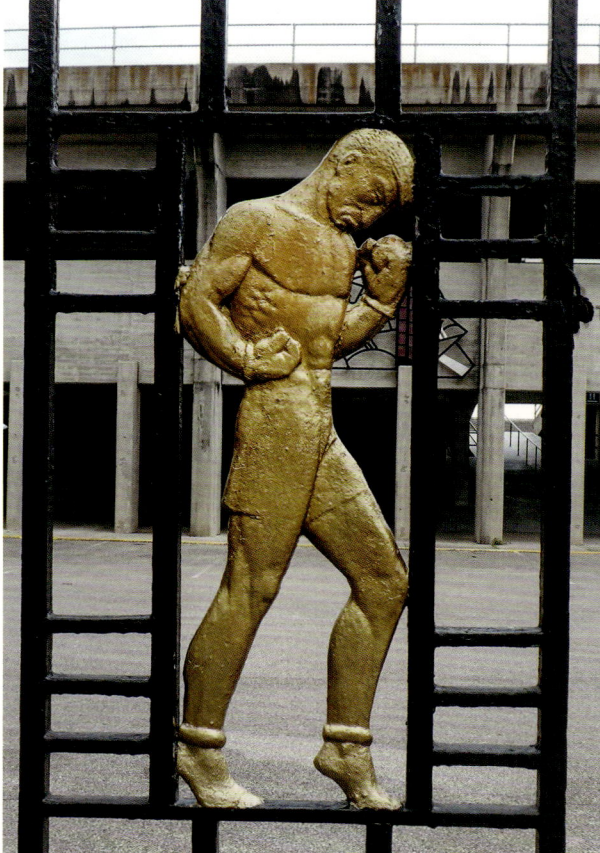

Plaster maquettes for works designed for
(but never installed at) City Park Stadium [1936–37]

THNOC, GIFT OF SAMUEL WILSON JR., 1983.234.11

Cast metal boxer on City Park
Stadium gate [1936–37]

photo by Alison Cody

today has two plaster maquettes in its holdings that depict laborers: a fisherman, and a man with a pickax.[260] Alférez's artistic skill can be seen elsewhere at the stadium, however. Koch designed a fence and gate that surrounds the stadium featuring cast metal plates of athletes, including a boxer, baseball player, and basketball player, among others, all of which were created by Alférez.

In 1937 Alférez finished Popp Fountain, one of City Park's major landmarks, with a pool sixty feet in diameter, surrounded by twenty-six Corinthian columns, a terrace, and a trellis that, in its earliest days, was covered in wisteria. In 1928, the park received donations totaling $40,000 from Rebecca Grant Popp and her sister Isabel Grant.[261] In 1929 a representative for the Olmsted Brothers, a prominent landscape architecture firm with ties to numerous parks, public spaces, and universities across the United States, visited New Orleans to create conceptual designs for the fountain. But construction couldn't begin before completion of the Bennett, Parsons, and Frost master plan. Additionally, the project required more funding from the WPA. The fountain took more time to complete than anticipated: it wasn't finished until 1937.[262]

Alférez designed the central cast-concrete feature of the fountain: dolphins riding waves that rise from a low pedestal. He designed the water to spray thirty feet into the air, in proportion with the pool's sixty-foot diameter, and used the motion of light and water to create visual effects. When he visited the park to put some finishing touches on the fountain, he was surprised to come upon a celebratory opening to which he had not been invited. He held Koch responsible for this exclusion, and felt it was intentional—due to his race—rather than an oversight.[263]

In the fountain's earliest years, lights were submerged beneath the water, but they were eventually replaced with overhead lights. The fountain continued

Popp Fountain, City Park [1937]

photo by Works Progress Administration
COURTESY OF WPA PHOTOGRAPH COLLECTION, LOUISIANA DIVISION/CITY ARCHIVES,
NEW ORLEANS PUBLIC LIBRARY

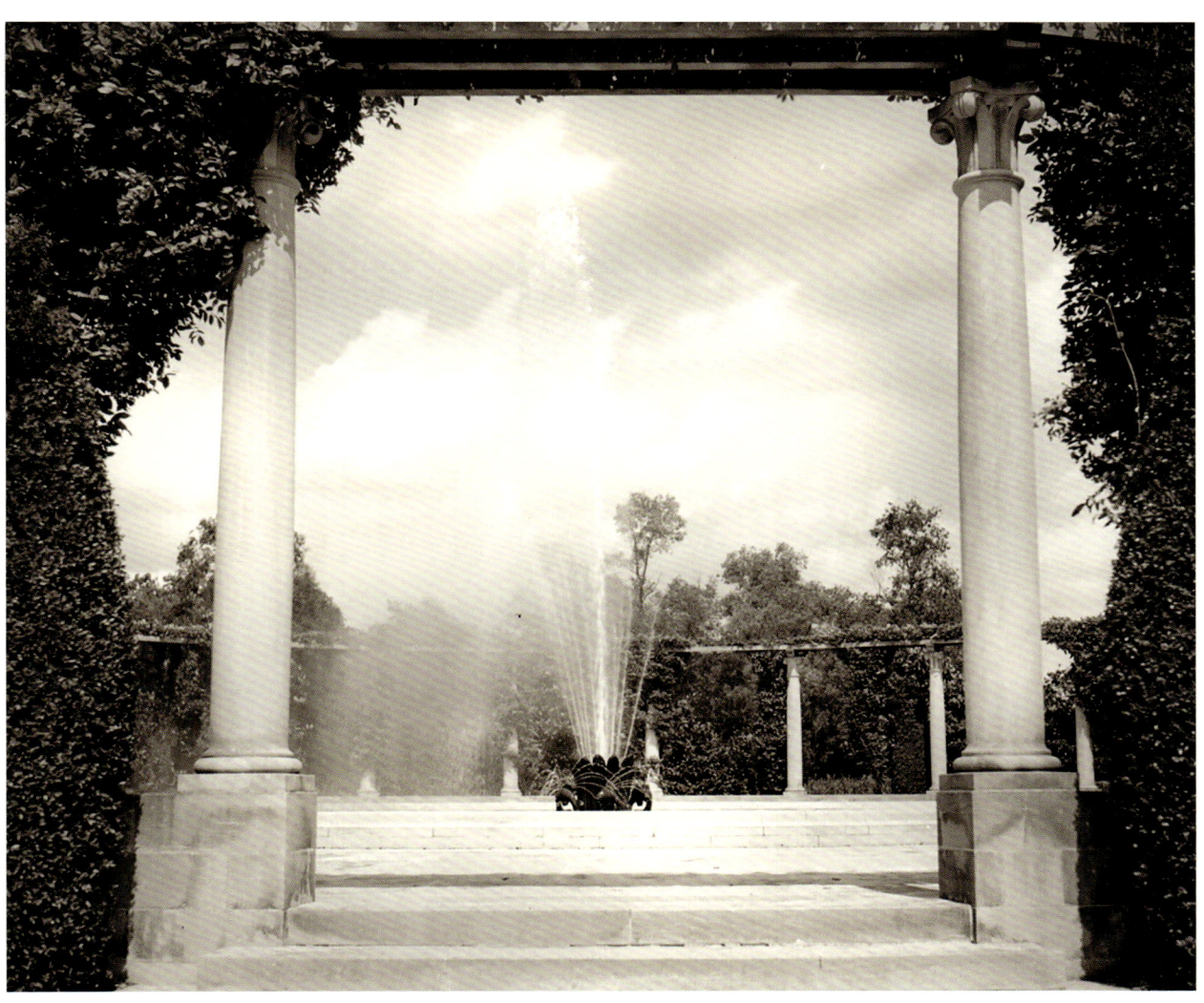

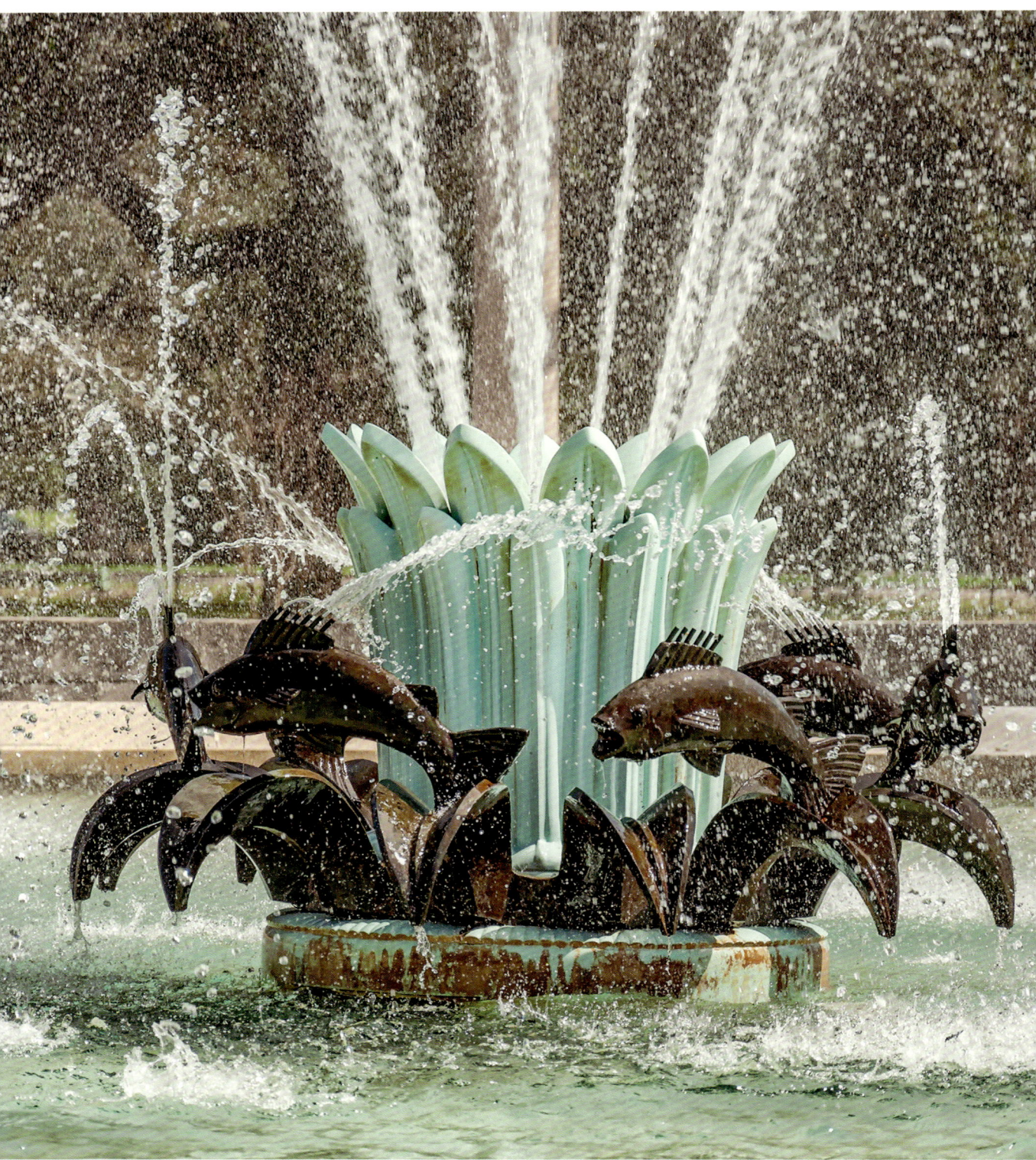

Popp Fountain [1937; dolphins recast in 1990s]

photo by Kathleen K. Parker

to deteriorate over the following decades, with damage caused by hurricanes and vandalism. In 1947, for example, a hurricane breached the nearby 17th Street Canal, and twenty-four of the twenty-six columns at Popp Fountain were damaged. By 1975, the cast-concrete dolphins had been smashed down to the reinforcement rods, and sections of the balustrade had been stolen. The grounds became overgrown and untended. A major restoration effort begun in the mid- to late 1990s resulted in the dolphins being recast in bronze. Today, the fountain is among the most beloved sites in the park, a frequent venue for weddings and celebrations.

Returning to City Park

By 1980 the Friends of City Park commissioned another master plan that would preserve the historic character of the park while also meeting more contemporary needs than could have been anticipated during the 1930s redevelopment. Margaret "Peggy" Read, inaugural president of the Friends of City Park and later president of the City Park Board of Commissioners, spearheaded the revitalization of the Rose Garden, turning it into what is now the Botanical Garden. Instrumental in these efforts was the hiring of garden director Paul Soniat in 1982.

Alférez was living in a house on Antonio Plaza in Santa María, on the outskirts of Morelia, when he was contacted about revisiting some of the works he had produced decades earlier that had fallen into disrepair. Alférez left his home in Santa María for another long journey to New Orleans to see what needed to be done in the garden. Read had hoped the garden could be in a more attractive state by the time of the opening of the 1984 world's fair, the latest world's fair to play a role in Alférez's life. He was hired both to restore figures and details in the garden and to design a new entrance gate with details reminiscent of leafy stalks of Louisiana grasses, created in cast iron. Soniat provided Alférez with space in a garden shed where he could work.

Alférez, who had left New Orleans and returned many times since his first arrival in 1929, had been spending more time outside the city than in it since the late 1960s. His invitation to return to the garden drew him back to living in New Orleans on a more permanent basis. By 1984, the year the world's fair opened, Alférez had completed his assignments for the Botanical Garden and had, for the first time in his life, bought a house in New Orleans.

The last major sculpture that Alférez created for the Botanical Garden is also among his distinctive works. The *Flute Player* was commissioned in 1994.[264] The garden's advisory board, chaired at the time by Genevieve "Gen" Trimble, selected Alférez because of the long influence he had on the garden and at the request of an old friend and benefactor, Doris Zemurray Stone.

Alférez modeled the ten-foot *Flute Player* at his home studio on Eighth Street. By then, age and injuries, including the 1971 stroke and multiple falls, had taken their toll. Alférez's hands were arthritic, and for years he had been struggling to open and close them in full. He often needed assistance when using power tools, due to the effect of the vibration and burden of the weight. He also had a limited range of motion in his right arm and was unable to lift it higher than his head, adding significant challenges to modeling a figure that was larger than life-size. Soniat had a hydraulic lift delivered to Alférez's studio so that he could reach the heights required to complete the piece.[265]

When the model was ready to be rolled out and sent to California to be cast, it was too tall to leave the house standing up. The *Flute Player* was tilted on its side and rolled through a doorway. From there, the work made the long journey to Piero Mussi's Artworks Foundry in Berkeley, California, to be cast in three sections under the guidance of Mussi and Karl Reichley.[266] Alférez and Peggy also traveled to inspect the process, although by then Peggy thought that they were getting "too old for such adventures."[267]

Reichley, who had been working with Alférez to refine his patinas since the 1980s, applied the silver nitrate patina to the sculpture, which was subsequently returned to New Orleans. The *Flute Player* was unveiled in May 1996, in accordance with Doris Zemurray Stone's wish that the camellias and azaleas be in bloom, and in time for a grand birthday celebration in the garden for Alférez, who had become more cherished in the city as the decades passed. The larger-than-life figure stands in a small fountain pond beside a live oak, her dark body occasionally turning green at the calves from a slight spray of water.

In 2015 the Botanical Garden opened The Helis Foundation Enrique Alférez Sculpture Garden, an 8,000-square-foot oasis celebrating Alférez's influence in the park. For many years, garden director Paul Soniat had hoped to create a sanctuary dedicated to Alférez. David A. Kerstein, president of The Helis Foundation, joined Soniat in the effort to bring together important statues and architectural details, in order to offer a proper treatment of Alférez's influence. Landscape architect Robin Tanner designed the space. The pergola at the garden's entry point is an introduction to Alférez's work, both in text panels as well as in the restored or reproduced artwork, such as restored gates from Tad Gormley Stadium and bas-reliefs that appear on bridges elsewhere in the park. The bas-reliefs were reproduced by master plasterer Jeff Porée Sr. The pergola opens into a wide path through palms, shrubs, and a live oak, and the garden features figures donated and loaned, including fourteen figures on loan from The Helis Foundation. The garden includes cast bronzes such as *La Soldadera* (1989–90), *Specter* (ca. 1985), *Repose* (1987–90), and *Pas de Deux* (ca. 1982). *Adam and Eve*, modeled in the 1930s and cast in stone in the 1980s, had

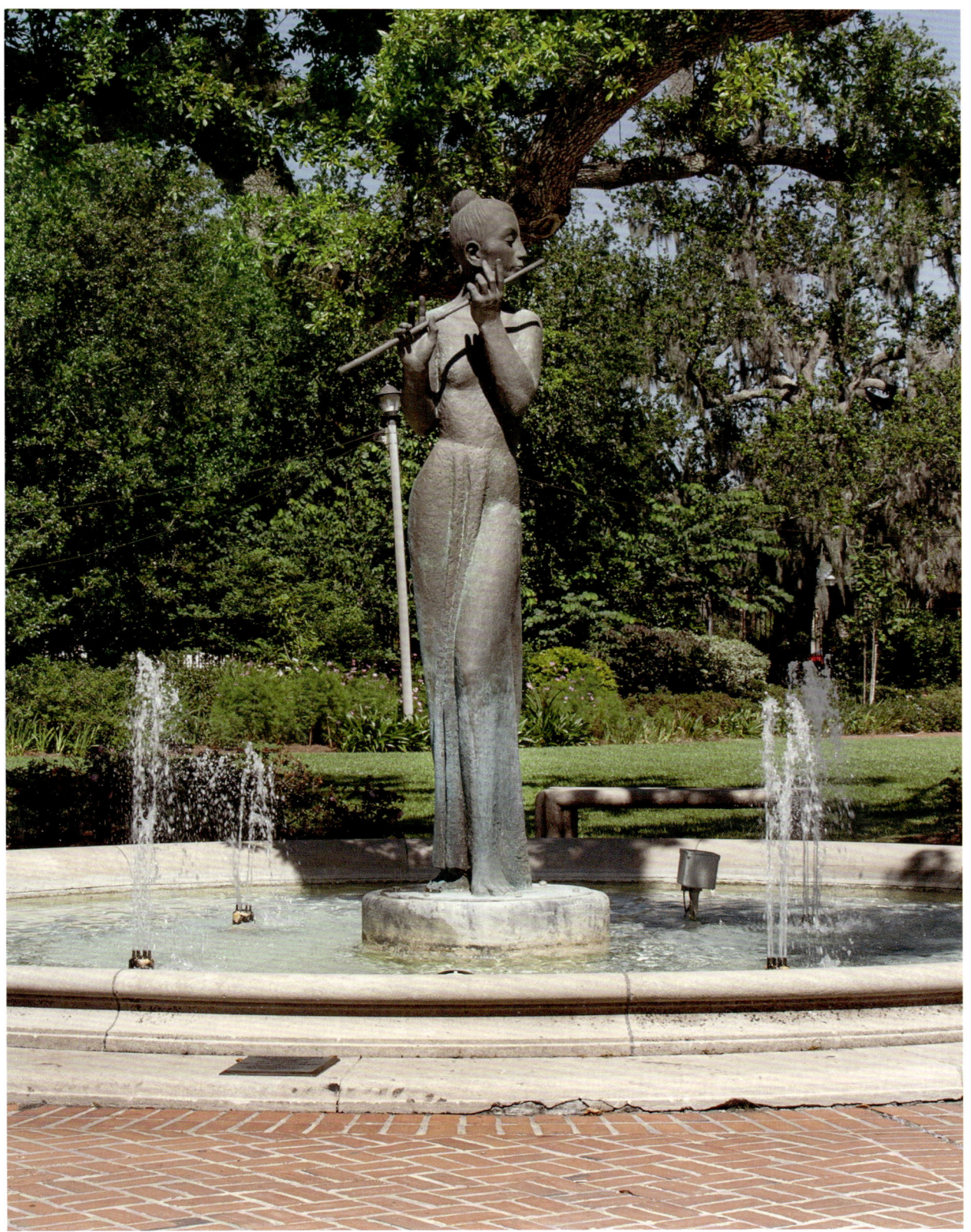

The *Flute Player* in the New Orleans Botanical Garden [1996]

photo by Ashley Merlin

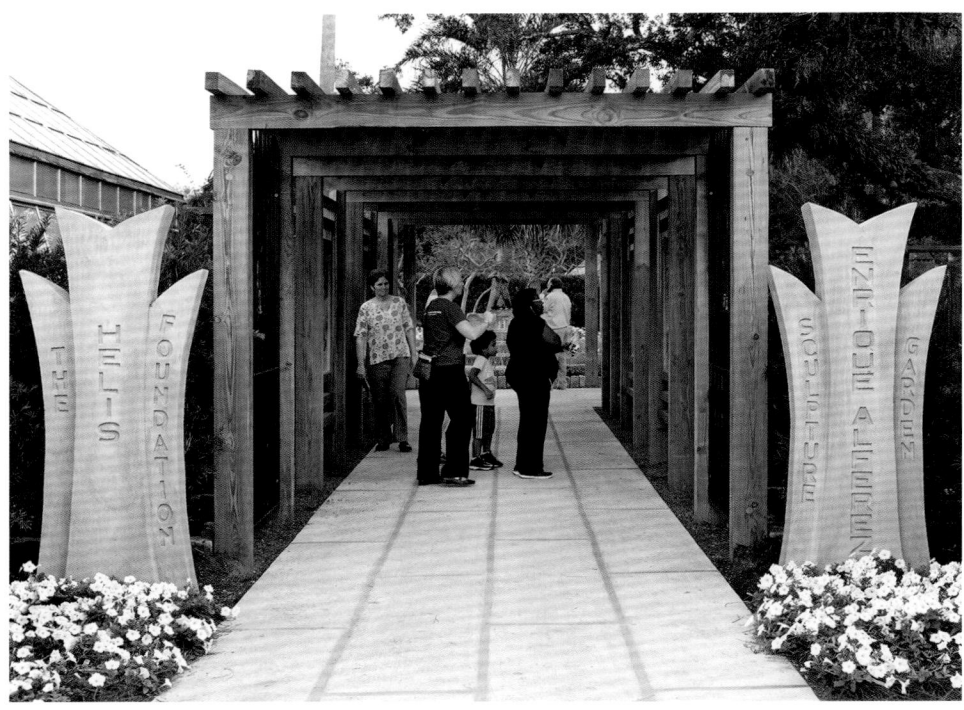

Entrance to The Helis Foundation Enrique Alférez Sculpture Garden
photo by Keely Merritt, THNOC

long been at the Alférez home until The Helis Foundation purchased it for display in the garden. Today Adam and Eve lie side by side in an embrace beneath a centuries-old live oak, their fated apple held overhead.

Alférez's daughter Tlaloc sees the support of Kerstein and The Helis Foundation as the fulfillment of the dream Peggy Read, Gen Trimble, Paul Soniat, and the Friends of City Park conceived in the early 1980s: to protect, maintain, and grow the body of Alférez's work at the park. Figures continue to arrive as New Orleans residents become inspired to share pieces that had once been in their homes or gardens. Among the contributors are Richard and Stacey Williams, who gave *The Bather* (cast stone, ca. 1951) to the garden, and the family of Mr. and Mrs. Alexander Charles Deneumoustier, whose donation returned *The Family* to public view for the first time in more than sixty years. In many ways, the value of *The Family* rests in its history, and its reemergence after being out of the public eye for so long was "an important discovery for the art community." Appraiser Stephen Woolford Clayton, who evaluated *The Family* in 2015, also saw its display as a way to recognize one of the "most highly regarded 20th century sculptors [of] the WPA era."[268]

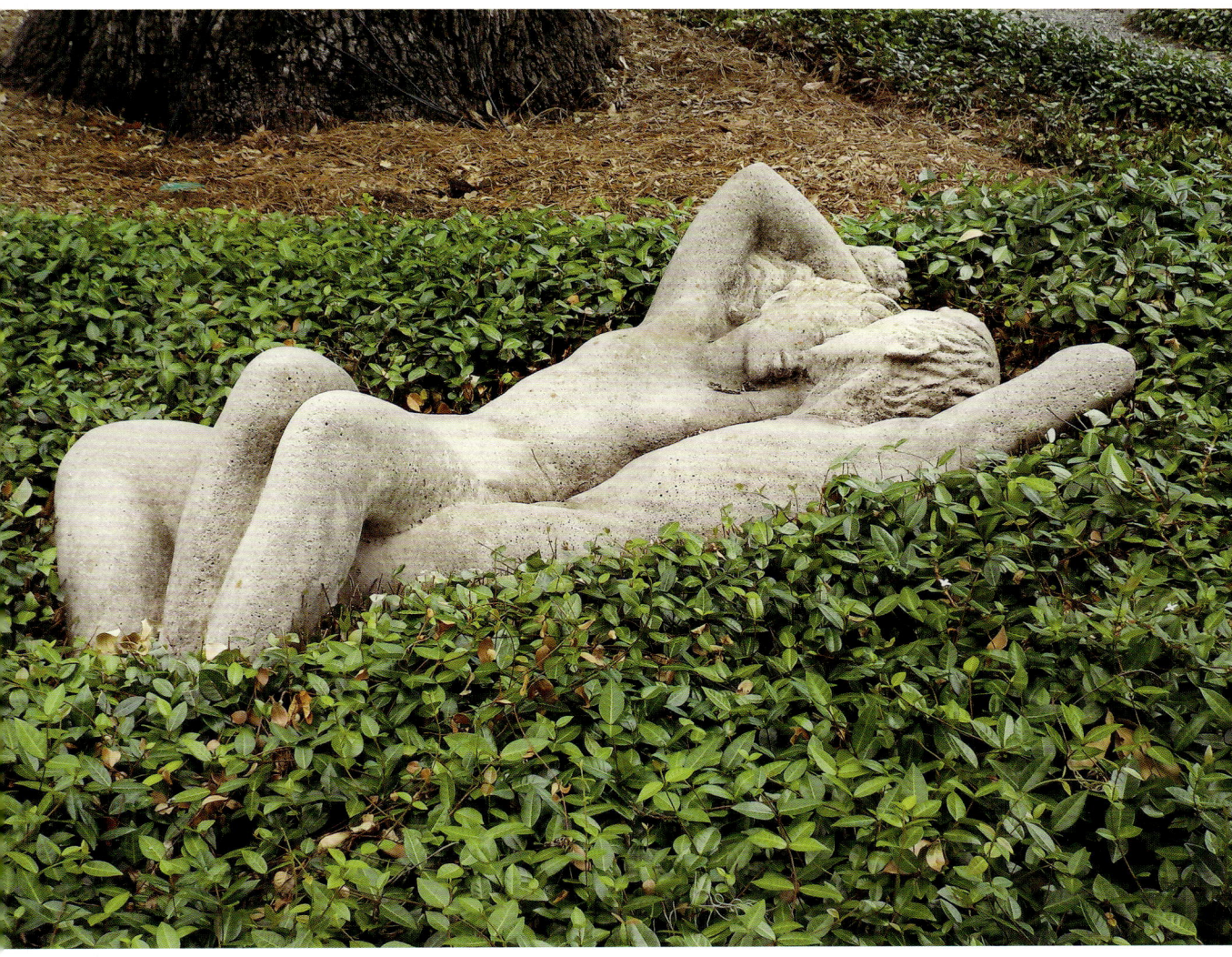

Adam and Eve, **New Orleans Botanical Garden** [modeled 1930s; cast 1980s]

photo by Alison Cody

THE HELIS FOUNDATION COLLECTION

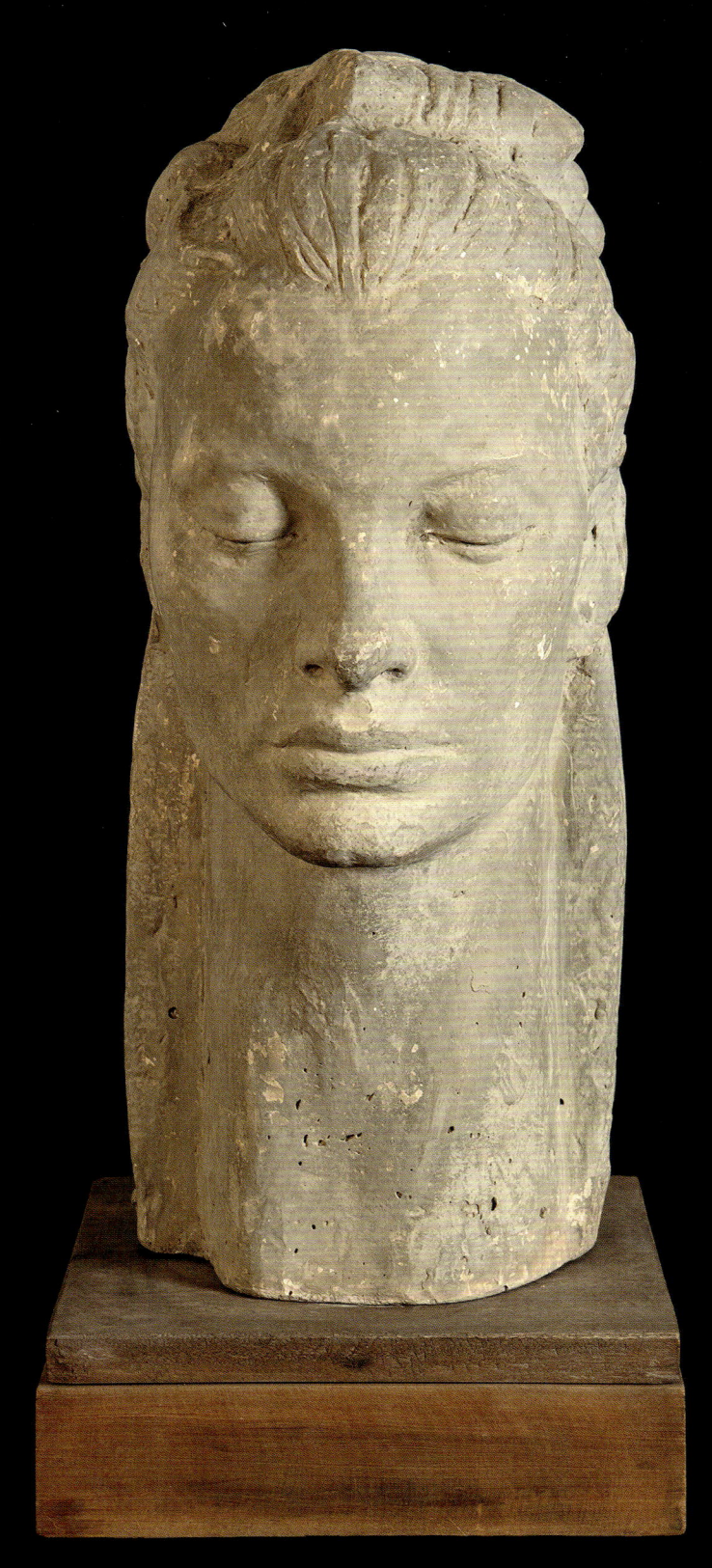

CHAPTER EIGHT

Recognition for a Lifetime of Sculpture

ENRIQUE ALFÉREZ WAS A PROLIFIC artist, one who focused more on drawing and sculpting than exhibiting or explaining his craft. Beginning in the early 1950s, when he met Peggy, her life too became dedicated to his art. She assumed a key role in shaping Alférez's career and legacy as a sculptor. In addition to her community service work, Peggy managed Alférez's business, researched techniques related to his sculpture, and organized with curators and gallerists in advance of exhibitions. Peggy understood the importance of retaining documents relevant to her husband's work. Within years of their marriage, she became a collector of news clippings, letters, photographs, and ephemera. She also took steps to rebuild records from the decades before she knew him. Over the years, envelopes arrived at their home from around the country: clippings and photos from Alférez's younger days, found in the attic or trunk of an old friend. She added these memorabilia to the family papers.[269] In addition to saving information about Alférez's public works, commissions, and sales, Peggy kept records related to his exhibitions: lists of exhibited sculptures, invitations, programs, catalogs, guest lists, congratulatory notes from friends, and other keepsakes.

Though exhibition was not at the forefront of Alférez's priorities as an artist, his work was shown in galleries, museums, and other venues. The first known group exhibition that he participated in was in El Paso in 1922.[270] His most active period of exhibiting was with the Arts and Crafts Club in New Orleans between 1932 and 1940, when his work was included in about a dozen group and solo exhibitions.

Alférez's first exhibition at the Arts and Crafts Club opened in February 1932 and featured a silver-finished plaster bust alongside paintings by Josephine Crawford and lithographs by David Alfaro Siqueiros. In a two-person show with Paul Ninas

Head of a woman [1936]
THNOC, 00.48

in 1936, Alférez showed a portrait of Bernard Szold, director of Le Petit Théâtre du Vieux Carré, and "strong, masterful drawings" he had completed as illustrations for Hermann B. Deutsch's novel *The Wedge*, based in part on Alférez's life.[271] Alférez often participated in group exhibitions with other Arts and Crafts Club teachers, including an outdoor exhibit "in the shadows of the old St. Louis Cathedral" in 1937 with Ninas, Julius Woeltz, and Xavier Gonzalez.[272] In 1938, he showed casts from a research expedition to Uxmal, most likely the 1930 trip with Frans Blom, and he also worked with students on annual Christmas window displays.

During the 1930s, Alférez was involved in the arts community in other ways, including serving as a judge for arts competitions held by Dillard University and Tulane's Middle American Research Institute, and was recognized among the city's leading artists. He was also part of art groups that were bringing the world's burgeoning artists to New Orleans—Siqueiros and Alexander Calder, to name a few. In 1939, he was among a number of artists whose works were included in the Louisiana section of the world's fair in New York, with his bust of Clayre Barr appearing alongside work by Caroline Durieux, Angela Gregory, Xavier Gonzalez, Paul Ninas, and Ellsworth Woodward, among others.[273] Despite the fact that the New Orleans art scene was growing in reputation, southern art was largely panned at the fair for not being responsive enough to socioeconomic problems of the time and for romanticizing "urgent social and economic problems." Critic Elizabeth McCausland, writing for *Parnassus* in 1939, criticized southern art for its representations of race, writing that it did not "consort well with the traditional American democratic ideal."[274]

That same year, Alférez joined with a new group taking shape to bring greater attention to southern artists.[275] A New Southern Group brought together Durieux, Gregory, Conrad Albrizio, John McCrady, Marion Souchon, Rudolf Staffel, and other artists, and they exhibited in New Orleans, Baton Rouge, and Dallas.[276]

This early, active period of exhibiting was coming to a close by the time Alférez left New Orleans for Mexico in 1942, and then moved to New York, where he focused on making furniture and leather goods. When Alférez returned to New Orleans around 1950, he turned his focus back toward sculpture although, on occasion, years passed between exhibitions. In November 1952, he opened an exhibition at Marc and Lucille Godchaux Antony's 331 Gallery at 331 Chartres Street, showing drawings and sculptures in a show with Paul Ninas. In a subsequent exhibition at the 331 Gallery in 1958, Alférez showed a dozen terra-cotta figures; critic Alberta Collier wrote that they were significant in demonstrating "the sculptor's best efforts." She also wrote that a show of "new work by Enrique Alférez is always an important event in New Orleans art circles" and noted "a blend of both Indian and classic motifs," combining the "life-force of the Mexican with the Greek feeling for pure line and ideal form."[277]

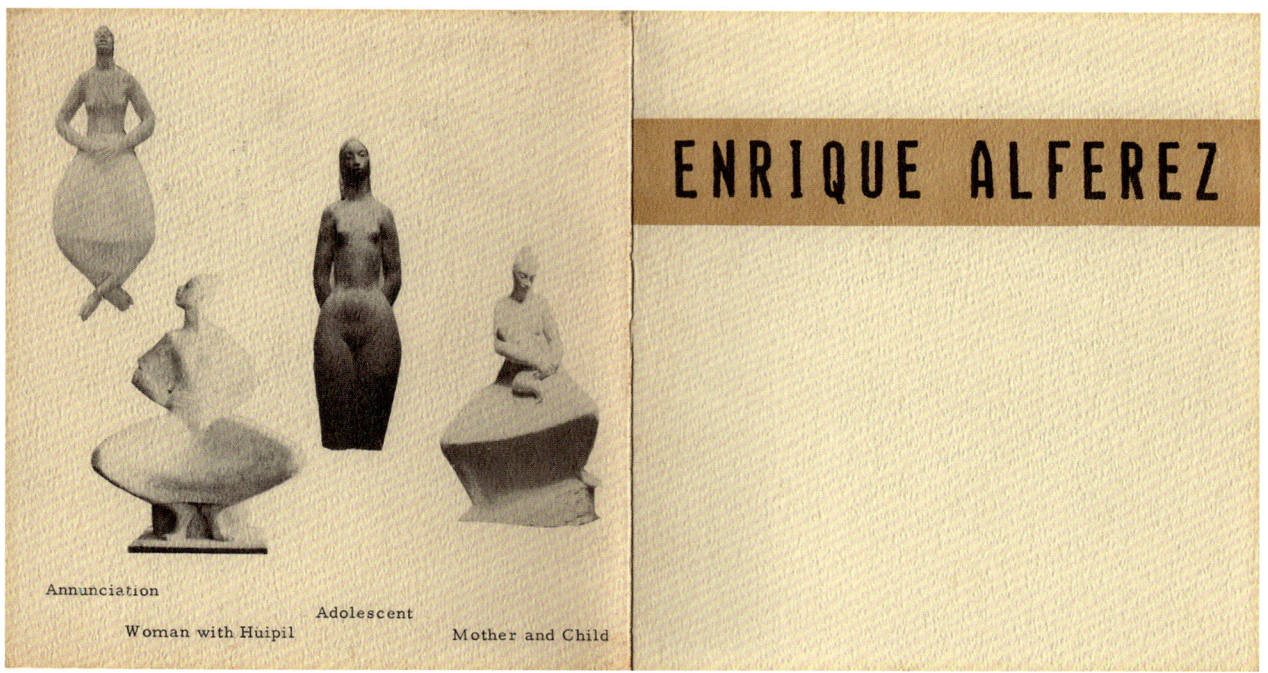

ENRIQUE ALFEREZ

Annunciation

Woman with Huipil

Adolescent

Mother and Child

Program for exhibition at El Paso Museum of Art, November 12–29, 1961
COURTESY OF THE TLALOC SELWAY ALFÉREZ PAPERS

Subsequent exhibitions often featured smaller works, in terra-cotta or bronze: charros, dancers, bathers, and lovers. His work was also shown at galleries including the New Downtown Gallery, Valerie Studios, Uptown Gallery, Studio Ten, Arthur Roger's 3005 Gallery on Magazine Street, International House, Galerie Simonne Stern, Downtown Gallery, and Circle Gallery, as well as the Marshall Art Foundation housed at Gallier Hall, where Alférez had a a studio alongside artist George Dunbar in the early 1960s.

In addition to gallery exhibitions, Alférez also exhibited in museums. The three most significant exhibitions during his lifetime were mounted at the El Paso Museum of Art (November 12–29, 1961); at the Evansville Museum of Arts, History, and Science (April 13–May 4, 1969); and at the New Orleans Museum of Art (February 21–March 29, 1981). His solo show in El Paso featured twenty-two sculptures, including a forty-five-inch plaster-and-cement *Woman with Huipil*, a precursor to the iconic bronze *Woman in a Huipil*, and multiple terra-cotta figures, *Mother and Child* and *Mourning* among them.[278] The artist Tom Lea, Alférez's old friend, facilitated his introduction to museum director Reginald Fisher, leading to Fisher hosting the exhibition.[279] After it closed, Alférez transferred some of the sculptures to Ferrell Galleries in El Paso for continued exhibition.

Alférez's Evansville exhibition was facilitated by museum director Siegfried Weng, whom Alférez met when Weng was a lecture assistant at Lorado Taft's studio in the 1920s. Weng was a visionary leader, credited with the greatest expansion of

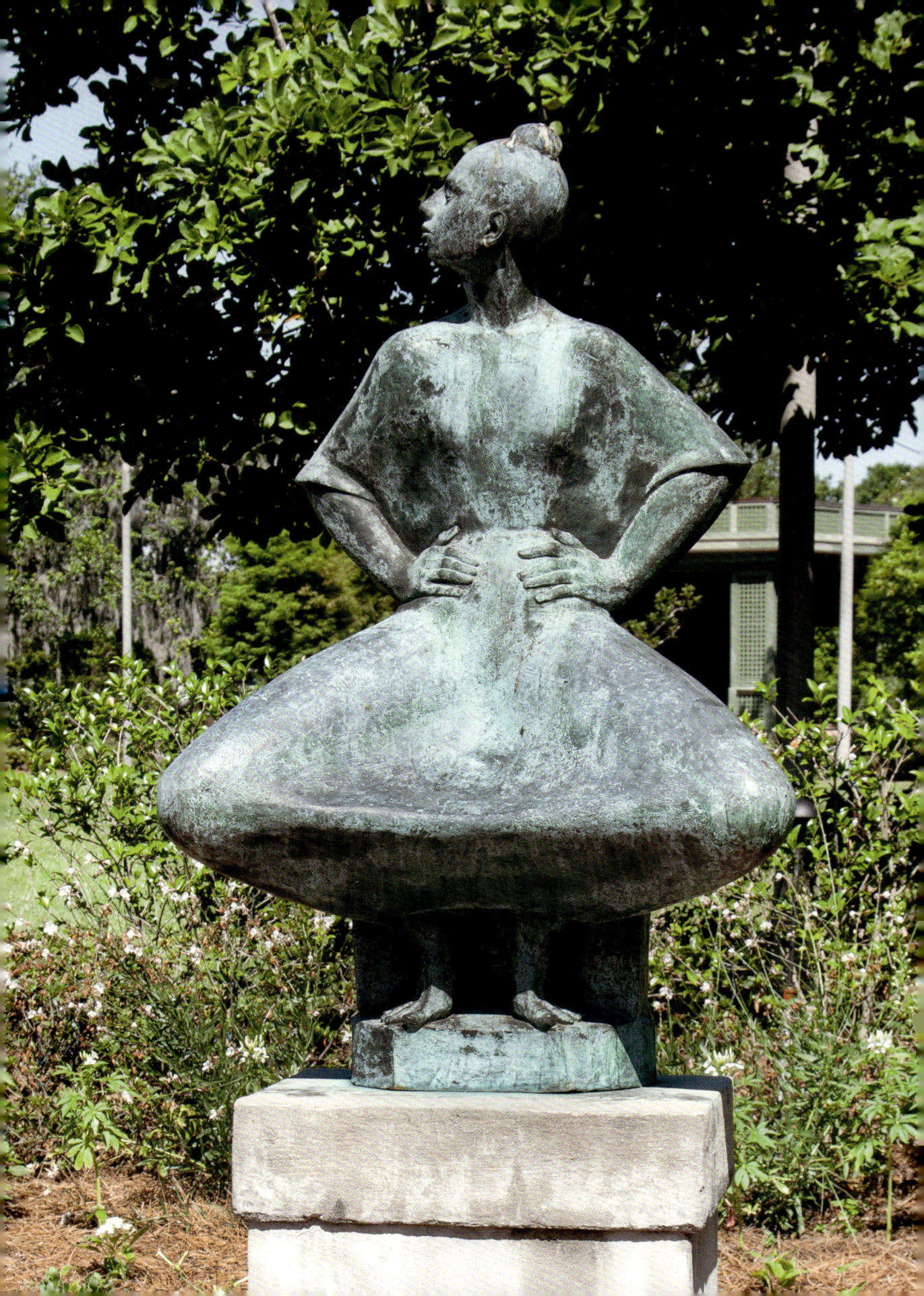

the museum's holdings over the course of its history.[280] Today, two of Alférez's figures are in the institution's permanent collection, a terra-cotta *Bather* and a plaster *Moses*.

Though he would have a handful of gallery and special exhibitions in New Orleans in the 1960s and 1970s, the final museum exhibit held during his lifetime was *Enrique Alférez: Drawings and Small Sculptures*, held at the New Orleans Museum of Art in 1981. Alférez had recently returned to New Orleans to discuss restoration of works at the Botanical Garden, and the extent of the assignment, coupled with the warm welcome received from the city, encouraged the family to buy its first house in the city. The exhibition, held during John Bullard's tenure as director, was organized by Valerie Loupe Olsen, senior curator of collections. The exhibition featured twenty-three of Alférez's drawings for *The Wedge* and sixteen small sculptures. Among the sculptures were bronze charros and bronze and terra-cotta female figures. Art critic Roger Green observed that the terra-cottas had a "pitted surface texture" that he considered "wonderfully suggestive and sensuous."

Green also singled out a figure that remains among Alférez's most important, *Woman in a Huipil*. Green acknowledged that *Huipil* was the "star" of the show, and its future as part of the museum's permanent collection was secured through the support of some of Alférez's friends and supporters, who were instrumental in raising the purchase funds. A matching gift from Robert T. and Doris Zemurray Stone allowed for the figure to be cast in bronze.[281]

Woman in a Huipil is integrally tied to Alférez's homeland. A pre-Hispanic traditional garment, the huipil is sometimes referred to as the mother of Indigenous Mexican textile art. Huipils are frequently worn at ceremonial occasions including weddings and funerals, and some women keep a single one their entire lives, with the expectation that it will be used as a burial garment. While the shape of the tunic itself is relatively simple—cloth woven on a backstrap loom and sewn together with openings for the head and arms—its decoration is often elaborate, with intricate designs, brocades, and embroidery. Folklorist Rodolfo Múzquiz Fuentes refers to the huipil—from the Nahuatl word huīpīlli—as a key part of a woman's ritual and identity, and also as a way of presenting herself to God.[282] *Woman in a Huipil* must have held much symbolism for Alférez when it was unveiled in February 1981—a true homecoming, through which he was able to bring a key aspect of his ancestral identity to New Orleans. Following the exhibition, the figure was moved to the north lawn of the New Orleans Museum of Art and later loaned to the Botanical Garden, where it can be seen today.

Woman in a Huipil in The Helis Foundation Enrique Alférez Sculpture Garden [ca. 1981]
photo by Ashley Merlin
ON LOAN FROM NEW ORLEANS MUSEUM OF ART

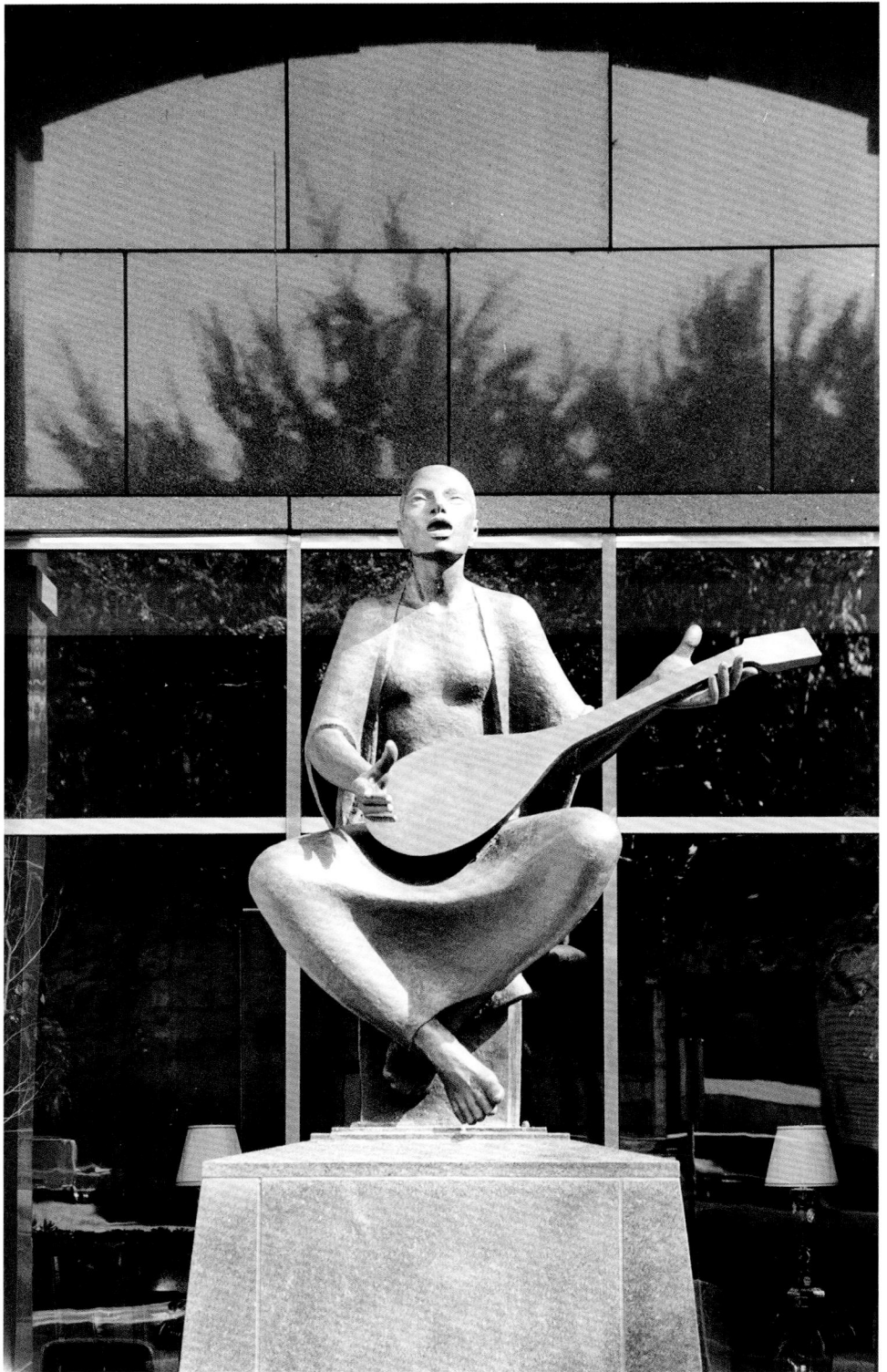

Lute Player [1986]

photo © Owen Murphy Jr., 1988

Outside of the exhibitions noted above, three larger-scale local shows warrant special attention: solo installations at the K&B Plaza at Lee Circle in 1975, the Academy Gallery at the New Orleans Academy of Fine Arts in 1986, and Longue Vue House and Gardens in 1996.

In 1975, Alférez was living in Mexico, but returned to New Orleans for the K&B Plaza exhibition. It was "a reunion of sorts," convening friends and benefactors for a show of twenty-two sculptures and six drawings. The exhibition confirmed the wisdom of Alférez's shift toward smaller-scale figural works. Critic Alberta Collier, long an admirer of Alférez's artwork, noted that "classic beauty [took] on warm life," and she singled out a number of pieces that moved her, including one in which a woman was sweeping the floor: "the swing of her body and the stance of her legs are something Edgar Degas would have appreciated."[283]

The 1986 exhibition at the Academy Gallery—one of many over the years at this venue to feature Alférez's work—is significant for the role it played in securing future commissions. *Enrique Alférez: Sculpture* garnered positive reviews, including Roger Green's comment that the figures on display that October and November were "in every respect equal, if not superior, to anything he has produced in the past."[284]

The exhibit included bronze and terra-cotta figures, wood carvings, and plaster friezes. Before visitors even entered the gallery, they first passed a larger-than-life cast-bronze *Lute Player* installed outside. Its placement created a stirring impact and inspired Joseph C. Canizaro, a New Orleans business leader and supporter of local artists, to commission *David* for the LL&E Tower he was developing on Poydras Street (now the First Bank and Trust Tower).[285] In conjunction with the unveiling, in 1988, Canizaro published a monograph on Alférez, *The Art and Times of Enrique Alférez*, with text by E. John Bullard and Sharon Litwin.

The last major exhibition during Alférez's lifetime was aptly named *An Abundance of Life*. Held from March to August 1996 at Longue Vue House and Gardens, it included more than sixty works. Drawings and figures in bronze, wood, and terra-cotta were displayed inside the house museum, and eight large bronze figures were placed

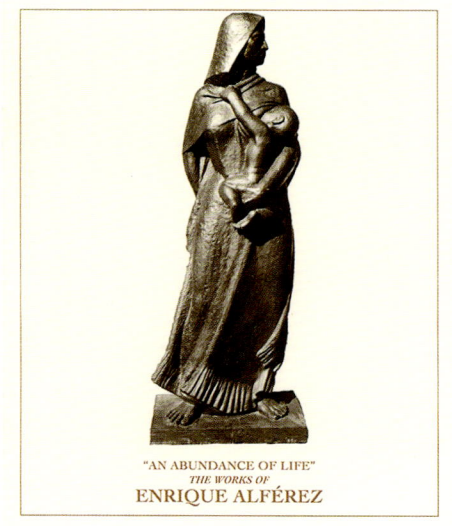

"An Abundance of Life": The Works of Enrique Alférez exhibition pamphlet

New Orleans: Longue Vue House and Gardens, ca. 1996
THNOC, 2003.0038.3

in the gardens. It was an impressive show, with pieces on loan from fifteen private collections, including *La Soldadera* from Alférez's own collection, numerous bronze dancers and gymnasts, and the startling *Vietnam*, a forty-seven-inch cast bronze mother and infant recoiling from the effects of war. Alférez gave a personal tour of the exhibition, which was complemented by a thirty-two-page catalog featuring thirty-seven photographs of exhibited works, introductory text by Jane Ferguson, and a map of twenty-five sites where Alférez's work could be seen throughout the city.

Alférez's family was usually with him at his openings; Peggy and Tlaloc were also instrumental in preparing for exhibitions, both during his lifetime and following his death. Thus far, there have been two major posthumous exhibitions of Alférez's work, at the Ogden Museum of Southern Art in New Orleans. David Houston, then chief curator, called the 2002 exhibition *Enrique Alférez: Art and Life* a "reintroduction to the remarkable life and art of Alférez, as well as an introduction to many works that have never been publicly exhibited."[286] And *Times-Picayune* critic Doug MacCash, reviewing the Ogden's 2012 exhibition *The Created World of Enrique Alférez*, noted the sense of emotion present in his figures. "The bravery, sadness, anger and eroticism that [Alférez] earnestly sought to communicate seem acute and

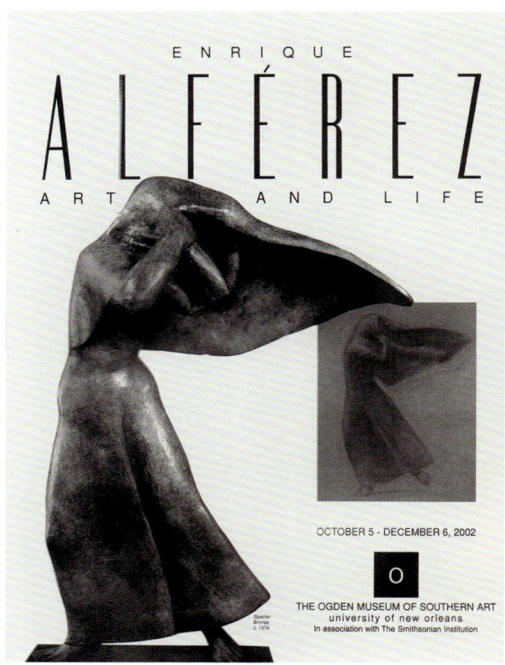

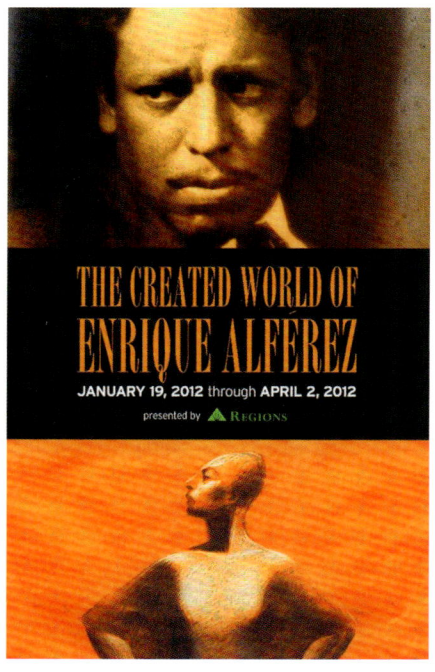

Enrique Alférez: Art and Life
exhibition postcard [2002]
Ogden Museum of Southern Art
COURTESY OF THE TLALOC SELWAY ALFÉREZ PAPERS

Online promotion for *The Created World of Enrique Alférez* exhibition [2012]
Ogden Museum of Southern Art

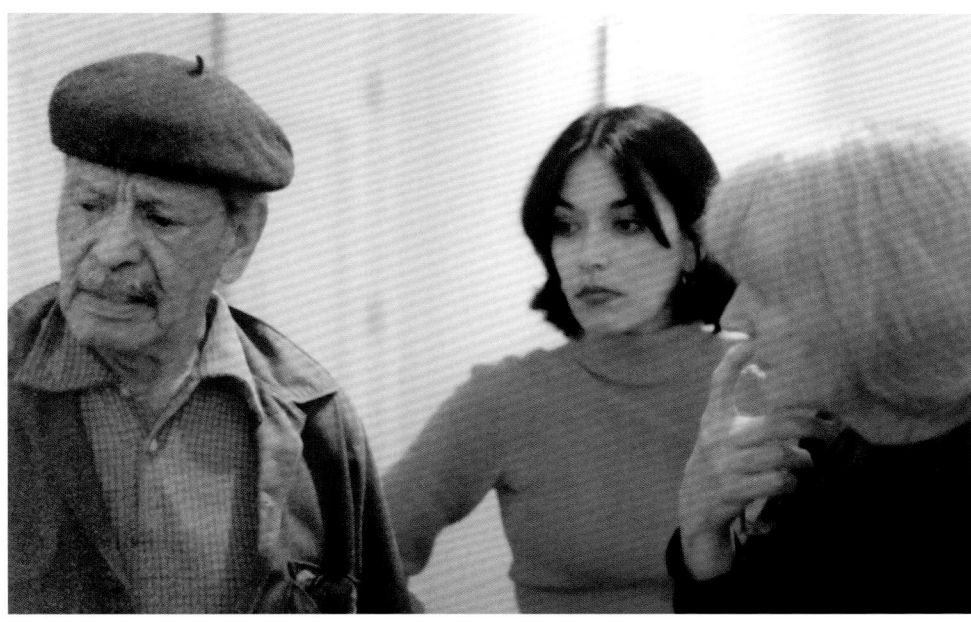

Alférez, Tlaloc, and Peggy
COURTESY OF THE TLALOC SELWAY ALFÉREZ PAPERS

authentic now," wrote MacCash, who also acknowledged that Alférez had become "the city's most celebrated public artist."[287] The authenticity that MacCash saw echoed Alférez's own goal of creating figures and their emotions "more honestly."

Additionally, Alférez's work was included in an important group exhibition at the National Museum of Mexican Art in Chicago, *Arte Diseño Xicágo: Mexican Inspiration from the World's Columbian Exposition to the Civil Rights Era* (March 23–August 19, 2018). The exhibition showed the influence of Mexican immigrants and artists in Chicago's art and design, and Alférez was among thirty-five featured artists.

During Alférez's life, Peggy represented her husband, frequently negotiating with clients, and she wanted him to be treated as a creator even if he saw himself as laborer. She was as tough as she could be with potential clients and was fiercely protective of him. Peggy's practice of keeping documentation related to his career provided the most extensive collection of papers about how Alférez imagined, created, sold, and exhibited. Late in Alférez's life, Peggy even started collecting his art, buying drawings and figures that were being sold at auction. Alférez found the process exasperating. What was she doing, buying art he had already sold? They didn't have money for that, he said. Nonetheless, she collected as much as possible and wrote notes about many other works.

On August 27, 2005, parts of southern Louisiana began receiving evacuation orders in advance of Hurricane Katrina. Radio announcements advised that anyone defying orders needed access to a second floor—and an ax with which to break

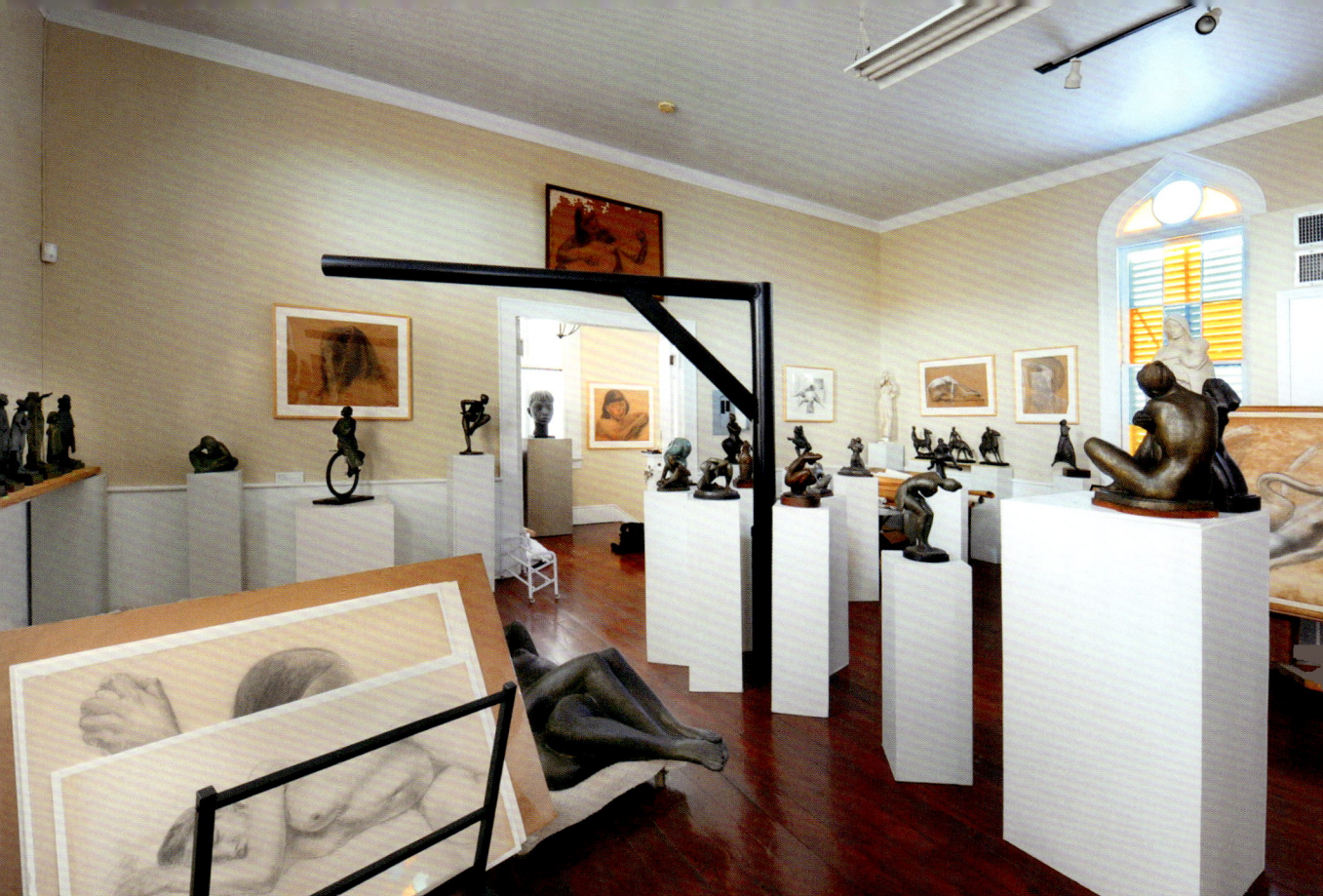

Gallery in Alférez's former home in New Orleans

photo by Donn Young, 2019

through the roof. Thousands stayed, for many reasons. Too many had too few options for where to go and how to get there; others stayed home to keep watch. Peggy also didn't leave. She stayed at the house she had shared with Alférez on Eighth Street since the early 1980s. As the rain came, and then the thunder, Peggy and Tlaloc relocated Alférez's busts and figures away from windows and into safer locations in the house, the weight of bronze in their arms. Peggy carried rolled drawings and tools that had once been in Alférez's hands. After the storm passed, Peggy, Tlaloc, and Tlaloc's partner Jim sat outside in a surprising calm. No electricity, but the crisis, they thought, had passed.

That night, Peggy went to sleep in the bedroom beside the studio where Alférez had worked. The false calm would soon lift. Did Peggy know that? Did she rise in the middle of the night to try to move more figures to safety? Perhaps the flashes of thunder and lightning combined with the weight she had carried placed an unbearable stress on her. The next morning, Tlaloc found her mother collapsed beside the bed.

Tlaloc and Jim put Peggy on an improvised stretcher and into the back seat of Tlaloc's car. They left their home on Eighth Street, uncertain of the condition it might be in when they returned, and headed toward the Crescent City Connection.

Tlaloc drove the car with Peggy in the back seat. They crossed the Mississippi River for a long drive west toward Baton Rouge, the city behind them while water rose among the flooded streets and people moved about in fear and need. Almost two thousand people would die in the storm's immediate aftermath. In many places overtaken by wind and water, Alférez's work overlooked disarray: quiet faces watching from the facades of historic buildings in the medical district, mythological figures near the lake brushed by harsh winds. His imprint was throughout the city: at the *Times-Picayune* headquarters on Howard Avenue, where his textured mural was in a building taking on water, the paper's staff evacuating to keep operations running from a safer setting; in Greenwood Cemetery, where a jagged maze led to a grave marked with a Buddha statue Alférez had cast to memorialize an old friend's husband; and at City Park, where Alférez's figure in Shriever Fountain stood alone in the empty and blackening Botanical Garden, still carrying a vessel for water on her shoulder.

When she fell, Peggy suffered a brain hemorrhage and never regained consciousness. She died September 10, 2005, in Baton Rouge.[288] Tlaloc has since become steward of her father's work and Peggy's collection of papers about him. Peggy died having no idea what a disaster Hurricane Katrina left—or how the storm created opportunities for rare pearls to surface, like the magnificent restoration of the Lakefront Airport, where her husband's art deco imprint, thought by Peggy and Alférez to be long gone, reemerged with splendor.

Peggy knew how the city of New Orleans settled in Alférez's heart, even with his memory of occasional rejections. She spent more than half a century creating a life that revolved around his art. She built the most extensive collection of his work and organized supporting documents in a way that said, *Look here, read, and remember.* In these ways, the collection Peggy created was an extension of the way she lived her life: preparing Enrique Alférez's art to live in perpetuity and preparing their daughter, Tlaloc, to take her place in preserving his work for future generations to enjoy and study.

Acknowledgments

THROUGH MY JOURNEY to get to know Enrique Alférez, I have met many of his friends and colleagues. They were generous with their time, reflections, and records. This generosity of spirit has been most warmly extended by Tlaloc Alférez and Jim Woods. My life was changed by the moments in which Tlaloc invited me over the thresholds of her family's homes in New Orleans and Morelia. I offer her my heartful gratitude for her support and for providing unrestricted access to her family's papers and collections.

For their work to preserve and document Enrique Alférez's art and life, and for their work to honor the many cultures of the region, I thank The Historic New Orleans Collection and The Helis Foundation. At The Collection, I wish to thank directors Priscilla Lawrence, who first supported this project, and Daniel Hammer, for making this book possible. Editor Dorothy Ball has been a creative and thoughtful partner whose close readings, suggestions, and challenges made my writing stronger. Hearty thanks to Jessica Dorman, Alison Cody, Siobhán McKiernan, Rebecca Smith, and to the family and friends of Sarah Doerries.

Many people opened their homes or papers to me, and all shared their knowledge or memories. I benefited from interviews and discussions with those who knew or worked with Alférez, as well as artists, architects, professionals, gallerists, and collectors. This narrative would have been incomplete without Jack and Mimi Davis, Karl Reichley, and Paul Soniat. I am also grateful to Joseph C. and Sue Ellen Canizaro, Auseklis Ozols, Elise Grenier, George Dunbar, Cornelio Campos, Cloe Roesler, Timothy Slater, Bridget Bishop, Wilma Heaton, Alton Ochsner Davis, Alexis O'Dwyer Navarro, and Donna Perret Rosen. I owe special thanks to Ed and Melissa Walker of Carolina Bronze Sculpture and the team at their foundry. Thank you, June Peay, for your correspondence.

I am indebted to many scholars and journalists. I offer special recognition to Allen S. Weller, biographer of Lorado Taft, whose work provided insight into Alférez's formal training. For their conversations, challenges, recommendations, and guided readings, I wish to thank Katie Pfohl, Louis A. Pérez Jr., Peter A. Coclanis, Anne Gilliland, Emiliano Corral, Roger Green, and Jonathan Hartlyn.

Among the many dedicated people with whom I worked at museums, libraries, archives, and historic sites, I want to acknowledge a few whose efforts were instrumental: Danny Gonzalez, Border Heritage Center, El Paso Public Library; Suzette Follette, Christ Church Cathedral, New Orleans; Adair Margo, The Tom Lea Institute, El Paso, Texas; Christine Hernández, Latin American Library, Tulane University; Florence M. Jumonville, Touro Infirmary and the Louisiana and Special Collections Department, Earl K. Long Library, University of New Orleans; Abbie H. Weiser, C. L. Sonnichsen Special Collections, University of Texas at El Paso; Kathe Lawton, Middle American Research Institute, Tulane University; Jon Schmitz, Chautauqua Institution; Liz Fuhrman Bragg, Evansville Museum of Arts, History, and Science; Hillary Bober, Dallas Museum of Art; and Lisa Rotondo-McCord, New Orleans Museum of Art. A very special thanks to Susan Brower and colleagues, Monroe Library, Loyola University New Orleans, for their technical assistance.

I am grateful to my research assistants, Juliet Demeter, Leslie Tate, and Sarah Huener.

Antonio García literally showed me the way, by bus and through the roads and music of Morelia. We all owe him thanks for his efforts to support and preserve Alférez's artwork and home in Morelia, Michoacán.

My husband and daughters have been alongside me every step of the way through this project. They have joined for research trips, read and listened to my drafts, and provided continuous encouragement. In many ways, my work became theirs. Thank you, Donn, Sophia, and Audrey. Other family and friends supported my research and writing, including my parents, Shirley and Mike.

Finally, and persistently, my gratitude to those whose guidance has helped me become a better writer: Debra Allbery, Joan Aleshire, Brooks Haxton, Martha Rhodes, Maudelle Driskell, Vievee Francis, and Maurice Manning. This book is dedicated to the memory Lee Ann Voorhies Vaught, an educator who saw writing as a tool to further our understanding of the world and our relationships to one another.

Notes

1. Matthew J. Martinez, "Enrique Alférez, Sculptor" (master's thesis, University of New Orleans, 1989). Video and text.

2. Don Lee Keith, "Cast in His Own Mold," *Louisiana Cultural Vistas*, Spring 1999, 25. In this interview, Alférez acknowledges that he was married four times.

3. Lorado Taft, *The Appreciation of Sculpture*, Reading with a Purpose (Chicago: American Library Association, 1927), 10.

4. Keith, "His Own Mold," 13.

5. Alférez, quoted in Keith, "His Own Mold," 14.

6. Alférez, quoted in Keith, "His Own Mold," 14.

7. Gina Cortez, "Enrique Alférez Revealed," *La Prensa* (New Orleans), May 1996, 27. Retrieved from Louisiana and Special Collections, Earl K. Long Library, University of New Orleans.

8. Judith H. Bonner, "The Power of Enrique Alférez," *New Orleans Art Review* 11, no. 5 (May–June 1993): 4.

9. I am grateful to gallerist Donna Perret Rosen for helping me sort out observations about the enduring value of Alférez's work relative to his contemporaries.

10. Katie A. Pfohl, *Mexico in New Orleans: A Tale of Two Americas* (Baton Rouge: Louisiana State University Museum of Art, 2015), 9.

11. "New Monteleone Lounge to Open," *Times-Picayune*, August 27, 1938, p. 17. This article makes note of Alférez's early work focusing on Leda.

12. In 1991, Alférez's wife Peggy sent family friends Jack and Mimi Davis a postcard from their travels to Italy, reflecting on Alférez's visit to see works of art that he began formally studying more than sixty years earlier with Taft in Chicago. In Florence, they went to the Galleria degli Uffizi and the Galleria dell'Accademia, home to Michelangelo's *David*. "Taft's studio began E's Florentine orientation. He often is close to tears," Peggy wrote of their visit to Florence. Peggy Alférez to Mimi and Jack Davis, October 1991, Mimi and Jack Davis Papers.

13. Bonner, "The World of Enrique Alférez," *New Orleans Art Review* 30, nos. 3–4 (March–May 2012): 13.

14. Keith, "His Own Mold," 14.

15. Benjamin Roja, *The City of Zacatecas: Zacatecas, Mexico* (Zacatecas: Grupo Azabache, 1991), 142.

16. Roger Green, "Rose Garden Sculptures Feel the Master's Touch," *Times-Picayune States-Item*, June 20, 1981, p. 3.

17. Martinez, "Enrique Alférez, Sculptor."

18. There is inconsistency in how Alférez's birth year is presented, with 1901 and 1903 referenced in separate instances. Alférez's birth date has been reported as May 4, 1901, in newspapers, magazines, and catalogs, and on plaques beside public sculptures. This conflicts with records related to his birth, baptism, immigration status, marriages, and travel, including shipping manifests, which record his birth date as May 4, 1903. Alférez's biographical sketch—which gives his birth

year as 1903—appeared in a catalog for his exhibition at the El Paso Museum of Art in November 1961. The Margaret "Peggy" Alférez Family Papers (hereafter Peggy Alférez Family Papers) include a copy of the catalog in which Peggy corrected a few errors in the margins by hand, but Alférez's birth year, 1903, stands uncorrected. There is a possibility that Alférez was uncertain about the year himself; through discussions with his daughter Tlaloc, I learned that he was unaware that his birth record existed.

19. Anne McArthur, Dick Allen, and Margery Wylie, interview with Enrique Alférez and Peggy Margaret "Peggy" Alférez, December 4-5, 1975, transcript, Peggy Alférez Family Papers; Tlaloc Alférez, in discussion with the author, March–April 2015.

20. "Enrique Alférez," *Arts and Antiques* 1, no. 1 (October 1938): 26; Tlaloc Alférez, in discussion with the author, March–April 2015; McArthur, Allen, and Wylie, interview with Alférez.

21. McArthur, Allen, and Wylie, interview with Alférez.

22. Alien case file (A-File) for Enrique Alférez, alien case files, 1944–2003, record group 566, United States Citizenship and Immigration Services (USCIS).

23. Martínez, "Enrique Alférez, Sculptor."

24. Divorcio del señor Enrique Alférez y de la señora Evelyn Kelly, Certificados de las actas del estados civil, año de 1930, Numéro 101, Ayuntamiento de Campeche, June 3, 1930, Peggy Alférez Family Papers.

25. Judy appears to have gone by the names Judy Barrett and Grace E. Duthie. Information about her identity and her death is scarce.

26. Details about delivering tugs to war fronts was included in a form completed for inclusion in the *Allgemeines Künstlerlexikon* (General dictionary of artists), June 10, 1985, Peggy Alférez Family Papers.

27. Alférez's library card, valid through May 13, 1951, Peggy Alférez Family Papers.

28. "Quits Art for Dishes: Rickey Alférez Home," *New Orleans Item*, December 27, 1946, Mimi and Jack Davis Papers; "The Shop of Leather," *Junior Bazaar* 2, no. 12 (December 1946): 96–97.

29. I have researched birth and death records through Ancestry.com, FamilySearch.com, and local or state records in places where Alférez lived or spent extended periods of time during the years of US engagement in World War II, including California and New York. I also researched local records in El Paso, Texas, with consideration for the unlikely possibility that a child might have been born when he lived there. No evidence of a son has been found.

30. Tlaloc Alférez, in discussion with the author, July 2015.

31. Doug MacCash, "Peggy Alférez, 1927–2005," Katrina's Lives Lost, *Times-Picayune*, November 18, 2005, sec. Living, p. 1.

32. Marilyn Hall, "N.O. Artist Fulfills Dream: Carves Mexican 'Firewood' Into Doors for New Church," *New Orleans States and Item*, August 15, 1959, Enrique Alférez artist file, The Historic New Orleans Collection.

33. Kate Doyle, ed., "The Dead of Tlatelolco: Using the Archives to Exhume the Past," *National Security Archive*, October 1, 2006. https://nsarchive2.gwu.edu/NSAEBB/NSAEBB201/. Early reports indicated a death toll of about twenty, but the number was long considered deceivingly low and believed to possibly have been in the hundreds. Over the course of Alférez's life, the Mexican and US governments provided incomplete information about the incident; in 2006, the National Security Archive documented forty-four deaths. Questions about the scale of the massacre persist. The incident left an indelible mark on Mexico City.

34. This detail, first noticed by immigration attorney Bridget Bishop, is apparent in Alférez's alien case file.

35. Details about this incident are drawn from numerous interviews with Tlaloc Alférez.

36. Jennifer J. Rose, in discussion with the author, August 17, 2016. See also emails from C. Warren Lewis (resident of Morelia) to Rose, January 2008, reproduced in "The Dragon of Santa María," *Red Shoes Are Better Than Bacon*, July 23, 2014, https://redshoesarebetterthanbacon.wordpress.com/2014/07/23/the-dragon-of-santa-maria/.

37. Cárdenas had three unsuccessful bids for the presidency of Mexico. His loss in 1988 has been recognized as the result of election fraud.

38. Tlaloc Alférez, in discussion with the author, April 2016.

39. Tlaloc Alférez, in discussion with the author, October 29–30, 2015.

40. Timothy Slater, in discussion with the author, January 23, 2015, and March 31, 2015.

41. George Dunbar, in discussion with the author, April 2, 2015.

42. Karl Reichley, in discussion with the author, June 9, 2016.

43. Montgomery Budd, "Montgomery Budd in Morelia," *News Mexico City*, April 8, 1984, sec. Travel/Vistas, p. 8, New Orleans Museum of Art Curatorial Files, 81.181, New Orleans Museum of Art, New Orleans.

44. Tlaloc Alférez, in discussion with the author, July 2015 and November 11, 2018.

45. Gina Cortez, "Enrique Alférez Revealed," 27.

46. Christ Church was the first Protestant church in the Louisiana Purchase territory, and it has undergone a series of new buildings and renovations since its founding in 1805. Samuel Wilson Jr., *The Buildings of Christ Church* (New Orleans: Louisiana Landmarks Society, 1997).

47. Suzette Follette, in discussion with the author, March 31, 2015.

48. In addition to searching Alférez's alien case file for evidence of the complaints, I submitted a Freedom of Information Act records request to the Federal Bureau of Investigation seeking any information about complaints against Alférez. No records were available.

49. Alien case file for Enrique Alférez. The examiner was referring to Section 2169 of the Revised Statutes of the Naturalization Act of 1790 (revised in 1870).

50. John W. Scott, *Natalie Scott: A Magnificent Life* (Gretna, LA: Pelican, 2008), 290.

51. "Alférez to Serve in Mexican Army," clipping from an unidentified newspaper, June or July 1942, Mimi and Jack Davis Papers.

52. Tlaloc Alférez, in discussion with the author, February 29, 2020.

53. Alien case file for Enrique Alférez.

54. McArthur, Allen, and Wylie, interview with Alférez; Enrique Alférez to Jack Davis, December 2, 1985, Mimi and Jack Davis Papers.

55. I investigated other specific circumstances in which Alférez was subjected to racism and bigotry; this comment struck me as similar to his everyday challenges and it has become a reminder of my own need to give careful attention to the language I use when speaking and writing about Alférez and the injustices he faced. I have tried, in the writing of this book, to avoid reinforcing stereotype and harmful power dynamics that are inherent risks for a white American writing about a brown person of indigenous Nahua origins. My desire to try to see through Alférez's eyes has had an immeasurable influence on my own continuous understanding of historic and contemporary injustices in our society—and of the dangerous, oppressive, and tender power of language.

56. E. John Bullard and Sharon Litwin, *The Art and Times of Enrique Alférez* (New Orleans: A Project of Joseph C. Canizaro Interests, 1988), 1. Tlaloc Alférez, in discussion with the author, March 29, 2015, confirmed the story and stated that Longinos studied for eight years.

57. McArthur, Allen, and Wylie, interview with Alférez.

58. "Enrique Alférez," *Arts and Antiques*; Tlaloc Alférez, in discussion with the author, March–April 2015; McArthur, Allen, and Wylie, interview with Alférez.

59. "Murió Anoche el Escultor Alférez Guzmán en Gómez," clipping from an unidentified publication, April 27, 1958, Peggy Alférez Family Papers.

60. Ed Walker, in discussion with the author, February 9, 2015, and June 26, 2015. Walker cast work by Alférez in New Orleans prior to establishing the Carolina Bronze Sculpture foundry in Seagrove, North Carolina.

61. Betty Jane Holder, "Jack of All Trades: Famous Sculptor Cooks, Too," *New Orleans Item*, January 3, 1951, Enrique Alférez artist file, The Historic New Orleans Collection.

62. Want Ad Reporter, "Up and Down the Street," *Times-Picayune*, July 16, 1937, p. 32; classified advertisement, *El Paso Herald*, March 1, 1922, p. 11. An El Paso city directory allowed me to cross-reference Alférez's address with the location cited in the classified ad.

63. Richard and Jules Cahn frequently provided such materials to Alférez from Dixie Mill.

64. Alférez, quoted in Daisy Anderson, "Concrete Sculpture to Decorate New Bridges in City Park," *Sunday Item-Tribune*, February 9, 1936, p. 5.

65. Much about Alférez's process is drawn from interviews with Karl Reichley and Tlaloc Alférez, in discussion with the author, 2015–16, and from a book by Alférez's friend and fellow sculptor Jules Struppeck, *The Creation of Sculpture* (New York: Henry Holt, 1952). I am also grateful to Reichley for helping me understand and articulate this process that Alférez commonly used; Ed Walker and his colleagues at Carolina Bronze Sculpture also helped me understand the difference between today's casting process versus standard practices during much of Alférez's career.

66. Arthur Halliburton, "Liquid Stone," *Times-Picayune New Orleans States*, May 4, 1941, sec. 2, p. 5.

67. "N.O. Artist Gets Mexico Commission: Enrique Alférez to Erect Huge Statue of Woman Near Border," clipping from an unidentified newspaper, May 15, 1932, Mimi and Jack Davis Papers.

68. Hector Galan, *The Hunt for Pancho Villa* (Alexandria, VA: PBS Video, 1993), videocassette.

69. Frank Tannenbaum, *The Mexican Agrarian Revolution* (New York: Macmillan, 1929).

70. Justino Fernández, *Mexican Art* (Mexico City: Hamlyn Publishing Group, 1967), 18.

71. Eileen Loh, "Sculpting a Long Life: New Orleans Artist's Works and Company Have Been Controversial and Legendary," *Fort Worth Star-Telegram*, August 6, 1995, sec. Texas, p. 30, Bulldog AM edition. McArthur, Allen, and Wylie, interview with Alférez; Tlaloc Alférez, in discussion with the author, April 2015; John Pope, "N.O. Sculptor Alférez Dies," *Times-Picayune*, September 14, 1999, sec. A, p. 1.

72. McArthur, Allen, and Wylie, interview with Alférez.

73. McArthur, Allen, and Wylie, interview with Alférez.

74. Tlaloc Alférez, in discussion with the author, March–April 2015.

75. Galan, *Hunt for Pancho Villa*.

76. Clipping from an unidentified publication published in conjunction with Alférez's work for Shushan Airport, ca. 1933–34, Peggy Alférez Family Papers.

77. Rubén De La Torre, "Un Raro Escultor Mexicano," *Revista de Revistas* (September 30, 1934), New Orleans Museum of Art Curatorial Files, 180.120.1-34; McArthur, Allen, and Wylie, interview with Alférez. Before the war, Gavira had a woodshop, and had been trained in arts and crafts at the Escuela Nacional de Artes y Oficios.

78. Friedrich Katz, *The Life and Times of Pancho Villa* (Stanford, CA: Stanford University Press, 1998), 714.

79. El Paso City Directories, 1921–24 and 1927, El Paso Public Library.

80. Alien case file for Enrique Alférez; Fourteenth Census of the United States, City of El Paso, 1920.

81. Alférez's recollection of the incident is primarily drawn from his interview with McArthur, Allen, and Wylie. It is puzzling how he came to know some of the details, since he said in the interview that he was standing outside the bar when the incident happened.

82. Facts about the barroom incident and Arévalo's artwork are primarily drawn from "Artist Shot in Juárez Dies; Body Sent to Durango," *El Paso Herald*, July 25, 1921, p. 2; and "Sigue el Desvarajuste en las Oficinas Municipales," *Excélsior*, July 26, 1921, p. 5.

83. El Paso City Directories, 1921–24, El Paso Public Library.

84. Advertisement for opening of Fine Arts Shop, *El Paso Herald*, September 21, 1918, p. 8.

85. McArthur, Allen, and Wylie, interview with Alférez; De La Torre, "Un Raro Escultor Mexicano."

86. Advertisement, *El Paso Herald*, September 27, 1919, p. 10.

87. McArthur, Allen, and Wylie, interview with Alférez.

88. "Paso Artist Employed for Shrine Work," *El Paso Evening Post*, February 2, 1928, p. 1; McArthur, Allen, and Wylie, interview with Alférez.

89. McArthur, Allen, and Wylie, interview with Alférez.

90. "Paintings by 33 Artists Displayed in Exhibition Here," *El Paso Herald*, February 11, 1922, p. 6.

91. Tom Lea, *Tom Lea: An Oral History*, ed. Rebecca McDowell Craver and Adair Margo (El Paso: Texas Western Press, 1995), 27.

92. Alférez returned to El Paso periodically throughout the 1920s and likely lived there again for some period of time in the late 1920s, at least long enough to establish a residency and become listed in a city directory.

93. Edan Milton Hughes, *Artists in California, 1786–1940*, vol. 2, L–Z (Sacramento, CA: Crocker Art Museum, 2002), 1154.

94. "El Paso People You Should Know," *El Paso Herald*, October 17, 1922, p. 14.

95. Staff photograph, ca. 1910–1915, Stout-Feldman Studio Photographs, PH 074, C. L. Sonnichsen Special Collections, University of Texas at El Paso Library, El Paso, Texas.

96. McArthur, Allen, and Wylie, interview with Alférez; Tlaloc Alférez, in discussion with the author, July 2015.

97. "Lorado Taft: Sculptor, Lecturer, Educator, Philanthropist," *Art Thoughts*, no. 6 (December 1936). First accessed through the El Paso Public Library Border Heritage Center Artist Files.

98. Barbara Hall and Robert Aaron Jones, "Time and Tide: Restoring Lorado Taft's *Fountain of Time*—An Overview," in "Conservation at the Art Institute of Chicago," *Art Institute of Chicago Museum Studies* 31, no. 2 (2005): 80–89, 111–112. Taft began teaching at the Institute in 1889 and was appointed nonresident professor of art at the University of Illinois in 1919.

99. Hall and Jones, "Time and Tide," 80–85.

100. Hall and Jones, "Time and Tide," 82.

101. "Noted Sculptor to Give Lecture in Liberty Hall," *El Paso Herald*, March 19, 1923, p. 4; Allen Stuart Weller, *Lorado Taft: The Chicago Years* (Urbana: University of Illinois Press, 2014), 61–64.

102. Joe Mears, "Taft Is Real Man, Wit, Philosopher; Crowd Enjoys Him," *El Paso Herald*, March 27, 1923, p. 8.

103. Ron Grossman, "Sculptor's Youth Is Written on the Skyline of Chicago," *Chicago Tribune*, December 20, 1985, sec. Tempo, p. 3.

104. Betty Luther, "Enrique Alférez, Illustrator of 'The Wedge,' Is Kiwanis Protege," *El Paso Herald Post*, September 2, 1935, p. 6, El Paso Public Library Border Heritage Center Vertical Files.

105. Pope, "N.O. Sculptor Alférez Dies."

106. McArthur, Allen, and Wylie, interview with Alférez.

107. Luther, "Enrique Alférez." The hotel was likely the Alamo, on South El Paso Street. El Paso City Directory, 1924, El Paso Public Library.

108. Luther, "Enrique Alférez."

109. Weller, *Lorado Taft*, 116.

110. Weller, *Lorado Taft*, 120.

111. Elizabeth Hazeltine, "Lorado Taft: Master Sculptor," *School Arts Magazine* 25, nos. 1–5 (January 1926): 260–62.

112. Lea, *Tom Lea*, 26.

113. Hazeltine, "Lorado Taft," 260–62.

114. Ruth Helming Mose, "Midway Studio," *American Magazine of Art* 19, no. 8 (August 1928): 417.

115. Mose, "Midway Studio," 421.

116. "Lorado Taft," *Art Thoughts*.

117. Weller, *Lorado Taft*, 4.

118. Sarah Kelly Oehler, *They Seek a City: Chicago and the Art of Migration, 1910–1950* (Chicago: Art Institute of Chicago, 2013), 36.

119. Details about Alférez's commute are from McArthur, Allen, and Wylie, interview with Alférez; details about his course work are from the author's email correspondence with Adam Torres (assistant director of registration and records, School of the Art Institute of Chicago), October 28, 2014.

120. Alastair Duncan, *Art Deco* (New York: Thames and Hudson, 1988), 7–8.

121. Weller, *Lorado Taft*, 116–17; Mose, "Midway Studio," 417.

122. The detail about shopping at a bakery for day-old pastries is from discussions with Alférez's daughter Cloe Roesler, October 28, 2015.

123. Lea, *Tom Lea*, 27.

124. Jeanette Almada's article, "Planners OK Palmolive Condos," *Chicago Tribune*, March 3, 2003, p. 5B, indicates the work was carved in walnut and oak. Alférez's ca. 1930 résumé indicates he created eighty-four panels. Louisiana State Capitol Project Plan No. 770, Box 13, Folder 5, Weiss, Dreyfous, and Seiferth Office Records, Southeastern Architectural Archive, Special Collections Division, Tulane University, New Orleans, LA.

125. John W. Stamper, *Chicago's North Michigan Avenue: Planning and Development, 1900–1930*, Chicago Architecture and Urbanism (Chicago: University of Chicago Press, 1991), 149, 154–55.

126. Alférez résumé, ca. 1930.

127. McArthur, Allen, and Wylie, interview with Alférez; Enrique Alférez to Jack Davis, December 2, 1985, Mimi and Jack Davis Papers.

128. Grossman, "Sculptor's Youth Is Written on the Skyline."

129. Alférez to Carl Sandburg, letter, ca. 1926, CARL 81932, Carl Sandburg Home National Historic Site, Flat Rock, North Carolina.

130. Details about Alférez improving his English by reading the comics are drawn from the author's discussion with Tlaloc Alférez, March 29, 2015.

131. McArthur, Allen, and Wylie, interview with Alférez; Martinez, "Enrique Alférez, Sculptor."

132. Lyle Saxon, "Pontalba Artist Colony Plan Gets Wide Approval," *New Orleans Item*, January 26, 1919, sec. 1, p. 12.

133. Anthony Wilson, "The Double Dealer," in *64 Parishes Encyclopedia of Louisiana* (Louisiana Endowment for the Humanities, 2010–), article published February 7, 2011, https://64parishes.org/entry/the-double-dealer.

134. Bonner, "The World of Enrique Alférez," 12.

135. John W. Scott, "William Spratling and the New Orleans Renaissance," *Louisiana History: The Journal of the Louisiana Historical Association* 45, no. 3 (Summer 2004): 317.

136. Scott, "William Spratling," 309–10.

137. Scott, "William Spratling," 311.

138. Pfohl, *Mexico in New Orleans*, 9.

139. John Shelton Reed, *Dixie Bohemia: A French Quarter Circle in the 1920s* (Baton Rouge: Louisiana State University Press, 2012), 60.

140. Irene Cooper, "Thriving Centers Are Established for Artists Here," *Times-Picayune*, February 5, 1937, p. 39.

141. Tlaloc Alférez, in discussion with the author, March 30, 2015; Rena Pederson (Evelyn Kelly biographer), in discussion with the author, November 7, 2016.

142. Joe Simnacher, "Evelyn Kelly Del Barrio Lambert—World Traveler Who Co-founded Annual Dallas Auction for Arts," *Dallas Morning News*, February 25, 2004, Metro, sec. B, p. 5.

143. Details about Alférez's work at Holy Name are drawn from Martinez, "Enrique Alférez, Sculptor."

144. Matthew Reonas, "Great Depression in Louisiana," in *64 Parishes Encyclopedia of Louisiana* (Louisiana Endowment for the Humanities, 2010–), article published December 17, 2010, https://64parishes.org/entry/great-depression-in-louisiana.

145. McArthur, Allen, and Wylie, interview with Alférez.

146. Alien case file for Enrique Alférez.

147. "Gay, Bold Sculptor, Famed for Adventures, Dead on Tulane Mission, Friends Hear," *Item-Tribune*, March 9, 1930, pp. 1, 4, Enrique Alférez artist file, The Historic New Orleans Collection.

148. "Gay, Bold Sculptor," *Item-Tribune*.

149. The 1930 US Department of Commerce US Census, Population Schedule, taken April 17, 1930, indicates that Huth was an "inmate" at the House of the Good Shepherd. The document is record-image_33SQ-GR4R-ZQ7, Ancestry.com.

150. Some of these details about Alférez's mysterious disappearance and rumored death are recounted in Jack Davis, "Enrique Alférez's Experiences with the Works Progress Administration," *New Orleans Art: The New Deal Era*, November 16, 1978, Jambalaya Program Records 1975–1980, New Orleans Public Library. Many details, including those about Bertha Rolfe and Tulane University, are from "Gay, Bold Sculptor." Additional information from Alférez's interview with McArthur, Allen, and Wylie. Beyond what is shared in Blom's field notes, Tlaloc Alférez provided more information about the nature of Alférez's illness in discussion with the author, July 2015.

151. Details about the site are drawn from Jeff Karl Kowalski, *The House of the Governor: A Maya Palace at Uxmal, Yucatan, Mexico* (Norman: University of Oklahoma Press, 1987), 241. Alférez's younger daughter was named for the Aztec rain god, Tlaloc, who corresponds to the Maya rain god, Chaac.

152. Details about the group are drawn from "Blom Declares Maya Expedition Reached Goals," *Times-Picayune*, May 20, 1930, p. 11; "Students Chosen by Frans Blom for Uxmal Trip," *Times-Picayune*, January 9, 1930, p. 7; Frans Blom, "The Uxmal Expedition," *Tulane News Bulletin* 10, no. 7 (April 1930): 111–14, Frans Blom Papers, 1919–1963, Latin American Library, Tulane University; and Robert Levere Brunhouse, *Frans Blom, Maya Explorer* (Albuquerque: University of New Mexico Press, 1976), 115.

153. Many details are drawn from Blom's field letters and notes in the Frans Blom Papers, 1919–1963, Latin American Library, Tulane University. Some of his field letters are handwritten, then typed and revised or included in *Tulane News Bulletin*. A second source of records of this research trip and related field letters, including copies, versions, and additional materials, is available through the Frans Blom Papers, ca. 1890–1942, Bancroft Library, University of California, Berkeley.

154. "Mayan Expeditions Add to Historical Knowledge through Tulane Department," *Times-Picayune*, February 4, 1932, p. 30.

155. At the time, Blom and his team believed this was the first use of night-lit photography, and there were newspaper reports celebrating the achievement. While they were indeed working during the early phases of new technology, they were not the first; they were just not familiar with Teobert Maler's photography from the late nineteenth and early twentieth centuries. Details from Brunhouse, *Frans Blom*, 118.

156. Brunhouse, *Frans Blom*, 118.

157. Frans Blom, "The 'Negative Batter' at Uxmal," *Middle American Papers,* Publication 4 (New Orleans: Middle American Research Institute, Tulane University, 1932), 565. The group visited other sites as well and observed the effect of negative batter at Labna, Sayil, Kabah, and Xlapak.

158. Brunhouse, *Frans Blom*, 139–40.

159. Brunhouse writes of a circumstance in which Blom's troubles were so significant that he neglected bills associated with an apartment in New Orleans; it is possible that Blom didn't get rid of Alférez's belongings, but that an eviction prevented their safe storage and return. Brunhouse, *Frans Blom*, 142.

160. Meyer Levin and Eli Levin, "Alférez Seeks Sandburg Mask," *Philadelphia Inquirer*, December 13, 1959, CARL 28274, Carl Sandburg Home, Flat Rock, North Carolina.

161. E. John Bullard to Mary Sefton Thomas, September 18, 1980, New Orleans Museum of Art Curatorial Files, 80.120.1-34.

162. "Blom Declares Maya Expedition Reached Goals." Also see Edward T. Hinderliter, "The Maya Temple of the 1933 Chicago World's Fair," in "Abstracts of Papers Presented at the Twenty-Fourth Annual Meeting of the Society of Architectural Historians," *Journal of the Society of Architectural Historians* 30, no. 3 (1971): 239–40.

163. Divorcio del señor Enrique Alférez y de la señora Evelyn Kelly, June 3, 1930, Peggy Alférez Family Papers; Ship manifest for SS *Munplace*, June 9, 1930, "Louisiana, New Orleans Passenger Lists, 1820–1945," affiliate film #135, NARA microfilm publications M259 and T905 (Washington DC: National Archives and Records Administration, n.d.), FHL microfilm 2,311,485. This manifest is also available through FamilySearch.org, https://familysearch.org/ark:/61903/1:1:KTTS-QMY (accessed March 12, 2018).

164. Alien case file for Enrique Alférez; marriage records of Rose Marie Huth and Enrique Alférez, June 13, 1930, Jefferson Parish Clerk of Court, Metairie, Louisiana.

165. Brunhouse, *Frans Blom*, 118.

166. Cheryl R. Ganz, *The 1933 Chicago World's Fair: A Century of Progress* (Urbana: University of Illinois Press, 2008), 130–31.

167. Martinez, "Enrique Alférez, Sculptor."

168. "Alférez, Sculptor, Sued for Separation," *Times-Picayune*, June 6, 1933, p. 24.

169. "Wife of Sculptor Is Granted Divorce," *Times-Picayune*, March 27, 1935, p. 11. Cloe's birth name was Clotilde Xochitl Alférez. She also went by Cloe Huth, before becoming Cloe Roesler by marriage. The name Xochitl is from the Nahuatl word xōchitl, for flower.

170. New Orleans Police Department arrest cards, TP35 1914–47, Roll 723B, New Orleans Public Library. Alférez was arrested June 22, 1929; March 10, 1934; November 28, 1936; and October 26, 1937.

171. "Alférez Granted Affidavit after Beating Charges: Sculptor Claims Policemen Slugged Him with Fists and Blackjacks," *Times-Picayune*, October 28, 1937, p. 1.

172. "Officer Exonerated in Beating of Sculptor Jailed for Drinking," *Times-Picayune New Orleans States,* October 31, 1937, p. 1.

173. Weiss, Dreyfous, and Seiferth were in partnership from the 1920s until Weiss was convicted of fraud in 1940 and imprisoned; Dreyfous and Seiferth continued their careers as architects and Weiss returned to architecture in 1952. Before he died in 1953, Weiss established a firm with Edward B. Silverstein, who also subsequently hired Alférez. Though Weiss, Dreyfous, and Seiferth's projects are extensively archived at the Southeastern Architectural Archive at Tulane University, it is not uncommon for building specs to include little information about the architectural details that Alférez or other sculptors contributed to the site, in part because the detail did not influence the soundness of the structure and was thus not rendered in drawings.

174. John Lachin created the portrait of Mrs. Miltenberger above the main entrance to the convalescent home. I include this detail to set the record straight; Alférez is occasionally given credit for this portrait.

175. Though Alférez worked on many projects for Weiss, Dreyfous, and Seiferth, he was notably not among the many sculptors, including his mentor Lorado Taft, who were hired by the firm to work on the State Capitol in Baton Rouge. Alférez submitted his résumé in hopes of working on the project in 1930, but he was not chosen.

176. Description of sculptural panel, Augustine I. Bloch Memorial, Project No. 837, minutes of the Board of Managers of Touro Infirmary, April 1935, 258, Touro Infirmary Archives, New Orleans.

177. Pope, "Art Deco Frieze Greets Students: LSU Health Center Displays 1931 Piece," *Times-Picayune*, November 15, 2009, sec. B, p. 1.

178. Cooper, "Pen, Chisel and Brush," *Times-Picayune*, January 29, 1933, sec. B, p. 5.

179. "Big Airport for South: Pan-American Air Races Will Open $4,000,000 Shushan Field," *New York Times*, February 4, 1934, p. 8.

180. Vincent Caire, *Louisiana Aviation: An Extraordinary History in Photographs* (Baton Rouge: Louisiana State University Press, 2012), 51.

181. Louisiana Board of Levee Commissioners of the Orleans Levee District, *Commemorating the Formal Opening of Shushan Airport* (New Orleans: Board of Levee Commissioners, 1933); Caire, *Louisiana Aviation*, 47–50.

182. "Shushan Airport, New Orleans, La.," *Architectural Forum* 61 (October 1934): 237.

183. Janna Eggebeen, "Airport Age: Architecture and Modernity in America" (PhD diss., City University of New York, 2007), 126.

184. The murals were restored by art conservator Elise Grenier from 2015 to 2018. One mural, "Flight Over Bali," was re-created because it was missing; as of the publication of this book, the original has not been found.

185. "Shushan Airport," *Architectural Forum*, 242.

186. Cooper, "Pen, Chisel and Brush."

187. Cooper's *Times-Picayune* column implies that Alférez completed three exterior panels, but in his interview with McArthur, Allen, and Wylie, he says he completed one panel and the central figure.

188. Cooper, "Pen, Chisel and Brush."

189. McArthur, Allen, and Wylie, interview with Alférez.

190. "Shushan Airport," *Architectural Forum*, 242.

191. Eggebeen, "Airport Age," 136.

192. Elise Grenier, in discussion with the author, July 3, 2019.

193. As discussed later in chapter 4, Alférez and Gonzalez's friendship was strained when Gonzalez played a joke on the sculptor in 1951, around the unveiling of *The Family*, which may have contributed to his unflattering description of Gonzalez's work.

194. Luba Glade, "Rique the Roisterer," *Figaro*, January 1, 1979, 18.

195. Martinez, "Enrique Alférez, Sculptor."

196. W. M. Darling, "Pen, Chisel and Brush," *Times-Picayune New Orleans States*, February 13, 1938, sec. B, p. 5.

197. Guillaume Hecht, dir., *Uxmal: Thrice Built* (New York: Films Media Group, 2001).

198. "Airport Fountain Lighting Signals Close of Two-Year Project for Improvement," *Times-Picayune*, July 9, 1938, sec. A, p. 1.

199. Darling, "Pen, Chisel and Brush," February 13, 1938.

200. Darling, "Pen, Chisel and Brush," February 13, 1938.

201. Darling, "Pen, Chisel and Brush," *Times-Picayune New Orleans States*, July 17, 1938, sec. 2, page 9.

202. Martinez, "Enrique Alférez, Sculptor."

203. Bill Grady, "Artist, Fountain Have Colorful Lives," *Times-Picayune*, October 13, 1991, sec. B, p. 1.

204. Glade "Rique the Roisterer," 18.

205. Martinez, "Enrique Alférez, Sculptor."

206. Eggebeen, "Airport Age," 140–41.

207. Martinez, "Enrique Alférez, Sculptor."

208. Bethany Villere (executive assistant to the president of the Orleans Levee Board) to Mr. and Mrs. Enrique Alférez, June 27, 1991, Peggy Alférez Family Papers.

209. Wilma Heaton (vice-chair of the Non-Flood Asset Protection Management Authority board and chair of its Lakefront Airport Committee), in discussion with the author, July 15, 2016.

210. Grady, "Artist, Fountain Have Colorful Lives." Some of Alférez's contemporaries have suggested he may have been pleased to destroy the globe, having been unsatisfied with it from the outset. This is at odds with how Alférez was said to feel about the addition of the globe in 1938.

211. Peggy Alférez to philanthropist and art patron Mary Catherine "Mickey" Easterling, July 22, 1994, Peggy Alférez Family Papers.

212. Jon Lash to Enrique Alférez, May 3, 1995, Peggy Alférez Family Papers.

213. Resolution 05-120513, adopted by the Non-Flood Protection Asset Management Authority, December 5, 2013. The document was provided by Wilma Heaton.

214. Peggy Alférez to Mickey Easterling, July 22, 1994, Peggy Alférez Family Papers.

215. Alton Ochsner Davis, in discussion with the author, December 31, 2015.

216. Darling, "Pen, Chisel and Brush," *Times-Picayune New Orleans States*, November 13, 1938, sec. 2, p. 7.

217. John E. Salvaggio, *New Orleans' Charity Hospital: A Story of Physicians, Politics, and Poverty* (Baton Rouge: Louisiana State University Press, 1992), 117.

218. Robert D. Leighninger Jr., *Building Louisiana: The Legacy of the Public Works Administration* (Jackson: University Press of Mississippi, 2007), 146.

219. Leighninger, *Building Louisiana*, 145–46.

220. Many of these details are drawn from Jack Davis, "Enrique Alférez' Tales Over Tequila," *Lagniappe*, November 22–28, 1975, and Davis's related recording of the interview in the Mimi and Jack Davis Papers, as well as Leighninger, *Building Louisiana*, 145. In Davis's recording, Alférez says that Richard W. Leche and Seymour Weiss (no relation to Leon Weiss) were at Leon Weiss's as well. Although this detail also appears in Davis's *Lagniappe* article, I am skeptical that they were in attendance.

221. Lanny Thomas, "Orleanians May be Ready to Drop the Fig Leaf Idea," *States-Item*, May 5, 1978, Peggy Alférez Family Papers.

222. Arthur Q. Davis, *It Happened by Design: The Life and Work of Arthur Q. Davis* (Jackson: University Press of Mississippi, 2009), 41.

223. The Historic New Orleans Collection Enrique Alférez artist file contains clippings of letters to the editor that appeared in the *New Orleans Item*, February 26, 1951.

224. Alonzo Lansford, "Nudity Nets New Orleans $600," *Art Digest* 25 (September 1951): 12.

225. Tlaloc Alférez, in discussion with the author, April 2016.

226. Thomas, "Orleanians May Be Ready to Drop the Fig Leaf Idea."

227. The Moore, Morrison, and Garofalo quotes can all be found in Lansford, "Nudity Nets New Orleans $600," 12.

228. Davis, *It Happened by Design*, 41.

229. Lansford, "Nudity Nets New Orleans $600," 20.

230 Thomas, "Orleanians May be Ready to Drop the Fig Leaf Idea."

231. Details about the purchase (by A. J. Truxillo or A. F. Truxillo) are drawn from Lansford, "Nudity Nets New Orleans $600," 20, and Howard Jacobs, "Remoulade: Nude Statuary Went Way of All Flesh," *Times-Picayune*, June 20, 1968, sec. 1, p. 9.

232. Shirley Deneumoustier O'Dwyer (Alexander Charles "Denny" Deneumoustier's daughter) and Alexis O'Dwyer Navarro (Denny Deneumoustier's granddaughter), in discussion with the author, October 2015.

233. Alberta Collier, "Lobby Wall Is Unique," *Times-Picayune*, January 28, 1968, sec. 10, p. 17, Sunday morning edition.

234. Collier, "Lobby Wall Is Unique."

235. Virginia Allred, "Molly Marine Restored," *Leatherneck* 71, no. 11 (November 1988): 79.

236. Kelly S. Ramsey, "'Molly Marine' Desperately in Need of Makeover," *Leatherneck* 82, no. 2 (February 1999): 56; Tlaloc Alférez, in discussion with the author, July 15, 2015.

237. Beck Pridemore, "Molly Marine Monument Dedicated at Parris Island," *Leatherneck* 83, no. 1 (January 2000): 35.

238. Pamela Gould, "'Molly Marine' Model, Like Statue, Fostered Role of Women in Corps," *Washington Times*, August 17, 2000, sec. C, p. 1.

239. "Little But O My!" *Times-Picayune*, September 9, 1961, sec. 1, p. 10; "Site Is Changed for Monument," *Times-Picayune*, September 13, 1961, sec. 3, p. 2.

240. Octavio Nuiry, "Approaching 87, Sculptor Alférez Still Young at Art," *Times-Picayune*, March 13, 1988, sec. C, p. 1.

241. Salvador Fuentes Salinas, "Obra y Fama de un Artista Singular: Enrique Alférez, Excepcional Escultor Mexicano," *La Voz* 21, no. 1158, January 25, 1981, sec. Supplemento Dominical, pp. 1, 3–5.

242. Eliana Guerreiro Bennett, "Mexican Artist Brings Skilled Hands to City," *Times-Picayune*, June 17, 1990, sec. Picayune, p. 1.

243. Fuentes Salinas, "Obra y Fama de un Artista Singular."

244. The monument at Conti and Basin Streets was created by sculptor Juan Fernando Olaguíbel Rosenzweig (1896–1976).

245. Budd. "Montgomery Budd in Morelia."

246. At ten feet, the works were slightly taller than Goliath, who, according to legend, was more than nine feet tall.

247. Sally K. Evans Reeves and William D. Reeves, with Ellis P. Laborde and James S. Janssen, *Historic City Park, New Orleans* (New Orleans: Friends of City Park, 1982), 49.

248. Reeves and Reeves, *Historic City Park*, 49–50.

249. Reeves and Reeves, *Historic City Park*, 59.

250. Reeves and Reeves, *Historic City Park*, 64.

251. Karen Kingsley, *Louisiana Buildings, 1720–1940: The Historic American Buildings Survey*, ed. Jessie Poesch and Barbara SoRelle Bacot (Baton Rouge: Louisiana State University Press, 1997), 332.

252. Reeves and Reeves, *Historic City Park*, 63.

253. Reeves and Reeves, *Historic City Park*, 66–67.

254. McArthur, Allen, and Wylie, interview with Alférez.

255. Green. "Rose Garden Sculptures Feel the Master's Touch."

256. Glade, "Rique the Roisterer," 18.

257. "Statuary Is Being Done by Alférez," *Sunday Item-Tribune*, June 14, 1936, p. 18, Mimi and Jack Davis Papers.

258. Martinez, "Enrique Alférez, Sculptor."

259. McArthur, Allen, and Wylie, interview with Alférez.

260. "Statuary Is Being Done by Alférez." When Samuel Wilson Jr. donated the maquettes to The Historic New Orleans Collection, he indicated that they had been for a project at City Park Stadium.

261. Carole Grout, "Popp Fountain Is Being Refurbished," *Times-Picayune*, June 25, 1998, sec. Picayune, p. 2.

262. Many of these details are drawn from Reeves and Reeves, *Historic City Park*, 115.

263. Alférez shared this experience with Paul Soniat. Additional sources indicate that Alférez had a complex relationship with Koch, including the interview with McArthur, Allen, and Wylie; the author's discussions with Tlaloc Alférez, July 2015, and George Dunbar, April 2, 2015; and Jeanette Hardy, "The Flute Player—Enrique Alférez Makes a New Sculpture for the New Orleans Botanical Garden in City Park, Scene of His Earliest Triumphs 60 Years Ago," *Times-Picayune*, September 26, 1995, sec. Living, p. 1.

264. The figure was a gift in memory of Eugenie and Joseph Merrick Jones, with support from Eugenie Jones Euger, Joseph Merrick Jones Jr., and Susan Jones Gundlach.

265. Soniat, in discussion with the author, March 30, 2015.

266. Reichley, in discussion with the author, June 9, 2016.

267. Peggy Alférez to Mickey Easterling, July 22, 1994, Peggy Alférez Family Papers.

268. Stephen Woolford Clayton, appraisal of *The Family*, issued December 2, 2015, Mr. and Mrs. Alexander Charles Deneumoustier and Family Papers.

269. Peggy Alférez to Mickey Easterling, July 22, 1994, Peggy Alférez Family Papers.

270. "Paintings By 33 Artists Displayed in Exhibition Here."

271. Cooper, "Pen, Chisel and Brush," *Times-Picayune New Orleans States*, April 26, 1936, sec. 2, p. 9. Alférez's drawings from *The Wedge* are in the holdings of the New Orleans Museum of Art.

272. Cooper, "Artists to Exhibit Paintings on French Quarter Streets," *Times-Picayune New Orleans States*, March 7, 1937, p. 16.

273. An image of the bust featured in the New York world's fair is included in a clipping in The Historic New Orleans Collection Enrique Alférez artist file. Additional details are from Darling, "Awards Granted in New Orleans Exhibits of Art," *Times-Picayune*, February 5, 1939, p. 14. Participating artists are also noted in Edith Norris, "State Painters, Sculptors Present Fine Exhibit Here," *Sunday Item-Tribune*, February 12, 1939, p. 7, Enrique Alférez artist file, The Historic New Orleans Collection.

274. Elizabeth McCausland, "Living American Art," *Parnassus* 11, no. 5 (May 1939): 25.

275. Darling, "Pen, Chisel, and Brush," *Times-Picayune New Orleans States*, March 5, 1939, sec. 2, p. 11.

276. "Arts and Artists: Lecture on Peirce at Museum on Friday Open to Members," *Dallas Morning News*, December 15, 1939, sec. 3, p. 2; *Bulletin of the Dallas Museum of Fine Arts*, January 1940, Dallas Museum of Art Archives.

277. Collier, "Alférez Exhibit," The World of Art, *Times-Picayune New Orleans States*, May 4, 1958, sec. 2, p. 8.

278. *Enrique Alférez*, exhibition catalogue, El Paso Museum of Arts, 1961. Available in Enrique Alférez Art and Artist Files, Smithsonian American Art Museum/National Portrait Gallery Library, Washington, DC.

279. Telegram from Reginald Fisher to Enrique Alférez, September 22, 1961, Peggy Alférez Family Papers.

280. Liz Fuhrman Bragg (registrar, Evansville Museum of Arts, History, and Science), in discussion with author, February 27, 2015.

281. Green, "Alférez Drawings and Sculptures Make a Stunning Exhibit," Vision: The World of Art, *Times-Picayune*, March 1, 1981, sec. 3, p. 6. Benefactors who paid for the purchase of the work include Timothy and Willa Slater, Arthur and Tiki Axelrod, and Miles and Nicole Friedlander.

282. "Exhiben en la UCSJ 'El Alma de México Entretejida en un Huipil," *NOTIMEX* (Mexico City), September 9, 2010. Mariana Gómez, "Revelarán Símbolos Del Huipil," *El Norte*, August 30, 2012, sec. Vida, p. 11.

283. "La Scene," *Times-Picayune*, November 15, 1975, sec. 2, p. 4; Collier, "Artist Immortalizes Subject with First Love, Lithography," The World of Art, *Times-Picayune*, November 23, 1975, sec. 3, p. 16.

284. Green, "A Rare N.O. Exhibit Offers Classic Alférez," Art, *Times-Picayune*, October 26, 1986, sec. L, p. 1.

285. Auseklis Ozols, in discussion with the author, February 26, 2015.

286. Ana Ester Gershanik, "Museum Features Local Artist's Works," *Times-Picayune*, October 24, 2002, sec. East New Orleans Picayune, p. 1.

287. MacCash, "Timeless Treasures—Elegantly Simple Sculptures That Exude Authentic Emotion Are Enrique Alférez's Legacy," *Times-Picayune*, March 27, 2012, sec. Living, p. 1.

288. Details about Peggy Alférez's death are drawn from discussions with Tlaloc Alférez, April 2016, and MacCash, "Peggy Alférez."

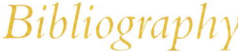

Bibliography

Archives and Records

Appalachian State University. Special Collections. Belk Library and Information Commons.

Chautauqua Institution. Chautauqua, New York.

Christ Church Cathedral New Orleans. Church Archives.

The Church of Jesus Christ of Latter Day Saints. FamilySearch.org.

Corporate Capital, LLC. Corporate Records; Ogden Museum File.

Dallas Museum of Art Archives.

Dirección del Registro Civil y Notarias de Zacatecas, Mexico.

El Paso Public Library. Border Heritage Center.

El Paso Museum of Art.

Evansville Museum of Arts, History, and Science. Artist Files. Evansville, Indiana.

The Historic New Orleans Collection. Williams Research Center. Enrique Alférez Artist File; Enrique Alférez Artworks and Artifacts; Arts and Crafts Club of New Orleans Records. New Orleans, Louisiana.

Jefferson Parish Clerk of Court. Metairie, Louisiana.

Jefferson Parish Library Special Collections. Metairie, Louisiana.

Library of Congress. Prints and Photographs Online Catalog.

Louisiana Secretary of State. Louisiana Public Vital Records; Orleans Parish Marriage Records.

Louisiana State University Libraries. Special Collections. Hill Memorial Library. Baton Rouge, Louisiana.

McNeese State University. Archives and Special Collections. Frazar Memorial Library. Lake Charles, Louisiana.

New Orleans Botanical Garden. Records of Director Paul Soniat. New Orleans, Louisiana.

New Orleans Museum of Art. Curatorial Files. New Orleans, Louisiana.

New Orleans Public Library. Louisiana Division (Vertical Files and Rare Vertical Files; City Archives); Special Collections; WPA Photograph Collection. New Orleans, Louisiana.

Ogden Museum of Southern Art. New Orleans, Louisiana.

Orange County Public Library. Ancestry.com. Hillsborough, North Carolina.

St. Martin's Episcopal Church Archives. Metairie, Louisiana.

School of the Art Institute of Chicago. Department of Registration Records.

Smithsonian American Art Museum/National Portrait Gallery Library. Art and Artists Files.

Tom Lea Institute. El Paso, Texas.

Touro Infirmary Archives. New Orleans, Louisiana.

Tulane University. Latin American Library. New Orleans, Louisiana.

Tulane University. Louisiana Research Collections (Frances Bryson Moore Papers); Special Collections. Howard-Tilton Memorial Library. New Orleans, Louisiana.

Tulane University. Middle American Research Institute. New Orleans, Louisiana.

Tulane University. Southeastern Architectural Archive. Richard Koch Papers and Photographs; Weiss, Dreyfous, and Seiferth Office Records. New Orleans, Louisiana.

University Hospital Records. Mobile, Alabama.

United States Citizenship and Immigration Services (USCIS).

University of New Orleans. Louisiana and Special Collections. Hermann B. Deutsch Collection; Don Lee Keith Collection. Earl K. Long Library. New Orleans, Louisiana.

University of Illinois at Urbana-Champaign. University Archives. Lorado Taft Papers, 1857–1953. Allen S. Weller Papers, 1860–1997.

University of California, Berkeley. Frans Blom Papers. Bancroft Library.

University of Texas at El Paso. C. L. Sonnichsen Special Collections. Stout-Feldman Studio Photographs. Tom Lea Papers.

US Army. National Personnel Records Center. St. Louis, Missouri.

US Census Bureau.

US Department of Commerce Census.

US National Archives at Kansas City, Missouri. Immigration, Emigration, and Naturalization Related Records.

US National Archives in College Park, Maryland. Records of the Works Projects Administration and Civil Works Administration; Louisiana Federal Emergency Relief Administration.

US National Park Service. National Register of Historic Places; Carl Sandburg Home National Historic Site.

US Social Security Administration.

USA Medical Center. Mobile, Alabama.

Whitney Museum of American Art. Artist File. New York, New York.

Windsor Court Hotel. New Orleans, Louisiana.

Personal and Family Papers

Margaret "Peggy" Alférez Family Papers

Joseph C. and Sue Ellen Canizaro Papers

George Dunbar Personal Papers

Mimi and Jack Davis Papers

Mr. and Mrs. Alexander Charles Deneumoustier and Family Papers

Donn Young Photography

Selected Primary and Secondary Sources

Alien case file (A-File) for Enrique Alférez. Alien case files, 1944–2003, record group 566. United States Citizenship and Immigration Services (USCIS).

Allred, Virginia. "Molly Marine Restored." *Leatherneck* 71, no. 11 (November 1988).

American Institute of Architects Chicago, Chicago Architecture Foundation, and Landmarks Preservation Council of Illinois. *AIA Guide to Chicago.* Edited by Alice Sinkevitch. 2nd ed. Orlando: Harcourt, 2004.

Antone, Evan Haywood. *Tom Lea: His Life and Work.* El Paso: Texas Western Press, University of Texas at El Paso, 1988.

Blaser, Werner, editor and translator. *Chicago Architecture: Holabird and Root, 1880–1992.* Basel and Boston: Birkhäuser Verlag, 1992.

Blom, Frans. "The 'Negative Batter' at Uxmal." In *Middle American Papers.* Publication No. 4. New Orleans: Middle American Research Institute, Tulane University, 1932.

——. The Uxmal Expedition." *Tulane News Bulletin* 10, no. 7 (April 1930): 111–14. Frans Blom Papers, 1919–1963, Latin American Library, Tulane University.

Blum, Betty J. Transcript: Oral history of Serge Chermayeff, May 23–24, 1985, Chicago Architects Oral History Project, The Art Institute of Chicago, 2001.

Bonner, Judith H. "The Power of Enrique Alférez." *New Orleans Art Review* 11, no. 5 (May–June 1993): 2–5.

——. "The World of Enrique Alférez." *New Orleans Art Review* 30, nos. 3–4 (March–May 2012): 12–15.

Brunhouse, Robert Levere. *Frans Blom, Maya Explorer.* Albuquerque: University of New Mexico Press, 1976.

Bullard, John, and Sharon Litwin. *The Art and Times of Enrique Alférez.* Edited by Sharon Litwin. New Orleans: A Project of Joseph C. Canizaro Interests, 1988.

Caire, Vincent. *Louisiana Aviation: An Extraordinary History in Photographs.* Baton Rouge: Louisiana State University Press, 2012.

Carter, Hodding, editor. *The Past as Prelude: New Orleans, 1718–1968.* New Orleans: Tulane University and Pelican, 1968.

Coffey, Mary K. *How a Revolutionary Art Became Official Culture: Murals, Museums, and the Mexican State.* Durham: Duke University Press, 2012.

Collier, Alberta. "Child, Crisis, Gratitude Inspire Statue." *Times-Picayune,* Sunday Morning Edition, November 18, 1962.

Courtney, Caroline R., and Hira Rashid. "Building Charity Hospital, Architect Leon Weiss." *New Orleans Historical.* Accessed November 1, 2015. http://neworleanshistorical.org/items /show/272.

Curtis, Penelope. *Sculpture 1900–1945: After Rodin.* Oxford and New York: Oxford University Press, 1999.

Davis, Arthur Q. *It Happened by Design: The Life and Work of Arthur Q. Davis.* Jackson: University Press of Mississippi, 2009.

Davis, Jack. "Enrique Alférez's Experiences with the Works Progress Administration." *New Orleans Art: The New Deal Era.* November 16, 1978. Jambalaya Program Records, 1975–1980, New Orleans Public Library. Audio recording.

De La Torre, Rubén. "Un Raro Escultor Mexicano." *Revista de Revistas,* September 30, 1934.

Deutsch, Hermann B. *The Wedge: A Novel of Mexico.* New York: Frederick A. Stokes Co., 1935.

Doyle, Kate, ed. "The Dead of Tlatelolco: Using the Archives to Exhume the Past." *National Security Archive.* October 1, 2006. https://nsarchive2.gwu.edu/NSAEBB/NSAEBB201/.

Duncan, Alastair. *Art Deco*. New York: Thames and Hudson, 1988.

Eggebeen, Janna. "Airport Age: Architecture and Modernity in America." PhD dissertation, City University of New York, 2007.

"Enrique Alférez." *Arts and Antiques* 1, no. 1 (October 1938).

Enrique Alférez. El Paso Museum of Art, 1961. Exhibition catalog.

Federal Writers' Project of the Works Progress Administration. *New Orleans City Guide*. Boston: Houghton Mifflin, 1938.

Fernández, Justino. *Mexican Art*. With photographs by Constantino Reyes-Valerio. Mexico City: Hamlyn Publishing Group, 1967.

Field, Corinne T., and Nicholas L. Syrett, eds. *Age in America: The Colonial Era to the Present*. New York: New York University Press, 2015.

Fonseca, Mary. *Louisiana Gardens*. Gretna, LA: Pelican, 1999.

Frank, Patrick, ed. *Readings in Latin American Modern Art*. New Haven, CT: Yale University Press, 2004.

Gaddo, Randy. "Molly Marine: From Assisting Recruiting in WWII to Recognizing Outstanding Leadership Today." *Leatherneck* 97, no. 7 (July 2014).

Galan, Hector, dir. *The Hunt for Pancho Villa*. Alexandria, VA: PBS Video, 1993. Videocassette.

Ganz, Cheryl R. *The 1933 Chicago World's Fair: A Century of Progress*. Urbana: University of Illinois Press, 2008.

Ganz, Cheryl R., and Margaret Strobel, eds. *Pots of Promise: Mexicans and Pottery at Hull-House, 1920–40*. Urbana: University of Illinois Press, 2004.

Glade, Luba. "Rique the Roisterer." *Figaro*, January 1, 1979.

Glassman, Steve, and Armando Anaya. *Cities of the Maya in Seven Epochs, 1250 B.C. to A.D. 1903*. Jefferson, NC: McFarland, 2011.

Grieve, Victoria. *The Federal Art Project and the Creation of Middlebrow Culture*. Urbana: University of Illinois Press, 2009.

Hall, Barbara, and Robert Aaron Jones. "Time and Tide: Restoring Lorado Taft's *Fountain of Time*—An Overview." In "Conservation at the Art Institute of Chicago." *Art Institute of Chicago Museum Studies* 31, no. 2 (2005): 80–89, 111–12.

Harvey, Chance, and Lyle Saxon. 2003. *The Life and Selected Letters of Lyle Saxon*. Gretna, LA: Pelican, 2003.

Hazeltine, Elizabeth. "Lorado Taft: Master Sculptor." *School Arts Magazine* 25, nos. 1–5 (January 1926): 260–68.

Hecht, Guillaume, dir. *Uxmal: Thrice Built*. New York: Films Media Group, 2001. Documentary film, 27 min.

Hinderliter, Edward T. "The Maya Temple of the 1933 Chicago World's Fair." In "Abstracts of Papers Presented at the Twenty-Fourth Annual Meeting of the Society of Architectural Historians." *Journal of the Society of Architectural Historians* 30, no. 3 (1971): 238–48.

Hughes, Edan Milton. *Artists in California, 1786–1940*. Vol. 2, *L–Z*. Sacramento, CA: Crocker Art Museum, 2002.

Katz, Friedrich. *The Life and Times of Pancho Villa*. Stanford, CA: Stanford University Press, 1998.

Keith, Don Lee. "Cast in His Own Mold." *Louisiana Cultural Vistas*, Spring 1999.

Kemp, John R. "Enrique Alférez." *64 Parishes Encyclopedia of Louisiana*. Louisiana Endowment for the Humanities, 2010–. https://64parishes.org/entry/enrique-alfrez.

Kingsley, Karen. *Louisiana Buildings, 1720–1940: The Historic American Buildings Survey*. Edited by Jessie Poesch and Barbara SoRelle Bacot. Baton Rouge: Louisiana State University Press, 1997.

Kirkland, Wallace. *The Many Faces of Hull-House: The Photographs of Wallace Kirkland*. Edited by Mary Ann Johnson. Urbana: University of Illinois Press, 1989.

Knight, Alan. *The Mexican Revolution*. 2 vols. Cambridge and New York: Cambridge University Press, 1986.

Kowalski, Jeff Karl. *The House of the Governor: A Maya Palace at Uxmal, Yucatan, Mexico*. Norman: University of Oklahoma Press, 1987.

Kubly, Vincent F. *The Louisiana Capitol: Its Art and Architecture*. Gretna, LA: Pelican, 1977.

Lanier, Henry Wysham. *Greenwich Village, Today and Yesterday. Photographs by Berenice Abbott*. New York: Harper, 1949.

Lansford, Alonzo. "Nudity Nets New Orleans $600." *Art Digest* 25 (September 1951): 12, 20.

Law, Hazel Jane. "Chicago Architectural Sculpture." Master's thesis, University of Chicago, August 1935.

Lea, Tom. *Tom Lea: An Oral History*. Edited by Rebecca McDowell Craver and Adair Margo. El Paso: Texas Western Press, 1995.

Leighninger, Robert D., Jr. *Building Louisiana: The Legacy of the Public Works Administration*. Jackson: University Press of Mississippi, 2007.

Locke, Adrian. *Mexico: A Revolution in Art, 1910–1940*. London: Royal Academy of Arts, 2013.

Longue Vue House and Gardens Advisory Corp. *"An Abundance of Life": The Works of Enrique Alférez*. New Orleans: Longue Vue House and Gardens, 1996. Exhibition catalog.

"Lorado Taft: Sculptor, Lecturer, Educator, Philanthropist." *Art Thoughts,* no. 6 (December 1936).

Louisiana Board of Levee Commissioners of the Orleans Levee District. *Commemorating the Formal Opening of Shushan Airport*. New Orleans: Board of Levee Commissioners, 1933.

Louisiana Writers' Project. *Louisiana: A Guide to the State*. American Guide Series. New York: Hastings House, 1941.

——. *New Orleans City Park: Its First Fifty Years*. New Orleans: Gulf Printing Company, Inc., 1941.

Martinez, Matthew J. "Enrique Alférez, Sculptor." Master's thesis, University of New Orleans, 1989. Video and text.

Mavigliano, George J., and Richard A. Lawson. *The Federal Art Project in Illinois, 1935–1943*. Carbondale: Southern Illinois University Press, 1990.

McArthur, Anne, Dick Allen, and Margery Wylie. Transcript of interview with Enrique Alférez and Margaret "Peggy" Alférez. December 4–5, 1975. Margaret "Peggy" Alférez Family Papers.

McCausland, Elizabeth. "Living American Art." *Parnassus* 11, no. 5 (May 1939): 16–25.

McDonald, William Francis. *Federal Relief Administration and the Arts: The Origins and Administrative History of the Arts Projects of the Works Progress Administration*. Columbus: Ohio State University Press, 1969.

Mérida, Carlos. *Modern Mexican Artists*. Freeport, New York: Frances Toor Studios, 1937.

Mizell-Nelson, Michael. "1929 Streetcar Strike: Part 1," *New Orleans Historical*. Accessed July 7, 2017. http://neworleanshistorical.org/items/show/514.

Mose, Ruth Helming. "Midway Studio." *American Magazine of Art* 19, no. 8 (August 1928): 413–22.

Mraz, John. *Looking for Mexico: Modern Visual Culture and National Identity*. Durham, NC: Duke University Press, 2009.

Museum of Modern Art. *Twenty Centuries of Mexican Art / Veinte Siglos de Arte Mexicano*. Mexico City: Museum of Modern Art in collaboration with the Mexican Government, 1940.

Naggar, Carole, and Fred Ritchin. *México Through Foreign Eyes / México Visto por Ojos Extranjeros, 1850–1990*. New York: W. W. Norton, 1996.

Newman, Arnold. "Sitting Book." https://arnoldnewman.com/sitting-book.html.

Oehler, Sarah Kelly. *They Seek a City: Chicago and the Art of Migration, 1910–1950*. Chicago: Art Institute of Chicago, 2013.

Official Guide: Book of the Fair, 1933. Chicago: A Century of Progress, 1933.

Oles, James, and Marta Ferragut. *South of the Border: Mexico in the American Imagination, 1917–1947 / México en la imaginación Norteamericana, 1917–1947.* Washington, DC: Smithsonian Institution Press, 1993.

Perales Garay, C. Rigoberto. *Historia Monográfica, Municipio Miguel Auza, Zacatecas.* Accessed May 24, 2015. https://miguelauzazac.net/cronista/cronista.html.

Pfohl, Katie A. *Mexico in New Orleans: A Tale of Two Americas.* Baton Rouge: Louisiana State University Museum of Art, 2015.

Poesch, Jessie, and Barbara SoRelle Bacot, eds. *Louisiana Buildings, 1720–1940: The Historic American Buildings Survey.* Baton Rouge: Louisiana State University Press, 1997.

Powers, John E., and Deborah Powers. *Texas Painters, Sculptors, and Graphic Artists: A Biographical Dictionary of Artists in Texas before 1942.* Austin, TX: Woodmont Books, 2000.

Pridemore, Beck. "Molly Marine Monument Dedicated at Parris Island." *Leatherneck* 83, no. 1 (January 2000).

Ramsey, Kelly S. "'Molly Marine' Desperately in Need of Makeover." *Leatherneck* 82, no. 2 (February 1999).

Reed, John Shelton. *Dixie Bohemia: A French Quarter Circle in the 1920s.* Baton Rouge: Louisiana State University Press, 2012.

Reeves, Sally K. Evans, and William D. Reeves, with Ellis P. Laborde and James S. Janssen. *Historic City Park, New Orleans.* New Orleans: Friends of City Park, 1982.

Reonas, Matthew. "Great Depression in Louisiana." *64 Parishes Encyclopedia of Louisiana.* Louisiana Endowment for the Humanities, 2010–. Article published December 17, 2010. https://64parishes.org/entry/great-depression-in-louisiana.

Ride, James L. *Chicago Sculpture.* Urbana: University of Illinois Press, 1981.

Roja, Benjamin. *The City of Zacatecas: Zacatecas, Mexico.* Zacatecas: Grupo Azabache, 1991.

Rose, Jennifer J. "The Dragon of Santa Maria." *Red Shoes Are Better Than Bacon.* July 23, 2014. http://redshoesarebetterthanbacon.wordpress.com/2014/07/23/the-dragon-of-santa-maria/.

Salvaggio, John E. *New Orleans' Charity Hospital: A Story of Physicians, Politics, and Poverty.* Baton Rouge: Louisiana State University Press, 1992.

Sánchez, George J. *Becoming Mexican American: Ethnicity, Culture, and Identity in Chicano Los Angeles, 1900–1945.* New York: Oxford University Press, 1993.

Sandburg, Carl. *Chicago Poems: Unabridged.* New York: Dover, 1994.

Sartisky, Michael, J. Richard Gruber, and John R. Kemp, eds. *A Unique Slant of Light: The Bicentennial History of Art in Louisiana.* New Orleans: Louisiana Endowment for the Humanities, 2012.

Schmeckebier, Laurence. *Modern Mexican Art.* Minneapolis: University of Minnesota Press, 1939.

Schrenk, Lisa D. *Building a Century of Progress: The Architecture of Chicago's 1933–34 World's Fair.* Minneapolis: University of Minnesota Press, 2007.

Scott, John W. *Natalie Scott: A Magnificent Life.* Gretna, LA: Pelican, 2008.

———. "William Spratling and the New Orleans Renaissance." *Louisiana History: The Journal of the Louisiana Historical Association* 45, no. 3 (Summer 2004), 287–322.

"The Shop of Leather." *Junior Bazaar* 2, no. 12 (December 1946).

"Shushan Airport, New Orleans, La." *Architectural Forum* 61 (October 1934).

Stamper, John W. *Chicago's North Michigan Avenue: Planning and Development, 1900–1930.* Chicago Architecture and Urbanism. Chicago: University of Chicago Press, 1991.

Struppeck, Jules. *The Creation of Sculpture.* New York: Henry Holt, 1952.

Taft, Lorado. *The Appreciation of Sculpture*. Reading with a Purpose. Chicago: American Library Association, 1927.

——. *The History of American Sculpture*. The History of American Art. New York, London: Macmillan, 1903.

——. *Modern Tendencies in Sculpture*. Freeport, NY: Books for Libraries Press, 1970.

Tannenbaum, Frank. *The Mexican Agrarian Revolution*. New York: Macmillan, 1929.

Weeks, John M., and Jane A. Hill. *The Carnegie Maya: The Carnegie Institution of Washington Maya Research Program, 1913–1957*. Boulder: University Press of Colorado, 2006.

Weller, Allen Stuart. *Lorado in Paris: The Letters of Lorado Taft, 1880–1885*. Urbana: University of Illinois Press, 1985.

——. *Lorado Taft: The Chicago Years*. Urbana: University of Illinois Press, 2014.

Wilson, Anthony. "The Double Dealer." *64 Parishes Encyclopedia of Louisiana*. Louisiana Endowment for the Humanities, 2010–. Article published February 7, 2011. https://64parishes.org/entry/the-double-dealer.

Wilson, Samuel, Jr. *The Buildings of Christ Church*. New Orleans: Louisiana Landmarks Society, 1997.

Index

[PAGE REFERENCES FOR ILLUSTRATIONS APPEAR IN ITALICS]

About the Author

Katie Bowler Young is the author of *Through Water with Ease* (Louisiana Literature Press, 2019) and *State Street* (Bull City Press, 2009). Her poetry and prose have appeared in journals including the *Southern Review*, the *Midwest Quarterly*, the *Carolina Quarterly,* and *Louisiana Literature.* Her work often focuses on art, culture, and perspective. Young is director of global relations at the University of North Carolina at Chapel Hill, responsible for international programs and partnerships. She has been an adjunct faculty member in poetry in the creative writing program at Warren Wilson College. Among other honors, she has earned a Fulbright–Nehru International Education award and was a finalist for the Marble Faun Prize for Poetry. Young earned degrees from the University of New Orleans and the Warren Wilson College MFA Program for Writers.

About the Publisher

The Historic New Orleans Collection is a museum, research center, and publisher dedicated to the study and preservation of the history and culture of New Orleans and the Gulf South. We have been publishing award-winning nonfiction for nearly four decades, striving always to put the regional and the global in conversation. *Enrique Alférez: Sculptor* is the latest entry in our Louisiana Artists Biography Series, and the first to center on sculpture and public art.

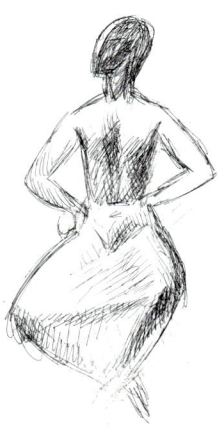

Generous funding for this book was provided by the 2019 Bienville Circle and Laussat Society, the premier membership groups of The Historic New Orleans Collection. Joyfully inspired by the arts, deeply informed by history, members of these groups provide integral support for THNOC exhibitions, acquisitions, and publications.

Untitled drawing
COURTESY OF THE COLLECTION OF TLALOC S. ALFÉREZ, MD

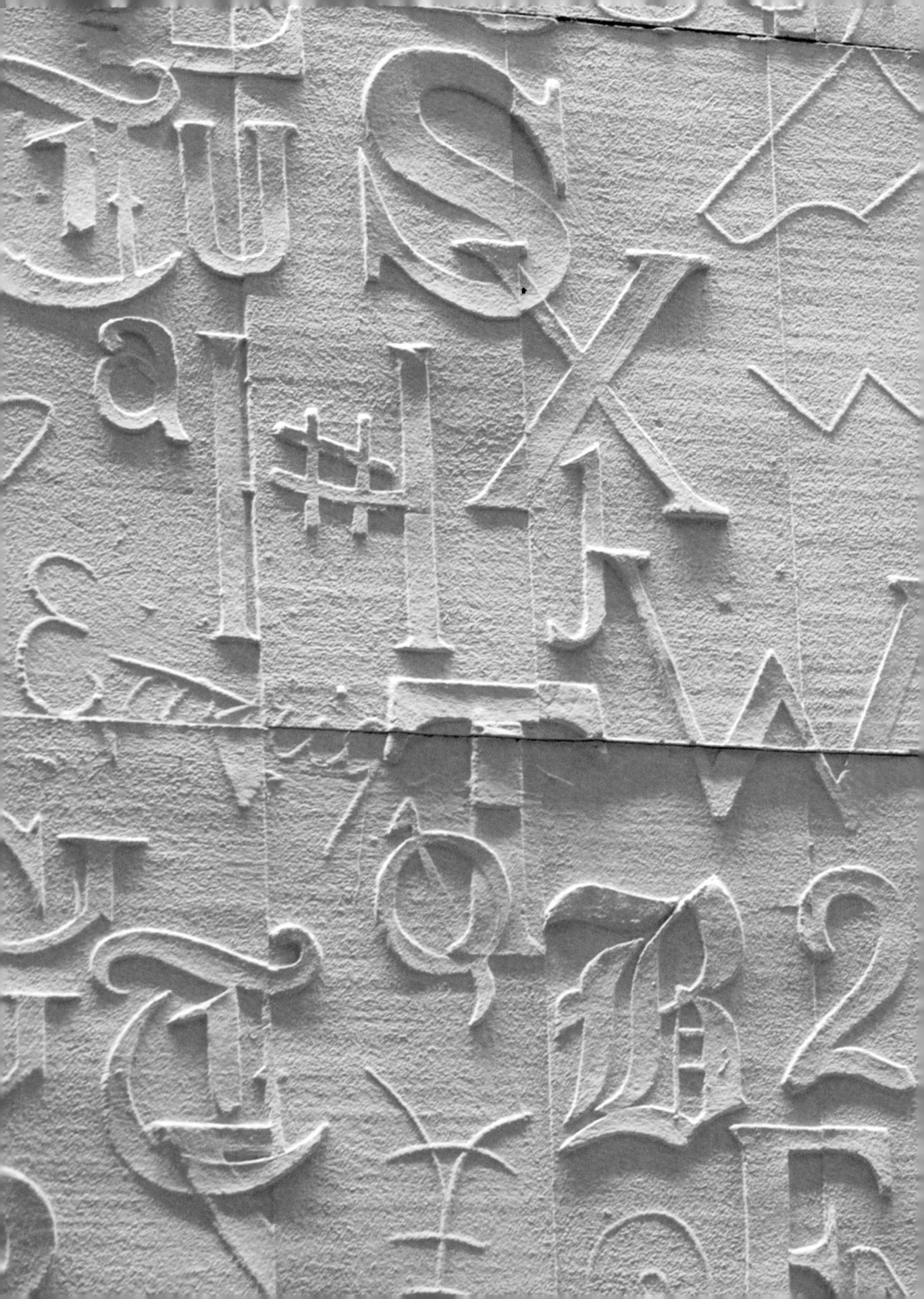